D1432042

Charles E. Cowman

Missionary : Warrior

CHARLES E. COWMAN

Charles E. Cowman

Missionary :: Warrior

With Portraits, Illustrations and Maps

By Lettie B. Cowman

(Mrs. Chas. E. Cowman)

Author of

"Streams in the Desert"

———

Printed in U. S. A.

———

The Oriental Missionary Society
900 North Hobart Boulevard
Los Angeles, California

"Unto me, who am less than
the least of all saints,
is this grace given,
that I
should preach among the Gentiles
the
unsearchable riches of Christ."
—Eph. 3:8

Fifth Printing

To His Mother

"Greatheart is dead they say;
  But the light shall burn the brighter,
  And the night shall be the lighter
  For his going;
  And a rich, rich harvest for his sowing.
                        —*John Oxenham.*

FOREWORD

The name, Charles E. Cowman, has become increasingly familiar during the past twenty-five years to those interested in foreign missions. As the founder and president of The Oriental Missionary Society, he won for himself and for the Mission a place in the respect and affection of a large number of Christians in the homelands, as well as in the mission fields of the world.

Many of his friends, believing that the origin and history of his work should be more widely known, requested him to write its story, but he felt a natural hesitancy in introducing a volume which would have had, in the very nature of things, a very personal touch, as it would have been written embodying much of his personal life and work. It was undertaken but, after several chapters of the manuscript were completed, he discontinued it, saying, "Let me be kept so busy *making* history that I shall have no time to write it. Should the time come *when it is necessary,* let the pen of another tell the story." The task has fallen to her who sits in the after-glow of that rarely beautiful life.

The biography is, in a sense, the history of a great missionary enterprise. So closely were his personality and the cause of missions linked, that it is impossible to separate them. His work was his very life.

"True biography," said one, "was never nor can be written. Fragrance cannot be put into picture or poem. There is a subtle evasive savor and flavor about character which escapes both tongue and pen. And, more than this, the very best things about such characters and careers are unknown, save to God, and cannot be revealed because they are among His secret things. [Like Elijah, the best men hide themselves with God before they show themselves to men.] The showing may be written in history, but the hiding has none, and after studying the narrative of such lives, even with the best helps, there remains a deeper, and unwritten history that only eternity can unveil."

What pen can fully compass or adequately portray the story of simple faith and mighty achievement; of faithful and heroic service of the subject of this memoir, the missionary whose life literally burned out, the man whose master-passion was missions? Such a life has a message for our day.

As he served Christ, so also ought we to serve Him, and surely we will serve Him better as we see what a noble service was rendered by this missionary. To young people his message was ever, "Find God's plan for your generation and get in line with it."

The world still has men in it whom they are pleased to term "spiritual geniuses"; but, should an examination be made to discover the secret, they would have to come to but one conclusion. They were men who set themselves to find and to do the will of God. That is the crux of the whole matter. "He that willeth to do His will shall know —and greater works than these shall ye do."

Important ends are served by the reputation which such labor sometimes acquires in this world, and by the good which they have done living after them in the records of earth and in the memories of men; for other hearts catch a kindred flame from their torch.

This volume has, like the life it sketches, just one aim. It is simply and solely meant, not to exalt a personality, but to show the reader what God can do with a humble instrument when fully and completely yielded to Him. He needs no praise for his work, but we need the impulse which his consecrated example gave to the world. Neither life nor labor has been in vain. What marvels may be wrought by the inspiration of a single life!

The book is a simple record of a real life, but it is a sacred romance, though the principal actor never dreamed that he was anything but a common man, not the missionary-hero that we see him to be. It is not a biography in the truest sense of the word; but a sheaf of memories gleaned at random from the harvest-field of his fruitful life.

In this work I would beg indulgence for many shortcomings of which I am painfully conscious, because of the fact that it has been written in the few leisure hours of an exceedingly active life. I have tried to paint impartially the portrait of my beloved husband as he lived, and if I have in any measure conveyed the lesson that a life wholly surrendered to God is the life that wins, I have not wholly failed in my task.

Lettie B. Cowman.

Los Angeles, Calif.
September 25, 1928.

CONTENTS

CONTENTS

ILLUSTRATIONS

ILLUSTRATIONS

"The humblest, in the sight of even the greatest, may admire and hope and take courage. These great brothers of ours in blood and lineage, who live a universal life, still speak to us from their graves, and beckon us on in the paths which they have trod. Their example is still with us, to guide, to influence, and to direct. For nobility of character is a perpetual bequest, living from age to age, and constantly tending to reproduce its like."—Samuel Smiles.

"The greatest gift a hero leaves his race is to have been a hero."

Charles E. Cowman
Missionary Warrior

CHAPTER I

IN THE BEGINNING

An old Bible, the treasured heirloom of succeeding generations, is in possession of the Cowman family. On a page discolored by age and in faded writing, making the record almost illegible, is the name, George W. Cowman, date of birth, October 16, 1810. Beneath his name, is that of his wife, Elizabeth, date of birth, July 27, 1820.

George W. Cowman's parents, a mixture of English and Scotch, came from Great Britain late in 1700 and settled in the Southern States during the slavery days. Very little of their history can be traced, as there were few records preserved, but stories have been handed down from one generation to another, from which one catches glimpses of life on an old Southern plantation, where cotton fields were a-bloom and ebony-skinned people played a great part.

George was the eldest of a long list of sons and daughters and the growing fledglings in his father's family crowded him out, so he migrated northward to seek his fortune in a newer and thriftier country. Years afterward, when sons and daughters were sent to bless his own home, he would take them upon his knee and relate to them stories of his boyhood days "away down South." He told them of the parting with his parents; of the way his sisters wept when he bade them goodbye; of the long journey which was made by wagon, over rough roads and through swollen streams; of the warm hospitality he found among the northerners; of how the North and South joined hands and hearts when he met their devoted mother, Elizabeth. The story usually concluded with something which they never tired of hearing—of the honeymoon which was spent on the long, long journey to the newer West, where they found their home among the pioneers in the State of Illinois. Upon their arrival they prayed, "May the God of our Fathers bless us and though, like Jacob of old, we have but a stone for a pillow and the canopy of Heaven for a covering, may we all find God in this place, and may it be to us as the House of God and the Gate of Heaven." How the prayers of these faithful pioneers have been answered, time has told.

There were neighbors scattered here and there, kind-hearted folk who had moved from New England and the Southern States to establish homes for themselves. Generally speaking they were fairly well-educated men and women who brought with them ideals of righteousness and truth, and the community might have been termed Christian.

There were tangled solitudes in their surroundings that challenged the courage of the bravest, but all was not dreariness in the life of a pioneer. They had their joys as well as their hardships and entered into the social spirit far more enthusiastically than much of the surfeited society of today. Out among the wilds, they were free to build after the inner pattern, to dream dreams and visualize their future. They proved to the world that "a man's

life consisteth not of the things which he possesseth."
Among the fine early pioneers were those who beheld the
beauty in the rainbow, in the sunset, and the thunder-
storms. There were books scattered about in the log
cabins, and around the flickering light of the fireplace they
read Dickens, Whittier, and Shakespeare.

Every year new settlers came; all were heartily welcomed. There were many "house warmings" when a new
house was completed, and "husking bees" when the
autumnal harvest was gathered.

A rare type of hospitality was developed and the
neighbors were acquainted with each other from Hickory
Hill to Four Mile Creek. Their interests were common;
"their fears, their hopes, their aims were one, their comforts and their cares."

Little children came to grace these humble homes and
the parents built log school houses in which they were to
receive their education. They also built churches, for
wherever these early pioneers went, they reared an altar
unto God. The settlers came from far and near to join in
the simple services that told the pioneer of the great hope
in the future which was for him, his wife and his children; that in spite of their lives of toil and deprivation,
there was something higher and better in another world
than this.

How much we owe to our rugged type of ancestry!
As we look at their pictures adorning the walls, the men,
with their stiffly starched shirts and ruffled collars, the
women, in flowing skirts and with their hair combed so
smoothly over their foreheads, we are inclined to look upon them with some scorn, but they are the stock from
which have sprung our courageous Americans.

To the home of George and Elizabeth Cowman, God
sent nine children. David Franklin was the second child,

2

one greatly loved by the mother; and what a mother Elizabeth Cowman proved to be! While the father would rise long before the dawn to feed the stock and do the chores, she would be preparing breakfast for the large family. There were no servants in those days, and every bit of cooking and baking had to be done by her own hands. The clothing had to be woven on a hand-loom, and made without the aid of a sewing machine; however, every Sabbath morning she, with her entire family neatly clad in their home-spun, was present at the church services.

What finer tribute could children pay to their mother than those of Elizabeth Cowman, who long afterward said, "We never saw our mother out of temper, or heard her speak a cross or harsh word." What was the secret? When about her hard work, she was humming some familiar hymn or meditating upon the rich promises from the Book of books. Her faith was in God and upon His strong arm she leaned.

David was very fond of books, early developing a gift for teaching, and his parents did their utmost to give him the best education which the humble schools afforded. He was a diligent student and his dollars, which were few, were spent for books. From his earliest youth he was a leader among the young people. He was a noble boy with fine, high ideals, and when his father died, leaving the mother with a family of nine to rear, it was to David that she looked for counsel.

The nearest neighbors of George and Elizabeth Cowman were a very congenial and companionable family, named Keyes. They, too, had moved from another state, following the lure of the West. The father of the family was named John, by his staunch Presbyterian parents. There were many Biblical names in the godly Cowman circle. It was not uncommon then to give the children

Bible names and often in one family were Matthew, Amos, Elijah, Hezekiah, Sarah and Hannah.

The Keyes home was a very hospitable one where a royal welcome was ever to be found. Their house, somewhat different from the others, was large and roomy. A wide open lawn led up to the doorway. There were trees with great overhanging branches inviting you to rest under their welcoming shade, when the thermometer registered one hundred degrees. The Keyes' farm had a beautiful river flowing at its edge and close by was a woodland, which for beauty was quite unsurpassed. Often during the summertime, the entire countryside would gather there for a campmeeting and the woods would ring and re-echo with songs of praise to God.

John and Sarah Keyes were the parents of three sons, Albert, William and Charles. There was an only daughter named Mary. When she was but thirteen years of age, the death-angel robbed the home of its dearest treasure, the mother, and henceforth it was upon this young girl that much of the care and burden of the home rested.

Mary was considered an unusual character. Everybody loved her sunny face and smiling eyes. Her jet-black hair was always neatly braided, her dresses and aprons spotlessly neat and clean. During the autumn and winter months she attended school, spending the evenings in study to keep up with her classes. Often at the midnight hour she would be found poring over her books and when she was but seventeen, she possessed a very thorough education for her day. Along with her studies the finest art which a woman can master was acquired, the art of homemaking, and Mary Keyes carried off the honor of being an ideal housekeeper. The neighbors loved her and named her "Our Mary."

The Cowman and Keyes families practically grew up together. They attended the same school, the same church; they vied with each other over the school prizes and David Cowman was often at the Keyes' home where there were boys of his own age; however, there was another magnet drawing him hither.

"Love took up the harp of life and smote on all the chords with might."

Emerson wrote: "Love is a fire, that, kindling its first embers in a narrow nook of a private bosom, caught from a spark of another private heart, glows and enlarges until it warms and beams upon multitudes of men and women, upon the universal heart of all, and so lights up the whole world of nature with its generous flames."

The happy schooldays and teen years for David Cowman and Mary Keyes were ended. They indulged in dreams of a home of their own; however, love's young dream was soon cut short by rumors of war. The North and the South became engaged in a deadly combat over the slavery question. The nation sent out a call to its men to shoulder arms. Thousands responded, other thousands enlisted; and one day an officer went to the home of Elizabeth Cowman, the widow, to inform her that her son David had volunteered for service, and would be expected to leave immediately for the battle-front.

Two days later a young man dressed in a soldier's blue uniform rode up to the Keyes' home to bid Mary farewell, and David Cowman left for the battle-front under Company G. 83rd Illinois Infantry, August, 1861.

Time passed slowly to the parents of the boys. The entire nation became weary and heartsick of the long-drawn-out struggle. The years between 1861 and 1864 dragged along, and the fourth year of the war was dawning. Letters had been exchanged between David and Mary and often she read and re-read them, then tied them with a bit of ribbon and placed them carefully away. Where is the person so devoid of sentiment that in his possession, somewhere, a package of old faded letters may not be found which tell of some wonderful moments in life?

On Sabbath days, at the little log church, prayer was offered for the safety of the loved ones at the front. Mary Keyes never failed to be present to mingle her petitions with the others, for was not David her soldier-boy and did not God hear and answer prayer, bringing many a lad home in safety?

One day Company G. was ordered out on a long march. It was in the month of August when the heat in the Southland was at its zenith. The route took them through a region where tall mountains reared their heads skyward. The air was stifling and David Cowman fell by the wayside, quite overcome. In the rear came the enemy in hot pursuit and they were compelled to march quickly. There was little time to pick up those who had fallen, but a kind-hearted soldier lad lifted David up, gently laid him under a tree and marched on.

A few hours later, another company came along this same route. In this company was Henry Cowman, David's brother. Henry noticed a soldier boy lying under a tree and he felt irresistibly drawn to step aside to see who it was, and there he recognized him as his own brother. In his canteen was left a cup of water; he pressed it to his brother's lips, life came back, and soon sufficient strength returned to David to enable him to return to his own camp. Thus the life of David Cowman was spared. Was God not planning then for the years ahead when his son would be marching through the mission fields of the Orient?

The fourth year of the war was drawing to a close when there came a glimmer of the dawn of peace; and one glad day there flashed over the wires from one end of the nation to the other, news that thrilled the hearts of all. Peace had been declared. The slaves had been freed. Company G. was ordered home.

Where did David Cowman go first of all upon his return? To the Keyes' home, most certainly, where his own dear mother and Mary were waiting to welcome him. Mary's father had given his consent to their early marriage and in the lovely month of September, the twenty-first day, 1865, David Cowman led Mary Keyes to the marriage altar.

It was a glorious autumn day, the maples were turning red and gold, a touch of Indian summer was in the air, peace brooded over hill and vale, and they were supremely happy. Was there ever a lovelier bride in her dress of soft grey, with its trim fitting bodice and sleeves of lace? Her skirt measured six full yards around the bottom and added to it was a fluting and a shirring, every stitch having been taken by the bride herself. How often, sitting by the fire-light with hands clasped in her lap, has "Mother Cowman," as she has been that to the writer for forty-one years, described that wonderful wedding day, sixty-three years ago, recounting the way the day was spent, naming the friends who were present, dwelling on the beautiful traits of her young husband and recalling to mind the new home where they began life together.

Their first home near Toulon, Illinois, was built on a knoll overlooking the hills and woodland meadows where in the early dawn the thrushes sang their sweetest songs. A brook ran close by and it was a picturesque spot. During the winter months David taught school and in the summertime he took care of the farm.

On August 1, 1866, "Our Mary" held in her arms a baby girl whom they named Cora Esther. Everybody loved the wee infant which had deep black eyes and delicate features. Their joy was complete when on March 13, 1868, there was given to them a little black-eyed son, whom they named Charles Elmer Cowman. The day of his birth seemed for awhile likely to prove the day of his death, for the evidences of animation were so slight, and the care which the mother required so absorbing, that the little infant was laid aside as dead; but soon afterwards, one of the attendants was providentially led to closer examination. A very slight heaving of the chest was observed, there was a low cry, and thus was saved to the world a life which proved to be of such incalculable value.

When he was but two weeks old, the parents took his little life and laid it in God's arms, dedicating him to His service. In that hour they claimed promises, writing his name across the best of them, and looked out into the darkness not knowing what the future held for him.

How often "Our Mary" would steal over to that little wooden cradle, gently lift the snowy cover and show the sleeping face of her baby to the neighbors who had dropped in for a call. In the hours of twilight when all alone, she would pray, "Oh, God, help my boy to grow up to be a good and useful man!"

"God oft hath a large share in a little house," runs the proverb, and His share was in that humble home, snugly nestled away in the cradle bed. His lullabies were old-fashioned hymns. As far back as they could trace, his ancestry, on both the father's and the mother's side, were virtuous and Christian people. Who shall estimate the value of such a pedigree? There were no lords or baronets in their ancestral line. None wore stars or crests, but behind him lay generations of clean and hardy living; in his veins ran the blood of men and women who had met life with stout hearts. They walked, their feet in the furrows, their heads among the stars. Beliefs were to them what houses and lands, bonds and stocks, are to some of their descendants, tangible possessions. By them they took hold of Heaven and swung it close to earth, until this life became its ante-chamber. Unseen, they stood about the cradle of little Charles Cowman, these alert, vigorous people of his race, and gave gifts to the child. What had been their own they gave to him,—a sound body, a dauntless spirit, a venturesome mind. In his hand were placed resourcefulness and courage. What greater gifts could they have brought? In the completed human history, heredity must be counted with environment. They had filled their place as pioneers and their dependence upon God, developed in the face of such conditions, laid the foundation for the character that is found in this book. They dreamed dreams, they saw visions. One of the early country orators said with much emotion as he stood in the open giving an address to the pioneers, "I have no doubt that somewhere in the wilds of this western land, whispering through the chinks of some log cabin, the wind is ruffling the curls upon the brow of a future son of fame."

How many homes, though seemingly insignificant, have furnished the background for some of the greatest moments of life, the turning point in the history of human events. "The mill stream that turns the world rises in solitary places."

Obscurity of birth is no obstacle to a life of noble service. Show us a list of men who have distinguished themselves in one department or another of philanthropy, literature, science, or art; of men who have proved to be the benefactors of their race; of men who have shone in the pulpit, or at the bar, or in the senate-house; and I will venture to say that no inconsiderable proportion of these sprang from a lowly level.

Dr. A. M. Hills once said: "Nothing is more remarkable than the surprising places in which God finds His great men, but it has been so throughout all ages. When God wanted to find the greatest king that ever sat on Israel's throne, the world's poet laureate, He passed by the city palaces and the families of the titled and the great, and all the stately brothers, and went out into the sheep pasture of a Bethlehem farmer. His mother was so unknown as never to have perpetuated her name. Even the prophetic vision of Samuel would have missed him. His own brothers saw nothing whatever of hope or promise in him, and rebuked him sharply for leaving the few sheep in the wilderness to visit the army. Not a soul dimly conjectured that the immortal giant-killer, the teacher of psalmody to our race, and the kingliest spirit his nation ever would produce stood before them.

"When the chosen people of God had touched the darkest hour of national backsliding, and the king and queen and courtiers had all forsaken the Lord, and none would speak for Him because of terror, it was then that God, hunting for a real hero to lift Jehovah's standard, one who would dare to rebuke crowned iniquity, and brave the wrath of the monster Jezebel, passed all the schools of the prophets, all the robed priests and Levites, and all the princes of the people, and found His man 'in the obscurity of the mountain village,' east of Jordan—'Elijah the Tishbite.' Here was a man who was to lock up and unlock the skies, slay the false prophets, and be the mouthpiece to a guilty nation of the God that answered by fire.

"And when this majestic character was approaching his translation, and must select his successor, nobody but God would have told him to pass all the sons of greatness and the men of renown, and select, as the great miracle-worker, the counselor of kings, and the guide of a nation's destiny, 'Elisha the plowman.'

"This same wonder-working God, whose ways are above ours as the heavens are above the earth, and who never sees as man sees, passed by all the strong and the great and the promising, and elected to a delicate and difficult mission 'Amos, the herdsman of Tekoa, and the gatherer of sycamore fruit.'

"Who but God would have ignored the claims of the titled and noble-born kings and princes of modern Europe, and passed unnoticed all the seats of learning and the heirs of power and wealth and culture, and would have gone to the miner's hut of a German peasant to find a boy who would throw all Europe into ferment, and make popes tremble, and launch upon the world a new civilization, a renewed Christianity, and all the tremendous forces of the Reformation? Modern progress, civil and religious liberty, and the teeming impulses of the foremost of all history came from that peasant hut where God found Martin Luther.

"This is not unusual; indeed it is almost the customary method of God in finding His most distinguished servants. If the wisest and the most far-seeing men in all America had been put to the work of discovering the birthplace of the child who should become the future president of the greatest Republic on earth, the greatest genius and the most unique character of all the presidents, the only one who would be the companion and peer of Washington in the enduring esteem of mankind, no one would have thought of the comfortless log hut, with its dirt floor, in the hills of Kentucky—the hut in which Lincoln was born. All these cases and thousands more that might be named, are God's surprises in history. He loves to laugh at human pomp and pride, and set at naught our calculations, and bring the unexpected to pass."

When the Lord has a great work to accomplish He frequently makes use of a very humble instrument that no flesh should glory in His presence.

"Thank God! a man can grow!
He is not bound
With earthward gaze to creep along the ground:
Though his beginnings be but poor and low,
Thank God! a man can grow!"

CHAPTER II

A BOY'S LIFE IN THE WEST

The training of youth for the battle of life is one of the most blessed ministries of parents. David and Mary Cowman expected to make the training of their children the supreme business of their lives and they began early to lay plans for their future. They prayed for divine guidance lest in their own planning they should make a mistake. Should they move to the city where the children could have educational advantages? Might the allurements and attractions be more than they would be able to resist? They knew that Satan would lay many a trap for their growing girl and boy and they recognized the need of having a Divine Guide. When, therefore, the way seemed clear to them, they moved to another place which afforded better advantages, but still kept them in the great open country during their formative years. In later years when taking a retrospect, how truly could they testify that "the kind hand of our God was upon us and led us in the right way."

"Christ spent His youth with field and hill and tree
And Christ grew up in rural Galilee."

The mother often said, "It was the very best of moves; we brought up our children by themselves and with us, as we never could have done in the city, and so they were saved the dangers and difficulties which they might not have been strong enough to meet."

A strange incident occurred during their journey from Illinois to Iowa, in the springtime of 1870. They arrived one evening at a place on the State Highway, known as the Burd Estate. The large house in a setting of eight hundred acres was a landmark for travelers. Isaac and Margaret Burd, Philadelphians, had also followed the lure many years before, and were among the early settlers "out where the West begins." They were not forgetful to entertain strangers, and David and Mary Cowman, with their two little ones, spent the night under their hospitable roof.

In the Burd home was a baby girl three months old, named Lettie. Little Charles Cowman was just two years of age. Did God whisper to the mothers that night that these two children were destined for each other, or did He keep it a secret until a few years later? Surely it must have been a special providence of God that directed them to that place!

It was the month of May, and the whole countryside was unspeakably beautiful—the fields, the hedgerows, the farms and the cherry trees in full bloom. Wild flowers draped every bank and knoll with beauty. In a picturesque region twenty miles from the Burd Estate, the Cowmans purchased their farm and established their new home. The location was by a river close to a forest and a deep lawn led up to the house. The place was known as "The Cedars" because of those stately trees that bordered the walk. It was a restful looking place. Many kinds of flowers grew in neatly kept beds; over the veranda were festoons of roses and honeysuckle. Back of the house was a fence, which in summertime was buried from sight 'neath the wealth of wild roses and hollyhocks. Back of the garden was an orchard. There was an abundance of pink and white apple blossoms and the breath of the morning was as perfume. Surrounding all were fields of corn, wheat, and meadow-land. Droves of cattle were seen lazily chewing their cud beneath the spreading oaks or maples; the meadow was deep in sweet-scented clover; the woods rang with bird song.

> "And life was sweet! What find we more
> In wearying quest from shore to shore?
> Ah! gracious memory! To restore
> Our golden West, its sun and shower,
> And that gay nest of ours
> Dropped down among the prairie flowers."

The boyhood days of Charles Cowman were spent in this rural magnificence. Isolated indeed, yet the mother had a way of making a homey atmosphere about her, and the parents were like two youthful companions to their children. Together they played, told stories, walked through the meadows, revelling in the beauty of flower, chirping bird, and cloudland. What an environment for a boy!

There was a charm in their mode of living and there was romance even in their surroundings. His great love for nature was doubtlessly implanted in his heart in these early years. How greatly he loved God's great out-of-doors! In later years when on the mission field, his letters home expressed a longing for a tramp in the woods, or an hour by the brook where the water purled over the cool, shadowed rocks. Until the day of his death, the country with its fresh-turned sod, its green fields of waving harvest, had a peculiar charm for his nature-loving soul.

The Cowman family was a component part of the community and their hospitable door had a gracious welcome for friend and stranger. The home had a gracious and far-reaching influence. The "olive plants" were under perpetual care and culture and nothing that would tend to perfect their miniature world was neglected. They reached out toward all the good that was attainable in their surroundings. Fortunate indeed were the children in being born into a home where there was neither poverty nor riches, so that they did not have the temptations of either.

To a community school more than a mile from the home, the two children would trudge along through the forest and across the ravine which had a log for a foot-bridge, making friends with the rabbits and squirrels, enticing them with crumbs saved from their lunch basket. On their return home they were allowed to spend some time looking for the hiding place of their favorite flowers, and great was their delight when they would carry a bouquet to their mother who was waiting at the doorway for them.

The father watched their progress in school with the same vigilance that he gave to his crops and herds. Every night they were examined in their studies and the parents of these two God-given little ones anticipated their development with as great an interest as a horticulturist gives to his rarest flowers.

Charles was a normal boy in every way, full of life and energy. An outlet for the overflowing life was found in helping his father with the work of the farm, doing chores, chopping wood, feeding chickens, and many other tasks. Undoubtedly this early discipline of work was wholesome for him, as it left neither time nor energy for mischief.

He was a hard working little boy and learned to fling the flail with the threshers in the barn, turn his swathe with the mowers in the field, and pitch hay with the hay-makers. Out in the freshness where things grew silently he was taught the worth of noiseless work, seeing to it that he never mistook clamor for force.

He relished with keen zest sports in God's great out-of-doors. What human gardener ever equaled the Divine in arranging a boy's playground in the pure air, under God's open sky, among the blossoming trees, singing birds and bumble bees, and down in the meadow by the brook? Who would not envy a childhood which left such memories?

Charles was a lad of character, endowed with high pressure, energy, and fire, capable of projecting his whole soul into any enterprise he undertook. Although much smaller in stature than his schoolmates, he was the acknowledged leader. It was he who planned the games and made the suggestions that others carried out. He led the way, but did it in such a selfless manner that his fellow schoolmates scarcely knew that they were being led, a gift of inestimable value for a leader.

Mental thoroughness early characterized him. Truthfulness and sincerity were part of his character; one could never connect him with any sham or subterfuge. There was a genuineness about him that everybody felt and he was trusted and loved. He was a thoroughly conscientious and noble-hearted boy; and as a child, Charles Cowman was what he was as a man, modest, capable, faithful, unselfish, conscientious, and entirely dependable.

In reckoning a man's present, a thousand past conditions and influences must be taken into consideration. Religious training was given first place to the children in those days and nothing was permitted to interfere with church duties. When Sabbath day came every one went to church, and it was never a debatable question whether Charles would go or remain at home. The world is languishing today for the old-time regime of parental authority. There was a very decided element of reverence and religion in the pioneer. Many thought nothing of walking five miles to attend Sabbath services.

The winters were bitterly cold, snow drifted the roadways, but the Cowmans seldom missed a service even when the thermometer registered many degrees below zero. The church which they attended was known as "The Centenary Methodist." It was a plain frame building painted white, and on the top was a belfry. Every fortnight a preacher of the old type came to hold services. He was filled with the Holy Spirit and tears would run down his cheeks while he preached, and a holy unction inspired his very tones. This made a lasting impression on the children.

The preacher usually accompanied them home for dinner, spending the afternoon in holy conversation, then in the evening all would walk back again to the services. The Cowman home was known throughout the country as a haven for the early circuit riders. There was about these itinerant preachers such a unique personality that they commanded reverence and an appreciation found nowhere else in Protestantism, and they who were permitted to entertain such men of God felt honored. These gracious influences became a rich endowment.

The life of this farmer boy might have been considered hard, but it gave to him vigor, strength, and courage. Moreover, life presented itself under this regime as something regular and fixed, with no uncertainties. It was settled that he labor, study, attend church, and enjoy certain pastimes. His elders had no uncertainties. They knew what they wanted, freely expressed it, struggled for it, obtained it.

David Cowman was a Methodist classleader, and during the week as the neighbors gathered in the different homes, for prayer, testimony, and reading the Scriptures, God met them in a gracious manner. The Bible was read daily in that humble country home. This early reading took Charles back and forth through the Bible several times, printing on his alert and impressionable mind a knowledge of the Book such as practically no child receives today. Before he was able to pronounce the long names, he had read the Gospels through and had committed many portions to memory. The large family Bible held something of reverence and awe and when it was taken down to be read, all play ceased and the children sat listening quietly.

Early impressions are the most enduring and lasting shape and trend are often given to human lives while children are yet in their infancy. A mother's prayers, a father's faith, the Christian atmosphere of the home, the place the Bible holds in the family, are vital influences in child training. The child who is taught to read the whole Bible, will be furnished, when he reaches manhood, with a complete armory of weapons with which to resist the devil. Half a century later the impressions made upon Charles Cowman through these influences had not left his mind.

When he was about ten years of age there was a rumor that a farmer living twenty miles distant had been to the city and, bringing home a keg of liquor, had become intoxicated. What consternation it caused! It was talked of in every home. The children were greatly excited as they listened to the comments made by their elders. Frequent references were made to this farmer's drunkenness. Sabbath school scholars were often strongly warned against the deadly drink. Around the family altars the parents prayed that their children might ever resist the temptation to taste the deadly poison. Is it any wonder that in later years when they were called upon to take their stand on the side of temperance, they voted one hundred percent for prohibition?

"Never go into debt" was an adage of the Cowman household. They adhered to it strictly because they

dreaded it as much as a contagious disease. Looking back
on those days, we can trace without difficulty the elements
of character that made his maturer life remarkable.

"This is not a world of chance or happen-so; behind
the heralded deeds of every man—such as have made
history and shaped the policies of men—there can be seen
in the dim background the shadow of *some one else,* or
something else."

It was the parents of Charles Cowman who implanted
in his heart the ideals that guided his life. A godly par-
entage is a precious boon; its blessing not only rests upon
the children of the first family, but has often been traced
to many successive generations.

David Cowman, the father of Charles, was a man of
few words. One of the things his son never could forget
was the father's utter sincerity and hatred of everything
mean and underhanded. He was the very soul of honor
and expected as much from everybody else.

The mother was the mainspring of his life. They were
great companions and it was in the heart-to-heart talks
between the young mother and son, that the foundation of
his character was laid. She had a power to draw her
children to her as the moon draws the tides. She seemed
to draw out all that was chivalrous and manly in a boy's
nature. Faithfulness, courtesy, and friendliness reappear-
ed in her son.

When one inquires into the life of a child, he must
take note of the mother who, more than any other on
earth, shapes infancy and adolescence into worthy manhood. Among the teeming ranks of the glorified, what
a special place in the van of the great army should be
assigned to Christian mothers! How many names would
we miss in the roll of Christian heroes but for them!

ABOVE—THE COWMAN FAMILY. FATHER, MOTHER, AND SISTER (1901).
CENTER—MOTHER COWMAN AT SEVENTY-EIGHT. CHARLES AT FIFTEEN
    AND FORTY-FIVE.
BELOW—THE LAD OF FIVE SUMMERS

There are two classes of women whom the Romans loved to honor—the few virgins who devoted themselves in perpetual virginity to keeping alive the vestal fires, and the mothers of heroes. When the lives of great men are written and Charles Cowman's name stands upon those pages, it will be the mother who made him what he was for the cause of Christ and humanity, who will stand emblazoned in the forefront of the army. To have given the world such a son is greater than to have conquered kingdoms.

Eight very happy years were spent in this home of the West. Although there had been numerous kinds of hardships and trials, these had been passed through victoriously. Life bloomed fair with cherished hopes. God had entrusted to their keeping another little child, a sweet baby named Lillian. Charles was exceedingly fond of her, and loved to carry her about in his strong arms, or sit by her cradle while he rocked her to sleep.

She was taken ill, suddenly, one day, when but a little over a year old. The family doctor was hastily summoned. After a careful diagnosis he beckoned the father from the room. When he returned his lips were pale, and his face ashen. The parents, grief-stricken, knelt by the little sufferer, imploring God to spare her life, but they remembered that she had only been loaned to them and He had a right to take her to the Home for little children above the bright blue sky. What did these God-fearing parents say? "His will be done! Let Him take what He will in His own royal way," and as a little lamb they laid her in the arms of the Good Shepherd.

A few days of anxious waiting and helpless watching followed, and then Lillian lay in her little white casket in the front room like a beautiful block of marble. Comfort came to the hearts of the parents as He whispered,

"She was Mine before she was thine, follow Me and thou shalt find thy treasure in Heaven." So the shaft of Heaven's glory seemed to fall on that silent crib and the sweet child was no longer dead, but sleeping.

> "We give thee back thy loan, Oh Lord,
> And praise thee while we weep."

When they carried her body away to the cemetery, Charles' heart was well nigh broken and he wept unconsolably beside the newly-made grave. *Why* had the God of love taken from them the one whom they loved so tenderly? Was He good to have done such a thing? How God can hurt where He loves was a puzzle to him. Rebellion rose in his young heart, but he kept it hidden, not daring to tell his dear mother. The summertime dragged by with its long, sad, and lonely days. No longer was the bird song sweet to his ears; the flowers had no message, earth seemed swept and desolate. The wintertime came with its bleak, bare, cold days, making the wound even deeper.

One Sabbath morning the Methodist preacher announced to his congregation that he expected to begin a revival meeting in their church. He asked that all the families pray especially for their children, so that every one of them might be brought into the fold. There was very little outbreaking sin in the community, but the preacher said, "We need an awakening."

These old-time preachers possessed a limited education, but they knew God, and the Bible plan of salvation was presented in a manner that even a child could understand. How very fortunate is the person who is reared in a community where the old-time mourner's bench is not a relic of by-gone days, an out-of-date, antiquated sort of thing. There can be no substitute for the altar of prayer, or a broken and contrite heart.

One night at the conclusion of the sermon, while the congregation was singing, "Come ye sinners poor and needy, weak and wounded, sick and sore," Charles Cowman, without persuasion, left his seat and walked down to the mourner's bench and wept out his sorrow. The imprint of that service remained on his spirit to the day of his death. Into his young heart stole a ray of light, and he seemed to see the Good Shepherd walking through the green pastures, while upon His arm He bore a little lamb. His kindly words quieted all the fears, as He said, "It is well with thy sister. We had need of her in the many mansions where she is adding new delight, and some day you will meet her again."

And as He spoke these comforting words there came into his heart a strange peace and resignation, a sunburst of light and revelation. He learned that not in cruelty, not in wrath, but in love, had He transplanted their loved one to a sunnier clime, where no rude blasts ever come. From that moment he thought of baby Lillian as being in the King's palace garden. On the way home that bitter winter night he sang for joy. The terrible tempest that had raged in his young heart was forever stilled.

The revival was thought by many to have been a failure as only one boy had been converted; but how little they realized what the conversion of that lad of thirteen would mean to thousands of heathen. How little did any one of that community dream that he would some day become a missionary and the founder of one of the greatest evangelizing forces on earth!

"A Hand
Always above my shoulder pushed me."—R. Browning.

CHAPTER III

BREAKING HOME-TIES

The years of his childhood were passing. The fledglings had outgrown their sheltered retreat. David and Mary Cowman realized that another change was inevitable. Charles had passed his fifteenth year and was in need of advanced schooling. Quite unconsciously an unseen Hand was leading him forward. Truly a Hand, other than his, was at the helm and the eternal forces had his life-plan in their mighty onward sweep. Another home was established, but how little did the parents dream of the changes that would occur during the months which were to follow.

There came to the town where they moved, a young telegraph operator. He was a winsome youth, one educated above his fellows. A warm friendship very soon sprang up between the two lads and Charles spent many an hour in the telegraph office, fascinated by the click of the instruments. During vacation he studied telegraphy with no thought whatever of anything but pastime. He never meant to make it his profession, but when he was able in several months, to send and receive messages and dispatch trains, the temptation became very strong to accept a position which had been offered him at a railway station some miles from home. He begged his parents to permit him to accept it until the opening of the autumn term of school. Very reluctantly they gave their consent and the boy of fifteen cut loose from his moorings and started out upon an unknown sea. This was a marked turning point which affected his entire life.

It was the first time that he had ever been away from home for a night and his parents were very anxious about him, fearing that he would fall asleep while on duty and allow the trains to pass by; but this wide-awake lad never slept at his post. Because of his youth he became quickly known from one end of the line to another as "the boy operator." The trainmen loved him, and the oldest conductors of the road said they had never met a more promising lad.

It was a new world in which he now lived; his boyhood days seemed ended and before him was the hard, serious business of life—the training school for the still greater days ahead. When autumn came, he had no desire to return to school, but he pursued his studies with an eagerness and interest that never waned. All times of transition are crises. The old is broken up, but what the new shall be is ours, under God, to determine.

Was it a grave mistake that he never returned to school? Who can think so in his particular case? When we see a person making such an outstanding success as did Charles Cowman, it were folly to wish that he had been a collegebred man.

A reminiscence of the writer's girlhood days will be pardoned. How true it is that all the ten thousand crossings and touchings of human paths have a divine purpose in them. There is no chance in this world. The smallest thing in our lives, the seemingly least important incidents are included in our Father's plan, in His care for us. "It chanced—eternal God, that chance did guide." again, God made our paths to cross—his and mine. My childhood home, the "Burd Estate," was a short distance from the village. One day my mother went to the village and on her return home said, "I met a dear lad today. He had such a frank, open countenance, but there was an air of loneliness about him and I thought he must be away from his home and parents for the first time. When I spoke to him I found that it was even so. His name is Charles Cowman and he is the night operator at the railway station. I invited him to the house, as I feel that he needs a little bit of mothering."

I was but a mere school girl, had just passed my thirteenth birthday. The village school was separated from my home by a small lake and a deep, rolling meadow. Morning and evening I had to cross the steps of the railway station to reach the roadway leading to our gate. Often Charles would accompany me home, opening the heavy meadow gates, and upon mother's invitation, would remain to evening tea. A warm welcome was found in our home and a great deal of his spare time was spent there when away from his office. We learned much of his boyhood and my mother was delighted to know that he was the boy who had spent the night with his parents and sister in this home some thirteen years before. A lifelong friendship sprung up between his family and mine.

The pupils of Madame Barnhart were giving a musical entertainment at the Methodist church in our village. I was her pupil and had a part on the program. Nearly every girl whose name was on the program, had a brother about her own age; mine were all grown up. The brothers were to accompany their sisters to the church and march down the aisle with them to the platform. Several days before the entertainment I received a brief note which read as follows:

"Miss Lettie Burd,

"May I have the privilege of accompanying you to the concert on Friday evening?

"Yours sincerely, Charles Cowman."

To this, mother gave her consent. The evening came, the church was filled to its limit, and down the aisle marched the pupils led by Madame Barnhart. Charles and myself followed immediately behind her. My dress was snowy white and I carried an armful of roses. Something whispered to mother at that moment, "Somewhere through the coming years, your little girl will be walking down the aisle with that boy to the marriage altar."

Some weeks later, a promotion was offered to Charles and he was transferred from the small station to a divisional center many miles away. As quickly as he received the news he came at once to tell my mother, but he told me something else. Our parents smiled at our childhood romance, but made no objection. From the first time we met we were sweethearts and to the last breath he drew, we were sweethearts still.

A year passed when another promotion was offered to him and when he was but seventeen he was occupying the position of train dispatcher at one of the largest divisional centers of the Burlington Railway. At eighteen he was transferred to Chicago, to fill a still more important position in the Railroad Office of the same company. One promotion followed another in rapid succession and he began climbing the ladder of success. At nineteen he was receiving the same salary as the employees who had been in the service for many years.

When Sabbath came, without any other thought, he went to church, just as he had been taught; but the great city congregation seemed entirely different from the humble village meeting-house, where all were acquainted with one another. He missed the familiar faces and the cordial manner of his former church friends. Again and again he listened to the same sweet gospel hymns, the same gospel story, but not finding the interest his young heart craved, he returned to his lodging with a touch of genuine homesickness. After a time his work kept him at his desk on Sabbath days, and little by little church attendance was neglected. This soon drifted into indifference, and the voice of God died out in his soul.

Temptations were present in his life as in the lives of other young men. The city streets were full of allure-ments, and companions were ever ready to lead him into forbidden paths; however, his early training, the example and prayers of father and mother, and the overshadowing mercy of God prevented his young life from being blighted. Many sought his companionship and tried to induce him to follow them into questionable amusements. Numbers had come from sheltered homes, just as he, but away from the godly influence they had given up church attendance and had fallen away entirely. He saw many of his young fellow-workers, ignorant of the ways of the world, wreck their lives through debauchery and drink. He resolved to keep away from them; and how graciously was he preserved from the sins of youth! He was living in an entirely new world; new experiences were the lot of the boy away from home. To be steadfast in such surroundings and under such influences, calls for the stuff of which martyrs are made.

There is no stronger force in a man's life than the memory of home and mother like that which belonged to Charles Cowman. He who has it, let him daily thank God for this incomparable blessing. It is an anchor to wind-ward, holding him fast whatever storms may arise or winds blow. The realization that he belonged to a family whose escutcheon has never been stained has held many a young man firm in the hour of testing.

The temptations which surrounded the young man of nineteen in the large city caused his parents much anxiety.

When a call came to him to accept the position as manager of the Western Union Telegraph Office at Glenwood Springs, Colorado, a lovely watering place in the heart of the Rockies, they strongly advised the change. He accepted the offered position.

But even there, he found himself in a strange environment which would have tested and tried many an older person. His dealings were chiefly with mining officials who gambled with mining stock losing and gaining fortunes overnight. These men admired the accuracy and carefulness with which the steady young telegraph operator handled their business. Often a bill would be slipped into his hand by men who wished to see some private telegrams which would have let them into the secret of the daily market, but the bill was quietly refused by this honest young man. Money considerations were not allowed to influence him in any way, although it might have become a great attraction and a snare, but he had no love for money. He lived in modest lodgings and from his monthly salary laid aside sufficient funds with which to purchase a home.

He remained in this position until his twenty-first birthday. On June 8, 1889, our childhood dream was realized, and a honeymoon began which increased in joy and love, lasting for thirty-six years.

Our first home was in the heart of the Rockies, where we lived for several years. It seemed that for us Heaven had begun. We were ideally happy together; but God whose ways are as much higher than our ways, as the Heavens are higher than the earth, had to stir up that cozy nest—that His purpose for the future might be carried out. The altitude proved too high for me, and several times it looked as if life itself would flicker out. Once a doctor was hastily summoned and memory will ever carry a picture of my loving young husband kneeling by my bedside, while the doctor tried to find my feeble pulse. How earnestly he prayed, "Oh, God, spare her life. Remember the boy who used to pray!" God did hear and He did restore. A change of altitude was necessary and he was granted a transfer back to the city of Chicago.

"The world's wealth is in its original men. By these and their works, it is a world and not a waste. Their memory and their record are its sacred property forever."—*Carlyle*.

CHAPTER IV

BEGINNING LIFE IN A NEW SETTING

"Thou camest not to thy place by accident,
It is the very place God meant for thee."

We shall have to pause here and penetrate below the surface of his life and surroundings, in order to understand God's workings and some of the details of His purpose, when He is forming a vessel for His special service.

The following is the story of the ten years of providential preparation for his life-work, and we shall see that God does not equip us for our work all at once, but trains His workmen in various ways, often in a very wide school.

These ten years were spent in the telegraph office in Chicago. They worked together for the last twenty-five which stand apart as the crowning years, "the last of life for which the first was made." The work then done demanded quality of mind and heart, insight, knowledge of character, and much besides which could not have been otherwise acquired. They were so ordinary in appearance, so commonplace, that one would have little dreamed them to be years which the world pauses to look at. One of the interesting things of the biography will be the tracing of the matchless hand of God, shaping this chosen vessel, and many doubtless will say, "Who but God could have formed it?"

We are fond of the saying that God can thrash a mountain with a worm. So He can, when it is necessary,

4

but there is nothing more certain than that He has always chosen great men for great work, not always what the world calls great, but those great in character and in Christlikeness. History reveals the fact that He has not placed pigmies in high places, nor appointed them to the leadership of great movements. Moses was a man of majestic mold whose personality, after thousands of years, still towers among the lordliest leaders of the centuries.

Martin Luther, John Knox, John Wesley, and Lincoln did not belong to the pigmy, but to the giant class. "The fiat of fate falls on the fittest." God lays His hand on those who are best prepared for His purposes, using every man and woman for just as great a work as their preparation will make possible. But may we ever keep in mind that this preparation is not always found in colleges or great universities.

His whole heart was thrown into his work and thoroughness was one of the most prominent elements of his character. What he did, he did with all his might. The position he occupied as Chief of the New York Division required a man of steady nerve and more than ordinary self-control.

The first year spent in Chicago proved to be one of great success. His new acquaintances among fellow-telegraphers numbered into hundreds, from officials to messengers. His genial manner and happy smile had won for him a place in their hearts. He was admired for his ability and loved by all. The sterling qualities which he exhibited and his considerate treatment of the men increased his popularity, and he held a power over them that did not consist of brawn or muscle. He permitted many of them to share some of the problems which often confronted him.

Life in the city held many attractions and one of the most alluring was the Grand Opera. Charles Cowman and wife, both lovers of music were often to be found in attendance. The fascinating entertainments were taking a firm hold upon their hearts and they drifted on with the multitudes who were walking in the broad way. But what of Christ's claim upon their hearts? What of the vow he had made to God when he prayed for the restoration of his loved one? His pen shall tell the story. Friends had asked him for the story of his life and shortly before the Home-call an attempt was made to write some of it but it was never completed. There are stray bits, however, and under the heading, "The Backslider's Return" are these lines.

"It is necessary here to relate first the conversion of my dear wife, who through a quarter of a century of Christian life has been my closest companion, beloved help-meet, and 'fellow-helper to the truth.' Our lives were thrown together providentially from early childhood, and when she was nineteen and I was of age, we were married, beginning life together. I had drifted away from God and from my earliest religious training, and both of us, after our marriage, were thrown into worldly society and continued therein until 1891, when I was transferred because of her illness to the Chicago Telegraph office, where I became traffic chief and later wire chief of the New York Division.

"Life went on much the same until one night shortly before Christmas, in 1893, a Christian worker called at our home inviting us to a meeting which was to be held for children in one of the churches of the neighborhood. A converted opera singer was to speak and sing. My wife, being interested in music, accepted the invitation. She attended the service and heard the noted lady sing.

" 'There were ninety and nine that safely lay
    In the shelter of the fold;
But one was out on the hills away
    Far off from the gates of gold.'

"It was like the singing of Paul and Silas in the jail at midnight and was accompanied by a spiritual earthquake which rent her heart from its worldly satisfaction. She went to the altar with a number of children and gave her heart to Christ. The change which immediately followed was a great surprise to me, for she at once separated herself from the world and testified that she was genuinely converted. She began dealing with me, but I told her that living a Christian life in a telegraph office was an utter impossibility; however her prayers and continued exhortations were rewarded by my conversion one month later.

"She became a member of Grace Methodist Church, which had a membership of six hundred, the majority being people of her own age. A revival meeting was in progress and she begged me to accompany her there on a Sabbath evening. Rev. Henry Ostrom was the evangelist. While he preached, there arose out of the misty past a vision of an old mourner's bench and revival scenes out in the dear open country, the remembrance of the blessed experience that had come to me, and of the tender way God had comforted my heart when but a lad. I thought of this one and that one who had gotten up out of his seat and with face aglow with that wonderful light that is not seen on sea or shore, had given their testimony to some blessed experience, and there came into my heart a deep, unutterable yearning to make it my own.

"Uppermost in my mind was the time when the life of my loved one had been spared through my humble prayer, and when I promised the Lord that if He would restore her I would henceforth serve Him. What of that unfulfilled vow? I could not lift up my head. Wife had invited me to accompany her to the altar, but I said, 'Not tonight,' and had stoutly refused her. That of itself almost broke my heart for we were rare lovers, and I could have readily laid down my life for her; but she left the pew where we were sitting and took her place with the newly converted who stood in one long line at the front of the pulpit. I felt absolutely alone without her as a great gulf seemed forever fixed between us and my heart was broken. But there arose in my mind the telegraph office with its associations, the place I occupied, and my future career. A battle raged, but peace tarried. How truly had I reached 'the place called Calvary.'

"A Voice seemed to say, 'Trust Jesus, surrender to Him, and let go,' but there was no power to do so. After the service closed, we started home. Being under deep conviction I could not utter a word but broke out in sobs. We walked twelve blocks, hastily entered our apartment, and without taking time to turn on the lights, we knelt by a chair and there I poured out my confession to God, asking Him to take back the prodigal. My dear wife, but a month old Christian, did her best to point me to the Saviour, and soon the blessed Spirit witnessed with my spirit that the past was all under the blood and that I was His child once more. The wanderer had returned to His Father's house. What joy was mine! Peace came flooding my heart and I wished to tell the world that Jesus had saved me. It was like a blissful new wedding day, for now I was able to walk by the side of my loved one, Homeward together."

And shall the writer ever forget that hour? The room became glorious with the presence of God. Charles Cowman's face was like that of Moses when he came down

from the Mount; joy and gladness too deep for words
filled his heart. The Spirit of God gave him such a witness, so real, so abiding, that for thirty-six years, amidst
all the testings and buffetings, it held him firm as the Rock
of Ages. In after years when he visited Chicago he
wished to go at once to the spot where Jesus had so wondrously revealed Himself to him, welcoming him home
to His fold.

It was a new and wonderful world that dawned with
the coming of the morning light, for old things had passed
away and all things had become new. He was converted
through and through, and the change in him was marked
because it was so radical. His first question to his newly
discovered Lord was that of Paul, "What wilt thou have
me to do?" Nay, that was his constant inquiry from the
day of his conversion onward; and the record of his life is
the record of his obedience to the directions which, in
response to that inquiry, he was constantly receiving.

He made it the *first thing* in his life to be a Christian,
feeling that if he would fulfil his discipleship, he must
concentrate all of his energy and strength upon it. It was
quickly noised about in the telegraph office that Charles
Cowman had become a Christian and there he stood, quite
alone, among the hundreds of men for whom he felt God
would hold him personally responsible. Having now come
into a place of victory and blessing in his own life, he was
anxious that his fellow-telegraphers should enter the
enjoyment of a similar triumph. Applied Christianity was
the track along which the energy of his nature was driven
by the Divine Spirit.

Immediately he began witnessing for Christ; conviction seized a number of his men and he became a soul-
winner from the day of his conversion. He knew practically nothing about dealing with seekers and when they

came to him with their questions, some under the deepest conviction for sin, others filled with doubts, wondering if they were included in "whosoever will," he would say to them, "Go home and pray," as there was no place for quiet in an office where hundreds of instruments were clicking continuously. Many came to him with difficult questions regarding the Scripture, and he found himself in a strange parish which would have troubled many an older and more experienced Christian.

The questions asked were written down in a notebook and he would go into his small study on his return from the office and, taking his Bible from the desk, would search for hours, often away into the early morning, to find a Scriptural answer. Methinks there was rejoicing in heaven as the angels bent over that earnest young soul. He learned from practical experience the value of the Word of God, and the following evening his seekers would find an answer to their questions in a word of Scripture. It was God's own Word and therefore could not fail.

An old fisherman, from long experience, knows just how to bait his hook, but Charles Cowman's knowledge of the Bible was limited to what he had been taught as a child; and where to begin and how to lead a soul to Christ appeared to him one of the most difficult of problems. Did not the Master say, "Follow Me, and *I will make you to become fishers of men?*" Difficulties fall before determined men, and this one, like a Jericho wall, needed to be marched around and taken, so the first thing he did was to begin reading the Word, ever keeping in mind that if he was called upon to speak to his men about divine things, he must have a knowledge of it himself. He had no one to guide him and was quite ignorant of the fact that there were splendid books on the subject of "Personal Evangelism" which would have been helpful for the time; but he struggled on alone, praying, reading, looking to the Lord to guide and direct him.

In the after-years when called upon to address assemblies of Christian workers and Bible students on the subject of "Soul-winning," in response to their earnest inquiry "How shall we do personal work?" he would invariably say, "Just begin and do it and let the method unfold of itself."

His first attempt to win a soul is a never-to-be-forgotten one. He went to his office one evening as usual with the determination to speak to some of his men that night about their souls' welfare. The operators had been at work at their respective wires for several hours when there came a lull which he interpreted as his opportunity for dealing with some soul.

In one corner of the long room sat a man at his desk, who apparently had a few spare moments. Back and forth through the length of the room he walked before he could summon up enough courage to speak to him. Finally the effort was made and for half an hour he stood beside his desk, engaged in a one-sided conversation. Doubtless this young man was astonished to find someone talking to him about his soul, as he never made a reply.

Charles Cowman left his office that night feeling downhearted over his first attempt at winning a soul; but the following night when he returned home, almost the first words he said were these: "Oh, I have something wonderful to tell you! The young man with whom I talked last night, came to me just as soon as I entered the office, saying, 'I went home last night after our conversation and did just what you told me. It is all settled and I gave myself to Christ.'"

The name of the young man was Ernest A. Kilbourne. The joy over that one soul was as great as that of an evangelist who has led hundreds to Christ during some special campaign.

On that day Charles Cowman and Ernest Kilbourne began a lifelong friendship and Christian partnership. Their hearts were knit together. He had the unique experience of leading to Christ his colleague and successor before he himself had left his native land for those romantic scenes amidst which his subsequent years were spent.

His heart was greatly encouraged through finding this one soul, so the next night he waxed bold and talked to another telegrapher who had once been an earnest Christian, but who, since coming to the Chicago telegraph office, had drifted away from God. Had he known how to deal with backsliders and how to have given them the right texts of Scripture he would have been happy, but he was devoid of such knowledge.

Murray McCheyne once said, "It is not so much great talent, or knowledge that God blesses, as likeness to Himself. Therefore love, divine love for God and man, and entire dependence upon the power of the Holy Spirit are the great essentials."

His men were dear to him, he loved them and they knew it. It was love that won Robert Fisher back to God that night. He also had a part to play in the future of the Oriental Missionary Society. Two souls had been won for the Master in less than a week. What encouragement from so little effort! His soul took fire from that very week and he became a soul-winner of the rarest and most original type. When God can grip a man, He always makes him a missionary, a witness, an ambassador, and a winner of souls, and this he made of Charles Cowman. In his business-like manner he began a systematic effort

to win his men, recognizing that men are not saved in
bundles, but *one by one*. There has never been any im-
provement on the methods used in Apostolic times. Philip
finds his man and the work spreads in Samaria and elsewhere. A Christian's best work is personal, and as Henry
Drummond has written: "The true worker's world is the
unit. Recognize the personal glory and dignity of the
unit as an agent. Work with units, but, above all, work *at*
units. But the capacity of acting upon individuals is now
almost a lost art. It is hard to learn again. We have
spoiled ourselves by thinking to draw thousands by public
work—by what people call 'pulpit eloquence,' by platform
speeches, and by convocations and councils, Christian conferences, and by books of many editions. We have been
painting Madonnas and *Ecce Homos* and choirs of angels,
like Raphael, and it is hard to condescend to the beggar
boy or Murillo. Yet we must begin again and begin far
down. *Christianity began with One*. We have forgotten
the simple way of the Founder of the greatest influence the
world has ever seen—how He ran away from cities, how
He shirked mobs, how He lagged behind the rest at
Samaria to have a quiet talk with *one woman* at a well,
how He stole away from crowds and entered into the
house of one humble Syro-Phoenician woman, 'and would
have no man know it.' In small groups of twos and
threes, He collected the early church around Him. One by
one the disciples were called—and there were only twelve
in all."

Charles Cowman made opportunities to speak to his
men about their souls' welfare. He did not wait for a con-
venient season, but prayed and made an advance toward
them. He kept a list of several hundred who were daily
remembered in prayer. This was followed by personal
effort and few escaped heart-to-heart talks over the sub-

ject that matters most. Such faithful and systematic work produced results. Each case was so different, so delicate, that it had to be dealt with by a method all its own; but brave, steady, unremitted work is that which pays best, both here and hereafter. Spasmodic effort, brief fervor wins no enduring honor either in this world or in that which is to come. His enthusiasm was not that of a moment, that blazed and then died, but a steady unabated force that entered into every part of his being. Like the Master Himself, to lie in wait for men with a wisdom and skill that is born from above and to catch them in the Gospel net is the highest calling of the surrendered and consecrated Christian. Weitbrecht's Memoirs have these lines: "While you aim at great things for the Lord, yet keep in view the arithmetic of heaven's exultant joy" (joy over one).

In less than six months he had personally led seventy-five of his fellow-workers to the Lord. All were hand-picked fruit. This personal work was done in odd moments, as he felt that his time belonged to his Company, and not once was there the slightest bit of criticism that business was being neglected. His was a mind farthest removed from the dogma that when a man becomes religious he must close his ledger, put an arrest on the wheels of industry, and bid his neighbor and his work farewell; but there were odd moments every night when it was not necessary for the men to be kept steadily at the telegraph key, and he kept an open eye for those moments. He who hoards and turns into account odd moments, half hours, gaps between times, achieves results which will astonish those who have not mastered the secret.

He was absolutely faithful at his post of duty. How very little do we know the importance in the Master's eye of the hidden positions we are set to occupy, or the inconspicuous work we are set to do. It may be the vital element in some providential movement. To fail in the lowliest place was to leave a flaw in God's great plan for him.

Charles Cowman capitalized every minute, made it count for something and kept on sowing the seed with the fullest assurance that there was a harvest in a grain of wheat with the power of God behind it. Oh, the marvelous results which come from faithful sowing! God often permits His children to see much of the fruitage from their sowing, but far beyond the seeing is the indirect influence. Unknown to us, the seed which we have imagined lost, has been blown hither and thither by the winds of God, planting itself by the way-side and in stony places. It will still be growing when we are in heaven for it has taken root in human hearts. When our sickles are laid aside forever, others may be reaping the golden grain we have sown.

The Holy Spirit carried on His work most successfully in the telegraph office. A real revival of religion was going on steadily without the aid of a preacher, and without a prayer room. One humble soul with a passion for winning the souls of his men was quietly praying and working, and of him it might be truly said, "As a prince hast thou power with God and men." The winning of a soul was to him what the winning of a battle is to a soldier; what the winning of a bride is to a lover; what the winning of a race is to an athlete. Charles Cowman lived for just one thing—to win souls for Christ. This was his sole passion, and in a very extraordinary manner God set His seal upon it. His resourcefulness was extraordinary and none felt that he was simply trying to force religion upon him. As love had made a pathway to the hearts of his fellow-workers, they enjoyed having him speak to them, knowing that their interests were dear to him. "Sympa-

ABOVE—MRS. CHAS. E. COWMAN AT TWENTY-FIVE.
CENTER—THE LITTLE BROWN HOME IN THE WEST.
BELOW—GRACE M. E. CHURCH CHICAGO.
MRS. COWMAN BEFORE HER MARRIAGE.

thy," wrote someone, "is two hearts tugging at the same load." What an infinite blessing to have a friend in whom you can confide, one who takes an interest and understands! Such a friend was Charles Cowman and faithfully did he fulfil the injunction, "Bear ye one another's burden and so fulfil the law of Christ." Because of his personal interest he was very approachable, and many said of him, "We felt drawn to him and could tell him everything—the good and the bad—and he would understand."

If the river of living water is flowing out from us, depend upon it people will not be in contact with us without effect. There was a quick sympathy in his manner that spoke to one's heart. Combined with a warm and tender heart, he had great energy of character and a countenance beaming with intelligence and love, God's own gifts to aid him in winning souls. What a strange and beautiful thing is heart sympathy! Untransmutable, undefinable, and yet the greatest thing in human life! Without choosing or knowing the reason why, how our hearts leap out to some understanding soul who has "let the hungry find his heart." The person who possesses this subtle gift of sympathy is in possession of the most precious thing on earth. But it is a rare gift. Happy the worker who possesses it!

He had a remarkable faculty of entering into the perplexities of his fellow-workers. They would come to him with their heart difficulties and he would seem able, as it were, to place himself in their particular situation, to enter into their feelings, to see the difficulty from their standpoint and then together they took it to God in prayer.

One of his operators told him of his overpowering temptation to drink. Instead of reprimanding him, he put his arms about him and with tears pleaded with God to destroy his thirst for drink and to give him deliverance. Long afterward that man testified that it was the tears of loving sympathy that had won him.

One morning another of his fellow-workers came from the office to his home. He had made a start heavenward some weeks before, but the enemy had taken advantage of him and his breath told the sad story of drink. Charles Cowman took him into his study, closed the door, and there the two remained all day long. Now and again voices could be heard, especially his voice in pleading, importunate prayer. Following it was a snatch of

> "Break down every idol, cast out every foe,
> Now wash me and I shall be whiter than snow."

There was a pause, then some more prayer, and soon voices were heard singing in unison,

> "He takes me as I am, He takes me as I am,
> He brings His full salvation nigh and takes me as I am."

There was a sound of praise and the two men emerged from the study, arm in arm. Their faces were wet with tears. Another prodigal had found a welcome home.

He tried to keep his men from drinking and waylaid them when they left the office. First and foremost he tried to bring them to Christ, for he believed that only as they were born again could they live overcoming lives.

There are no friendships like those made under the shadow of the cross. His whole affection went forth to those who were passing through sorrow. One of his workers lost his little ten-month-old babe and his heart was fairly crushed. This dear bereaved parent came to his work as usual throughout the child's brief illness, as money was needed to meet the doctor's bills. Charles Cowman saw tear stains on the telegraph blanks, and going to the man's side, he quietly slipped his arm around him saying, "I know all about it, for I, too, lost a sweet baby sister and my heart was broken until Jesus came with His healing balm." And there beside that desk another soul was won for the Master through tender understanding sympathy.

Someone has well said that "We need Calvary hearts for a Calvary ministry. We must be crucified men to proclaim our crucified Lord. We must bleed, to proclaim worthily the Gospel of the Blood. The passion of the Saviour needs passion-swept servants to apply its warm grace and power to the cold, dead hearts of unsaved men and women." To be a man of God, what a sacred thing it is!

Influence is something which distils from every life. It cannot be weighed, photographed, or measured, yet it is the most real thing about a man. It gathers unto itself all that belongs to the life. The whole of one's biography is condensed into it.

A noted writer states that the most searching and influential power that issues from a human life is that of which the person himself is largely unconscious. It flows from him in every form of occupation, in every relationship, in rest or in work, in silence or in speech, at home or abroad. There are hosts of men and women who are healers, teachers, helpers, almost without being conscious of it. Lights shine from them at times when they are utterly unaware that the hem of their garment is being touched.

A godly life is a popular commentary on the Bible. Men will believe the Scriptures when we live them. The world's greatest evangelizing force is Christian character and the only sermon that never wearies us is that of an eloquent life. It is that background of holy personality which gives such tremendous force and impressiveness to some men's work. The most masterly treatise on "evidences of Christianity" is a sanctified man or woman.

It was the character of Charles Cowman that counted above all else. It was what he was that constituted his real greatness for back of his wonderful smile was his wonderful soul. His life was a great revelation of Christian manhood.

Dr. Jowett has written: "There is a certain compulsory impressiveness of character which attaches to profound spirituality, and which is commandingly present in those who walk in the fellowship of the Holy Ghost. I know not how to define it. It is a certain convincing aroma, self-witnessing, like the perfume of a flower. It is independent of mental equipment, and it makes no preference between a plenteous and a penurious estate. It works without the aid of speech, because it is the effluence of a silent and secret communion. It begins to minister before you preach; it continues its ministry when the sermon is ended. It is endowed with marvellous powers of compulsion, and it sways the lives of others when mere words would miserably fail.

No finer tributes have been written than those which came from his old associates of the telegraph office after his Home-call.

"The most remarkable thing about Mr. Cowman," wrote one, "was the way he managed the men in his office. He possessed a certain power over us and those with the strongest wills bended to his way of thinking without one particle of friction. He made us feel, and believe, and desire to do what he requested. I could never quite analyze this power. As his beaming face looked down upon us at our tables at the key, as those sparkling eyes met ours, everyone of us felt that he sought our best, our highest good, and as we sat there before him, we were permanently changed in habits and character."

"He helped us to feel that we were stronger," wrote another, "and our work better than we had dared to believe. His sunniness brought hope to everyone about him; and the air of distinction which he carried was so manifestly an air of purity and not of pride, that it helped us to keep ourselves separate from that which was base and trivial. We felt that he was interested in us and his interest, being without officiousness, won our confidence and made us frank with him. We could tell him the worst about ourselves—the worst just as easily as the best—our ideals and ambitions, of which men are often as ashamed to speak as they are about their sins. His great, glorious calmness was the most powerful of all. Things settled themselves in his presence without as much as a word. He always spoke to us with a soft tone. He never shouted out his orders, and we breathed another air altogether when we were working for him."

Wrote another, "He caused us to look at religious matters from a new angle."

An official wrote, "We still feel the tingling touch of his personality."

Life in the telegraph office might have seemed commonplace, and to the majority of men it is given to lead humdrum commonplace lives. It was never commonplace to Charles Cowman for his daily task was an inspiration. The love of God shed abroad in his heart illuminated the commonplace.

He possessed a quiet compelling personality. He had power to transplant his belief, his enthusiasm, his courage into others. He created a type that reproduced itself. The converts won in the telegraph office were infected with his own consuming passion, for they too verily

5

"ached for souls." The hours of service required of the telegraphers kept many of them from attending church services and there came to his mind a plan for their spiritual upbuilding. The parlor of a downtown hotel in close proximity to the office was secured for an hour on Sabbath afternoons and here religious services were begun.

From among the converts and a few other Christians, a band was formed known thereafter as The Telegraphers' Mission Band.

The services were exceedingly simple. There was prayer, singing, the reading of God's Word, followed by a short exhortation from one of the newly converted; and all returned to the office with a firmer determination to let their light shine. They strengthened each other's hands and said one to another, "Be of good courage." "Who hath despised the day of small things?" The busy world took no notice of this insignificant little company, but it was the mission's Bethlehem. This "Telegraphers' Mission Band" was destined to be the foundation of a great missionary society, one of the greatest evangelizing forces in the Far East. They met once each month on Sabbath afternoon and gave their humble offerings amounting to $20.00 (£4), for missions. Shall we call it the wave offering of the several millions which have since been laid on the altar of the sacred task? Small? Insignificant? "Little is much when God is in it."

Great blessing followed these simple services and Charles Cowman said to this company of young Christians, "Why not reach the telegraphers in other cities and towns?" He had never been the kind of a man simply to follow in the beaten tracks, but was ever ready for new ventures that required courage and faith. A plan was formulated. Letters were sent to the Telegraph officers all over the United States, Great Britain and Australia. In the letters were Gospel tracts explaining the way of salvation and the results were most encouraging. Christians were found here and there who were set to work among those of their own profession and friendships were formed among the fellow-telegraphers which continue until this day.

It was not possible for a man with a strong nature such as the subject of this memoir, to do things by halves. Having come boldly out for the Lord, he could not keep from taking up active work in the harvest fields of the world. Personal work, open-air services, Sabbath School and mission work,—all engaged his energies.

He became deeply interested in the welfare of the men who frequented mission halls, but he had little faith in any but spiritual methods as a means of helping and elevating them. Indeed, his one idea in all of his intercourse with his fellow-men was to bring them into personal contact with the living Saviour.

His first attempt at giving a Gospel message was made some months after his conversion. He thought it might be well to get in touch with various classes. One Sabbath evening he attended a service in a district in Chicago known as "Little Hell." The leader, mistaking him for a minister, invited him to preach for them on the following Sabbath evening. With the conviction that every opportunity which presented itself should be "bought up," the invitation was accepted. During the following week he prepared his first sermon.

Hours were spent in prayer and the study of the Word. Sabbath evening came and the walk of a mile and a half was made in silence. The hall was crowded to its limit with men and women of the worst class. Some came reeling down the aisle in a drunken stupor; others were soon fast asleep from the effect of strong drink: the friendless were there, the homeless, the penniless. What a number of sin-marred faces looked up at the speaker! The carefully prepared sermon was forgotten and he talked to the hearts of that motley crowd, begging them with tears to give up their lives of sin and come to Jesus: and they came, a long altar full—weeping their way to Zion. He was there until midnight praying with them, and thus a definite work began with a limited amount of knowledge in the divine art of soul-winning. What a great encouragement he received from his labors in "Little Hell," where he spent every Sabbath evening thereafter. In the after years when he went to Japan as a missionary, many of these "down-and-outs" whom he had led to Christ became his faithful supporters in his new field of labor.

He had a marvelous influence over abandoned and desperate men, winning some from the gambling table to the altar of God's house. He disarmed men by trusting them. He dealt with hundreds at the crises of their lives. Thus when but a young man among men he saw all sides of life, learned the secrets of hundreds of characters and was trusted and loved. Men felt that he was not a voice merely, but a friend, and on his arms they were lifted up. He was always hopeful about the most hopeless, picked out some good points in the worst, and sent a man away feeling he was trusted once more, not only by a friend, but by Christ.

The affection which such treatment aroused was extra-ordinary. Often his trust was betrayed, but he mastered the lesson to trust and yet trust again, and many a Lazarus came forth from the grave of spiritual death and after-ward sat at meat with Him, and some of them went forth to preach the Gospel. He was prophet and priest to a host of individuals. They claimed from him the solution of their problems, they believed in his prayers for their souls' diseases and came away with fresh inspiration and hope. "Little Hell" thus became a training college for service in far wider fields than he had yet been called upon to occupy, thus early in his Christian life he drank deeply of the Master's spirit, and worked and prayed for the conversion of the most hopeless, the most degraded of his fellow-men.

In a small diary belonging to this period of his life, interspersed among notes, Gospel addresses, and illustrations culled from many quarters, we find some graphic accounts of the people with whom he came in contact and whom he tried to win as trophies for his beloved Master. Carefully preserved among his papers were some soiled old letters, each one of them the confession of a soul, or the sob of a broken heart, or the cry of a cold and starving one. His intense and crowded life of service was his own choice. We are certain that he does not regret it now; nor should we even in the midst of our keen sense of loss.

Someone placed in his hands, "The life of Charles S. Finney." It made a very deep impression upon him, especially the chapter that told of Finney passing through a mill and the people falling under deep conviction as he spoke to them of the Lord. He said, "My men do not do that when I witness to them," and he prayed, "Lord, show me what is the matter. I wish to become like Charles Finney." But his Lord said to him, "I wish you to be Charles Cowman, not Charles Finney."

He was not a reflector of other men's opinions, but was always just himself, a simple, straightforward, brotherly man, with no pose and no pretense of any kind.

"Have ye received the Holy Ghost since ye believed?"
This was the pass-word into the early Church.

To the question "Do you expect to be made perfect in love in this life? Are you groaning after it?" Methodist preachers who are candidates for admission into the ministry are expected to answer affirmatively, and Methodism does not recognize one law for the spiritual life for its ministers and another for its laymen.

CHAPTER V

ANOTHER LIFE CRISIS

We now come to another important experience in Charles Cowman's life. He had lived as a Christian for a year, and among the members of Grace Methodist church none were more zealous for souls than he. Quite unconsciously he had become a leader among the young people. Among the members was a very earnest brother, named George Simister. He, too, was a layman, a successful soul-winner, and very often he took Charles Cowman aside to tell him of a wonderful blessing which he had received, seeking to impress upon him that he was in need of the same experience, but as he never had lost the thrill of his first love, never had lost the wonder of the miracle of his conversion, never had waned in glad responsive gratitude to the Lord, he saw no need of being sanctified. But something happened in his office one night and the calm, quiet, self-possessed man became impatient and spoke harshly to one of his men. Quickly he asked the man's forgiveness, but peace left his heart and he continued in this state of mind for almost a week.

He sent for George Simister who came and said, "Brother Cowman, you need to have your heart cleansed from all sin." In the simplest manner he explained to him that after conversion, "the old man" of sin still remains and the only remedy is cleansing through the precious Blood.

Vouchsafed to most there are tide-times of the soul which should be "taken at the flood." It is possible to permit an ebb to take place, but Charles Cowman seized the opportunity. He regarded nothing as important as having his heart cleansed from all sin, and he began to seek it with a full purpose of soul. He formed a habit of jotting down his thoughts and during this time he penned these lines which breathed out his inner heart:

"I was profoundly impressed and powerfully sustained, almost absorbed by the Word, 'This is the will of God, even your sanctification.' 'He that willeth to do His will shall know of the doctrine.' These words cannot be too deeply engraved upon the heart. I will ever seek to have my will one with the will of God."

"What is the end of life?" wrote Drummond. "The end of life is not to do good, although many of us think so. It is not to win souls, although I once thought so. The end of life is to do the will of God. That may be in the line of winning souls or doing good, or it may not. To the individual who asks the question, 'What is the end of life?' there can be but one answer, 'To do the will of God, whatever that may be.' Spurgeon replied to an invitation to preach to an exceptionally large audience, 'I have no ambition to preach to ten thousand people, but to do the will of God,' and he declined. If we could have no ambition past the will of God our lives would be successful. If we could say, 'I have no ambition to go to the heathen, I have no ambition to win souls; my ambition is to do the will of God, whatever that may be,' that makes lives equally great or equally small, because the only great thing in life is what of God's will there is in it. The maximum achievement of any man's life after it is all over is to have done the will of God."

In Charles Cowman's notes were these brief lines:

"I have committed myself and my all into God's hands, and He has accepted the offering. Life henceforth can never be the same."

The fact that it made his ministry what it was, is equally certain, and those who knew him before and after this experience could not question that he had found a new secret of power for his own life and work.

He came into a fresh experience, a second definite work of grace,—a crisis as radical and revolutionary as the crisis of regeneration. A new union began with his Saviour, new victories enriched his life, and a new power marked his service from that day. The great need in his soul had been met by the greater power of God and he began an unbroken walk with his Lord. From that hour he felt that he must lose no opportunity of leading others to that overflowing fountain of mercy and truth. It was his life-long task and even death could not interrupt it. The witness of the Divine Comforter proved not a transient but a perennial grace. He had come to abide forever; and the Day-star had risen upon his heart with an unsetting light. It was his determination to live as a blood-washed man and to seek to bring others under the power of the same soul-cleansing Blood. Multitudes will praise God, in that sweet Morning-land, that Charles Cowman sought and obtained the blessing of "Full Salvation," but not one fraction of the result will be known until that glorious morning.

God was henceforth first in everything and a penciled note in his Bible beside the words, "Suffer me first" shows in these interesting steps his consecration.

God first.

Wife and home second.

Telegraph office third.

He was truly sanctified and Holiness had in him not only an advocate, but an illustration. He was manifestly crucified unto the world and the world unto him. His life was one simple long fulfillment of the will of God as he apprehended and understood it.

Out from his life flowed a stream of power, not the power of eloquence or great scholarship, but the power of the Spirit of God, pouring its life-giving stream through the life of a man who was wholly abandoned to Him, one who was content to be a channel only.

Holiness on fire! Is not that one of the great needs of the day? The man who has seen the essential need of holy living, and believes that he has found, in union with the Lord Jesus, the secret of its realization, should he not burn up with desire to spread the glad tidings among his fellow Christians as well as to exhibit its power in holiness of conduct? We want everywhere the most intense glow of Christian zeal. When Elijah had built the altar of God, placed the wood in order, and the sacrifice on the wood, he knelt and prayed for the fire. All else had been in vain without that. *"Then the fire of the Lord fell."*

How many men not remarkable for their natural ability, have done noble things by their burning zeal!

There comes a point of time in the history of every soul when, if he wishes to become a sanctified vessel, "meet for the Master's use," he must choose whether he will take the heavenly inheritance or the earthly. The latter may look exceedingly brilliant, but it must be dropped if it prevents a holy career and a life of perfect service for the Lord.

"Though the life through which God has prevailed is profoundly humble, it is yet conscious that God's Almightiness belongs to it, and moves upon its mission as though the destinies of earth depend upon its effort, as they do." A more profound truth was never uttered and never did it find a better illustration than in the life of Charles Cowman.

The days of small things were now past; henceforth he was to open his mouth wide that He might fill it. Little by little was he led out to possess more territory until God could entrust him with the "wealthy place" where he stood with steady nerve and unfaltering faith throughout the years that followed.

He witnessed faithfully to the twos, the threes, the crowds in Mission Halls, the hundreds in the telegraph office; and now and then came invitations from the pastors of the large city churches asking him to address their congregations. He was introduced to their audiences much after this fashion: "We have with us tonight, a devoted layman, a business man, who will relate some of his experiences in winning souls in a telegraph office;" or, "A Methodist brother noted for his aggressiveness, will give us a glimpse of his strange parish, the telegraph office in our city."

In a simple, straightforward manner he would go to the pulpit, dressed in his neatly fitting suit of gray. His messages were seldom more than twenty minutes long and took the form of a simple testimony of what God was doing among the telegraphers of his office. Many a man went home from the service with a fresh vision of what could be done in witnessing for Christ in his own place of business. Several leaders of large business concerns whose light had been hidden under a bushel, entered their offices the next day not only to transact their own business, but also to look after the King's business.

The day of his conversion never faded from his memory, but stood out in sharp relief, and his simple heart-gripping messages, usually contained his testimony. "Saved to serve" was ever his life's motto.

A preacher noted for his oratory invited him to speak at his Sabbath evening service, as he, too, had heard of the revival in the telegraph office and longed to know the secret of this business man's success. After the service he called Charles Cowman to his study for a heart-to-heart talk. In the course of the conversation he said, "I try to win souls, but fail every time. Can you tell me the reason?"

The two men were alone, the key was turned in the door, and the janitor was notified not to disturb them, nor to admit anyone. Ten o'clock came, then eleven, and the clock in the tower struck twelve. One, two, and three tolled the bell; the two walked out into the street, wending their way homeward. They had met Someone during those hours and the next Sabbath evening there was a new man in the pulpit with a new heart and a new message.

"What has happened to our minister?" was whispered from pew to pew.

A man sitting in one of the fashionable pews could have given an answer to their inquiry, for he knew the struggle of that popular preacher, of the midnight battle, as he faced the question whether he would yield himself wholly to God and become just a plain soul-winner or a pulpit orator. Weeks afterward, when a great revival broke out in that church, none rejoiced more over "the spoils won in battle" than did Charles Cowman.

The great learned man, having several degrees attached to his name, came down from his pulpit one night, slipped his arm about a man and said, "God bless you, Brother Cowman, for your faithfulness to me that night. I would rather have the love of God shed abroad in my heart and witness the scenes of the past two weeks than to have the world at my feet."

Some of Charles Cowman's most spiritual triumphs were won where we least expected them. There is no limit to the victories possible to that soul which lies as a helpless worm before the mercy-seat, utterly surrendered to the crucified Christ.

One impressive trait of character was his ability to become all things to all men. It did not matter who the individual was, whether rich or poor, young or old, educated or illiterate, worldly or spiritually minded, he understood them and their need.

During the weeks which followed, he received invitations from numbers of pastors to address their congregations. These he accepted as the voice of the Lord; and relying upon Him who said, "I will be with thy mouth," he ventured forth into this new field, saying, "My preparation must come directly from Him upon whom my soul continually feeds." Thus without any human authority or professional training, this layman became a minister of the Word. And if He who inspires and fulfils the Word orders a man to preach it, what man or what convocation of men shall dare dispute the ordination or the call? From that time, Charles Cowman, without assuming any clerical dignity, continued to preach the gospel; "the Lord working with (him), and comfirming the Word with signs following."

"Does it pay to be an out-and-out Christian?" was frequently asked him. Does it pay the river to scatter blessings along its course? Does it pay the rose to fling its sweetness to the world? Does it pay the wheat to grow and feed the hungry millions? It does pay a thousand fold to live a life that counts and it may be lived in the hardest place, but that life is not found on a bargain table. Remember what Jesus said to the young ruler, "Sell *all*"—"all that thou hast and come, follow Me."

"Who is conscious of possessing little in Christ, the same loveth little, and is little disposed to make Him known. Our experience of Christ is the fountain, our missionary zeal is the stream. The one measures the other."—Egbert W. Smith.

"It is something to be a missionary. The morning stars sang together and all the sons of God shouted for joy when they saw the field which the first missionary was to fill. The great and loving God, before whom angels veil their faces, had an only Son, and He was sent to earth as a Missionary Physician. It is something to be a follower, however feeble, in the wake of the great Teacher and only model Missionary that ever appeared among men, and now that He is Head over all things, King of kings, and Lord of lords, what commission is equal to that which the missionary holds from Him? May I venture to invite young men of education, when laying down the plan of their lives, to take a glance at that of missionary? We will magnify the office! For my own part, I never cease to rejoice that God has appointed me to such an office."
—David Livingstone.

CHAPTER VI

THE VOLUNTEER

A national Epworth League Convention was held at Chattanooga, Tennessee, to which Charles Cowman and wife were sent as delegates from Grace Methodist Church. It was an epochal time as Bishop Joyce had just returned from his world tour, his soul having been mightily stirred as he had looked upon the fields white unto harvest. The thousands who were assembled in the great tabernacle erected for the special occasion, were swayed by his message. Charles Cowman's soul took fire that day. Hitherto he had given little or no thought to the great regions beyond. His "world" was bounded on the north by the telegraph office, on the south by his church, on the east and the west by his home; but he had not made explorations beyond these boundaries. There had been no intimation whatever that he would ever see the foreign field, but now he caught a vision.

This was his first missionary awakening and when a plea was made for the support of native workers it strongly appealed to him. He was never influenced by excitement or carried away from his position by epidemical impulses, but gradually the Holy Spirit was gently awakening him and he was receiving an unconscious preparation for the years ahead. God prepares his heroes in peculiar places and when opportunity comes, he can fit them into their places in a moment and the world looks on wondering from whence they came. The unlikely instruments used by our Lord in carrying out His purpose of love ever proves an interesting study.

At this convention a tract on the subject of tithing was handed to him. He saw its truth and on New Year's Day, one year after his conversion, he opened his first account with the Lord. When his monthly salary was received, a tenth of it was laid aside and an entry made in his notebook, "The Lord's Tithe." On the flyleaf was written, "The tithe is the Lord's" and "The connection between man's tithes and God's windows."

From that day to the end of his life, nothing ever came into his hand that was not first of all tithed. He felt that if the Lord was interested in this, he was also interested in the *way* money was expended and his mind was greatly exercised upon the subject.

How was the remaining nine tenths to be spent and what did the Word mean by "offerings?" In his tithing account book was also a page for his "offerings." It would be a convincing argument for those who are not acquainted with tithing to note the increase in his salary. However, the tithing was not undertaken with any thought of selfish gain, but God has promised to honor them who will honor Him with their substance.

When special needs arose in the church and the members were at their wit's end, when bazaars and fairs were talked of by the "Ways and Means Committee," it was Charles Cowman who usually took the floor and made a ringing speech telling them that he did not agree with that method of helping maintain the house of the Lord, that the Scriptural plan was tithing. A "Tithers' League" was formed, carried out successfully, and there was no longer a need for festivals and fairs to raise money. Best of all, the spiritual life of the church began to increase and a revival of religion broke out at once.

Very few, if any, outside of his immediate family knew just how much he gave each month, but God was training

His child in various ways for the work He was preparing him for, though he was yet wholly unconscious of his destined task. Later on he decided that he would give all his income to God, excepting the amount needed for actual personal need. The *needs* and *wants* were placed on a scale and carefully weighed. "How much can we do without each month? Just what do we actually need, and what can be spared for the Lord's work?"

He kept all of his accounts for the Lord's inspection knowing that he must give an account of the way he expended money, thus he was having a training for the leadership of a great missionary movement. Even back there, God was training His child for a life of faith.

When the call came to leave all and go to Japan, had he not given away all his income, he would have had more than sufficient to have supported himself and his wife; but God had another plan and to others He had entrusted the honor of paying the steamer fare and lending a hand.

He made no investments excepting those in the work of God. He was unconsciously trained for the pathway of a missionary. "Lay not up for yourselves treasures upon earth," was early impressed upon his mind; and in later years when several personal gifts came to him as an inheritance, they were not tithed, but given outright for the work so close to his heart.

He felt definitely called to self-denial for Christ and missions and thus God kept him always at a place where heroic exercise of faith was necessary. His life was one unbroken record of self-denial. Self-sacrifice began very early in his Christian life. Nothing was ever reserved for himself, and he resolved that everything that flowed *into* his life should, in still greater volume flow *out* of it again.

Said Dr. Jowett: "We begin to operate with vital forces when we cross the border into the land of sacrifices.

The things that we can spare carry no sacrifice blood. The things that we cannot spare carry part of ourselves and are alive."

Charles Cowman lived in a beautiful, well furnished home, but this was exchanged for a small apartment in order that he might support another native worker in Africa. Often was he asked the question, "How can you afford to support so many native workers?" The inquiry usually received this reply, "I cannot afford it, I can sacrifice it."

In replying to an inquirer on the subject of tithing, he wrote these lines:

"The man who begins to tithe will have six genuine surprises. (1) He will be surprised at the amount of money he has for the Lord's work; (2) at the deepening of his own spiritual life in paying the tithe; (3) at the ease in meeting his own obligations with the nine-tenths with God's blessing; (4) at the ease in going on from one-tenth to larger giving; (5) at the preparation this gives to be a faithful and wise steward over the nine-tenths that remain; (6) at himself in not adopting the Biblical plan sooner."

"Bring ye all the tithes into the storehouse and prove me herewith." In no other duty commanded with promise of blessing resulting, does God challenge us to test Him as in this. We recommend tithing for those whose faith is not strong enough for unconditional surrender, but who are willing to accept God's challenge for a year and prayerfully observe His leadings. Seldom do any such ever recede from the covenant. "Honor the Lord with thy substance; so shall thy barns be filled with plenty and thy presses burst out with new wine."

God does not promise great wealth to the man who pays the tenth, but we do have the promise that if we pay

the whole tithe into the storehouse, God will give us more
financial success than we could obtain without it.   And
we are challenged to put it to the test.

"Nine-tenths of your income with God's blessing will
go further than ten-tenths without, just as you can accomplish more on six days by consecrating the seventh to Him
as commanded."

"God's Word says, 'bring ye all the tithes into the
storehouse, and I will *pour* you out a blessing (not sprin-
kle, rain down, but *pour*) so that there will not be room
enough to receive it.   And I will rebuke the devourer for
your sakes, and he shall not destroy the fruits of *your*
ground.'   There is the signature to the contract.   Do we
want any better security than that?"

A great Missionary Convention was being held in the
Moody Church, Chicago, in 1894.   Dr. A. B. Simpson was
the principal speaker.   A large number of missionaries were
present, Forder of Arabia, Leleacheur from the Tibetan
borders, and others from various corners of the world.
Charles Cowman's heart was strangely moved when Dr.
Simpson told of a young business man who, with his wife
and small child, had gone to the heart of Africa in simple
faith, trusting God for the supply of their needs.   He had
never heard of such an extraordinary course of action
and the self-denial of these servants of God gripped him.
Enthusiasm ran high, and when the missionary offering
was being taken, a roll of bills representing his monthly
salary, together with his beautiful gold watch, was laid
on the collection plate.   After the offering, came the call
for volunteers.   The appeal was in substance as follows:
"If there are any young people here who will offer themselves to go out as missionaries to the heathen providing
God calls and opens up the way, please stand."   To his
wife sitting beside him he said, "That means you and me;

so let us stand and show our colors." Charles Cowman was on his feet in an instant. These lines were found in his diary!

"September 3, 1894. Attended Dr. Simpson's missionary convention and was searched through and through and bared and exposed and searched by God's searching Spirit. I took another step toward God."

Missionary literature was placed in his hand and he began reading of India's millions. It made a deep impression upon him and on his heart was rolled a burden that would not leave him, even after much prayer. He believed that God was calling him to India, but he did not know what step to take to reach this dark land. His wife did not feel called to India and the family physician said she could not live in such a trying climate. In the providence of God, he at this time met Dr. Arthur T. Pierson, who had heard of his work in the telegraph office, and of the influence he was exerting in his own church among the young people. He said to him with much emphasis, "Wait, young man, wait God's hour." His whole soul sought earnestly for a word from the Lord, a word from the Book of books sealed by the Holy Spirit's power. He prayed, waited, watched, expected; suddenly the word came, *"Stay thou there, till I bring thee word"* (Matt. 2:13). Said the good Phillips Brooks, *"The highest attitude of any man's life is to stand waiting for God,—for what God will choose to make of him."*

The Holy Spirit is our never-failing Guide, our Leader. There are times when He presses us forward into service, into new experiences, new duties, new claims of faith; but there are times when He arrests us in our activity, rests us under His over-shadowing wing, and quiets us in the secret place of the Most High, teaching us some new lessons, breathing into us some deeper strength,

CAPTAIN ROBERT C. DALTON

A

Baptist Chaplain

TESTIFIES

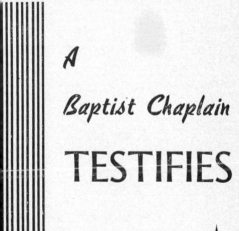

*I*N THE winter of 1934, in Seattle, God laid His hand upon me, and I consecrated my life to Him. From that time forward God has graciously led me step by step into the knowledge of the experience known as the Baptism in the Holy Spirit.

I was brought up in the Midwest, in a strict Baptist family, in which there were numerous Baptist preachers. My father was a leading layman in his church. At my mother's knee I was told of the Blood that saves from sin and of the coming again of Jesus. This teaching of the return of the Lord Jesus Christ has done more than any other doctrine in the Bible to keep me walking in close fellowship with Him.

When God definitely laid His hand upon me in 1934, I was a student, and I came to certain conclusions, based upon my study of the history of revivals, as follows:

1. That real religious revivals are seldom recognized as such by the established denominations at the time they occur.

2. That in religious revivals of the past many peculiar manifestations occurred, such as quaking, shaking, and falling prostrate on the ground.

3. That even though well-meaning people affected by these revivals often went to extremes and excesses, yet by far the greatest majority became sane, moral citizens, whose lives influenced their communities in some cases for two or more generations.

4. That we ought not to limit God as to how He must work in the event that His Spirit again begins to move in genuine revival.

5. That we ought to expect some of the same manifestations in the present.

After my experience in Seattle I returned to Wheaton College and there heard of the

the Holy Spirit: held meetings in all the churches. In the space of a year and a half I baptized in water some sixty-five people, the greatest number of whom were over twenty-one years of age and of the male sex. All this time, to those who were spiritually ready for it, I opened up the truth of the Baptism in the Spirit, and after I left in November, 1941, to go on active duty in the U. S. Army as a chaplain, several members of these Baptist churches received their Baptism in the Holy Spirit with the Pentecostal phenomenon.

All of this time I had been desperately praying for my own Baptism in the Holy Spirit. It was an exceedingly dry period in my life. At times it seemed as though I could hardly go on in my ministry, for even though God blessed in His exceeding love and mercy to the salvation of many souls, I felt myself an utter failure before God. Many times Satan tried to destroy me. He put every obstacle and temptation conceivable in my way, but I clung to the blessed Rock, Christ Jesus, and the precious truth of the Promise of the Father.

Throughout my experience in the U.S. Army I clung to the knowledge that God would fill my hungry heart with the glorious Holy Spirit. From Fort Riley, Kansas, where I went on active duty, to the Isthmus of Panama, back and forth across America, I sought the face of God. Whenever I could find time from my duties as chaplain I attended Pentecostal churches, staying for the after-meeting and praying at their altars. At the Mount Rainier Ordnance Depot, Tacoma, Washington, where I was a depot chaplain, after morning and evening services in my own chapel, I would take my wife and baby and go into Tacoma, to the Gospel Tabernacle on 12th and G Streets,

7

and tarry for the Baptism. I had also set aside Tuesday nights for the seeking of God in the same place.

Finally, after I had received orders to leave Tacoma and go on Army Transport duty, while I was in Seattle waiting for my ship, in the Christian Servicemen's Club I was having a cup of coffee in the kitchenette, and discussing the Lord Jesus Christ and His death on the cross for our sins. There God graciously and wonderfully filled me with His Spirit to the point of overflowing, and I myself received the promise of the Father according to Acts 2, with like signs.

This was on March 28, 1944. From this time forward there has been a new presence of God in my life. Whereas before I had walked entirely by faith, I now had within me a glorious supernatural proof of the fact of His walking with me.

As I went about my duties at sea on an army transport, I had wonderful peace, continually enjoying the welling up within me of this precious supernatural presence of the Lord. My cabin was a little heaven. I had no fears of any kind. God's constant presence was sufficient hour by hour. To this day I have only one desire—to be filled constantly with His Spirit. I know then that I can win many precious souls to Christ.

Tract No. 4640—60c per 100
Sample package 4675 (2 and 4 page)
Sample package 4676 (6 and 8 page)
50c per package

Gospel Publishing House, Springfield 1, Mo.
PRINTED IN THE U.S.A.

FULL GOSPEL ASSEMBLY,
LANDIS AVE. WEST OF CIRCLE
VINELAND, NEW JERSEY

Pentecostal phenomenon for the first time. The professor was speaking on 1 Corinthians 14, and quoted certain verses as proof that this particular phenomenon could not occur, and if it did occur it was of Satan. As he read and taught I followed him with my own Testament, and the same scriptures which told him that it could not occur told me that it could.

After graduating in 1936, I went to the Eastern Baptist Theological Seminary in Philadelphia, where I put my whole soul into my studies and into the practical work of presenting the gospel in that great metropolitan area, in Sunday school classes, in street meetings, and in whatever churches gave me opportunity to preach.

From the beginning of my call to the ministry I believed that God would send a mighty Holy Ghost revival on a world basis, so in every message I preached and in my discussions with individuals I attempted to uphold the cause of Christ as I saw it. In the practical work of witnessing for Christ to individuals and in my regular ministry as pastor, I realized an exceeding great lack of power in my life to be an effective witness for the Lord Jesus Christ.

In the spring of my middle year in the seminary I read Day's book, "The Shadow of the Broad Brim," which is the life of Charles Haddon Spurgeon. As I read how that young preacher stood in his London pulpit and proclaimed the precious truth of the gospel, until people came by the thousands and until thousands were converted, I broke before the Lord, realizing the lack of such ministry in my life. I made a vow that somehow I would find what was lacking.

A month or so later, after school had closed, I mentioned to a fellow student

something in connection with my heart's cry for more power to proclaim God's message. He said, "Come with my wife and me to West Philadelphia." I went. Before the young lady began her message, I realized that I was close to finding someone who could give me the secret of my own lack. At college and seminary I had heard some of the greatest preachers from both America and the British Isles, but I had never heard anyone teach the Bible with such great authority and power.

At the close of this meeting two or three of us made an appointment with the young lady for the next day at the seminary, where she opened up to us the blessed truth of the Promise of the Father. I was so eager and hungry that I could not help reading two or three verses ahead of her all the time, and I believed with all my heart in the Pentecostal experience even before she arrived at the particular scriptures relating to it.

Although for my stand I bore various types of persecution, I never for one moment doubted:

1. That down through history, a religious experience subsequent to regeneration has been experienced by various individuals.

2. That a genuine experience of this nature appears today among many devout Christians.

3. That the experience is for each of us today, including me.

4. That the world needs a revitalized Christianity, based upon the individual Christian's experiencing the promise of the Father, as spoken of in Acts.

5. That I myself must have this experience at any cost.

A short time after the above events, several students of the Seminary who were hungry for God and for power to proclaim the gospel, met by appointment at the High-way Gospel Tabernacle in Philadelphia, where Pastor Wesley R. Steelberg, out of the Scriptures and out of his deep well of experience, opened up to us more fully this greatly neglected teaching. Although I had no doubt as to the genuineness of the experience, I felt that I owed it to myself to face every possible argument that might be used in attempting to show error in the doctrine. I had to refute every argument that anyone could bring up to disprove the teaching.

Following this discussion there came a prayer meeting which certain students who were attending the Baptist Seminary at that time will never forget. A student whom I least expected to receive a genuine spiritual blessing received the Baptism in the Holy Spirit that night. Not only did I believe this teaching of the Holy Spirit in my mind and in my heart, but I saw one of my fellow students display the Pentecostal phenomenon, not only speaking in tongues but singing in a high soprano the most beautiful melody I had ever heard.

That fall when school opened, a young lady who was not in attendance at the meeting at the Highway Gospel Tabernacle, but who was a friend of one of the young men who had been with us, received the Baptism in the Holy Spirit at the altar in Highway Gospel Tabernacle.

It is not to be supposed that the prayer meetings we had continued to hold all summer, and our attendance at both Pentecostal churches and camp meetings, and the actual experience of those who had been baptized in the Holy Spirit, should go unheeded by the Seminary authorities. Shortly after school started, several of us received notice to appear before a select committee of the faculty to answer questions concerning our experiences of the summer. The professors were very kind. They asked each one to write a statement about the meeting in which the member of our group had received his Baptism. A short time after this we each received a note from the registrar's office placing each of us on probation pending our withdrawing from any further contact with the Pentecostal movement. Several months later, without having made any sort of retraction as to our personal belief in the experience of the Baptism in the Holy Spirit, we were removed from probation.

About the time I was to receive my Bachelor of Divinity degree, as I was writing my thesis on the Pentecostal phenomenon of speaking in tongues and its connection with the Baptism in the Holy Spirit, I was asked to present myself at the president's office. For the space of about one hour the president of the seminary with a great deal of persuasion attempted to lead me away from my "heretical views" on the Holy Spirit. On my leaving, he received the promise from me, that I would continue to search the Scriptures and ask the guidance of God in this matter.

I was called by five Baptist churches in Adams County, Ohio, to be their pastor. In this region began a most glorious and interesting experiment in the teaching of the Word of God to a hungry, spiritually half-starved people. I held revival meetings, and in one or two of the churches in particular there were numerous converts. Six months later the young woman who first opened the Scriptures to me concerning the Baptism in or fulness, and then leaving us again to wait for His bidding. He never sets His children to an impossible task, but standards must be reached in His school. God is never in a hurry, but spends long years with those whom He expects to use greatly, and never thinks the days of preparation too long or too dull. When He permits delays, He is not inactive. He is getting ready His instruments, ripening their powers; and at the appointed moment they shall arise equal to their task.

"If it be the Lord's will to bring you into His service for the ministry," wrote Spurgeon, *"He has already appointed your place and service, and though you know it not at present, you shall at the proper time."*

We read in God's Word of Paul and Timothy who tried to enter a certain door, but "the Spirit suffered them not." What a mistake would Charles Cowman have made if he had gone to India out of the will of God! He ever praised Him for the closed-up way. In the later years when he was called upon to deal with young people who felt they had received a call, he was most insistent that they should be called to a particular field, as he believed that a person could find God's perfect plan for his life. No other class of people interested him more than those who seemed at first bidden to go and yet who found before them a fast-barred door. "Thou didst well that it was in thine heart," was an oft-quoted Scripture.

He worked as hard and as unsparingly as ever. There was a very marked fresh zeal for God and His cause, a determination that He should be honored, loved, exalted and His name be praised in the earth. After this disappointment, which no doubt, God reckoned to him in his future career, he purposed that since he was not to be a missionary to India, he would joyfully carry on his work for the Lord in the telegraph office. He did not look back with a sad, lingering look as if to say, "Why could not I have gone to India? I am having God's second best." Nothing of the kind! He accepted it cheerfully. Notwithstanding his very heavy duties among his hundreds of men, his heart overstepped the boundaries of kindred and country to take in the whole wide world. A map of the world became a sort of prayer-book, and his heart was drawn out in intercessory prayer. He believed in the great, white-robed multitude who had washed their robes and were gathered from every nation, and kindred, and people, and tongue; and for the gathering out of these blessed ones he pleaded patiently and hopefully for years. At last came one of God's surprises, the call to the work for which God had been preparing him for a number of years.

He received many invitations to speak in city churches and began to feel his lack of Bible knowledge. Therefore he began the study of a special course offered by the Garrett Theological School of Evanston. He worked in the telegraph office from five o'clock until midnight and this schedule gave him an opportunity to attend morning classes at the Moody Bible Institute. Thus he spent the following six years in diligent Bible study. He reveled in the study of God's Word, ever keeping before him the one object, to qualify himself for personal soul-winning. His sound judgment, unflagging energy, and uniform urbanity of manner, would have secured for him a leading place in business circles and would have guaranteed pecuniary success, but God had another plan for His servant. How little did he imagine that in the providence of God he was to be called from his busy office and whirled out into the mighty outer world that lay beyond the Pacific! An elaborate training, such as hundreds of others receive now-a-days might have ruined him. Indeed, did he not have all the equipment needed for the task?

"It is a sacrilege of Christianity," said Dr. A. J. Gordon, "that the church has so often undertaken to manufacture missionaries by priestly ordination or by literary training. The prerogative of furnishing the ministry for His own church is sublimely accorded to Christ alone. It is His office to give the various orders of the ministry, ours to ask for them, to receive and recognize them when sent."

The supreme qualification for holy service is not intellectual but spiritual, and is therefore within reach of disciples of every age, of all varieties of temperament, and all degrees of education. The telegraph office was his college of missions, and Charles Cowman could say with the great Apostle to the Gentiles, "According to the grace of God which was given unto me" (Col. 1:25).

When honors came to Charles Cowman in the after years he refused them, and was wont to describe himself as only a shepherd dog, ready to run after the lost sheep and bring them into the fold of the Shepherd.

"It was a spark dropped from heaven."—James Montgomery.

CHAPTER VII

MEETING REV. JUJI NAKADA

The Sabbath morning service in Grace Methodist Church had just begun when a young Japanese walked down the aisle and took his seat directly in front of the Charles Cowman pew. At the close of the service there was a hearty handshake and Charles Cowman learned that the visitor, Rev. Juji Nakada of Japan, had come to America from his far-away island kingdom to seek help for his preaching, having, as he said, "run out of methods."

He was given a most cordial invitation to attend the Monday evening Holiness meeting led by Dr. J. R. Boynton, one of the leading physicians of the city, who, a few weeks previous to this, had been sanctified wholly. The invitation was accepted, and Rev. Juji Nakada listened for the first in his lifetime, to an old-fashioned Holiness sermon. He had become a student at the Moody Bible Institute previously, as the fame of D. L. Moody and his success as a soul-winner had reached Japan.

Dr. A. M. Hills was also staying at the Institute as a guest. He met our native brother and placed in his hand his very helpful book entitled "Holiness and Power." As he earnestly sought to be filled with the Holy Spirit, it was not long until his hungry heart was satisfied. Having come so definitely into the blessings, he soon felt strongly impressed that God would send him back to his people to preach full salvation to them. As yet it had not dawned upon the mind of Charles Cowman that God had chosen him to be the co-worker of this native Japanese and to find in the very city of Tokyo, Japan, his permanent home, the center of his life work. God was leading His child by a way that he knew not, and his hands were being gently loosed from the work in the telegraph office.

When our Lord awakens interest in objects dear to Himself, He invariably designs not only to stir their sympathies, but graciously to link them with some definite branch of service connected with the object in question, thus bestowing upon them a blessed life-work as well as drawing their hearts unto prayer, and into fellowship with His own desires and eternal purposes. Thus Charles Cowman's chief life-work came through a chain of events growing out of a friendship with Rev. Juji Nakada. The issues of this friendship will never be fully known until we are overwhelmed with the disclosures and surprises of eternity. Not more manifest the flaming pillar of old than the providential indications which guided him. Our life occurrences are not just a lot of accidental fragments.

The Telegraphers Mission Band assumed the support of our Japanese brother and sent him back to his own country rejoicing. He became their representative in Japan, traveling all over the land holding evangelistic services. His letters and reports were most eagerly read at the meetings of the Band; thus a missionary fire that was never extinguished was kindled.

If the Holy Spirit dwells in us there will be a strange accordance with God's working in the world around us. There is a divine harmony between the Spirit and providence. There is a double presence of the Lord for the consecrated believer. He is present in the heart, and is mightily present in the events of life.

"How marvelously," wrote one, "God can fit things together and His purposes meet without a shade of variation. Look at that beautiful scene in the temple when the infant Jesus was brought in to be presented before the Lord. Just at the right moment old Simeon was there to receive Him by the intimation of the Holy Ghost; and we read further still that, at the same instant, the aged Anna, also coming in, recognized her coming Saviour and joined in the welcome testimony.

"Look at Peter and Cornelius. Just the moment Peter had been prepared for the commission, messengers were waiting at the door to take him to Joppa. God had it all arranged and He had but to carry out the plan.

"The Acts of the Apostles is the book of providences under the control of the Holy Ghost. We see in that wonderful book how everything moves at the bidding of the ascended Christ and the Holy Spirit.

"Look at Philip and the eunuch of Ethiopia. In the height of his work in Samaria the evangelist is called away by the voice of God to go down into the desert. Everything looked the other way. The work seems to require him there, and yet he obeys and leaves thousands of seeking souls and a whole city moved to its depth by the Holy Ghost, to go down into a desert. So God sometimes calls us from the most useful position to what seems a waste of time. But God has stepped before him. This Ethiopian prince has been up to Jerusalem, seeking after the truth, and has not found the need of his heart. They meet on the way, but for a few moments, perhaps, or a passing hour; but in that hour an eternity has been decided for that man, and not for him alone, but, perhaps, for the whole nation to which he was to return with the strange and glorious tidings of salvation.

"Look at Paul's wondrous life. What a romance of providence, culminating in the marvelous voyage to Rome, which is a sort of picture in miniature of the whole church in her perilous journey through the seas of time. Everything tried to baffle and hinder, but through everything God led him, and used the very things that seemed to be against him for the furtherance of the Gospel, making all things work together for good to him and for glory to His own great name."

Everything is included in the plan of God. Not only all things in general, but everything in particular. The theologians love to call it the particular providence of God. That means His plan in reference to the minutest detail of human life, and the most significant things that happen.

In the beautifully written tract, "The God-planned life," are these lines, "Every child of God may find and enter into God's plan for his life," and along with the God-planned life is divine providence. It is interwoven with every page of the Holy Scriptures and every part of our Christian life. The God of the Bible is a Father and Friend, concerned in everything concerning us, touching with a hand of love and power all the ordinary affairs of life, and directing and governing the whole universe, from the minutest insect that floats in summer air to the mightiest star that rolls in immensity.

In the story of Eliezer and Rebekah, we have the finest illustration of God's particular providence. The servant goes forth to find a bride for Isaac, watching every indication of the will of God as he treads his unknown way; and as the maiden meets him at the well and every circumstance seems to point in the one direction, he recognizes the hand of divine guidance and utters that sentence which is the very embodiment of the whole philosophy of divine providence; "I being in the way, the Lord led me to the house of my master's brethren."

Still more wonderful is the story of Joseph. It begins with a vision of his future, and then with dramatic vividness everything is blotted out in the bitter trials and disappointments that blight the fair promise of his youth; but the hand of love leads unerringly through it all, and the day comes when every one of these sorrows is overruled for his good and he can say to his cruel brethren, "Be ye not grieved or sorry that ye sold me into Egypt. As for you, ye thought evil against me, but God meant it unto good to bring to pass, as it is this day, to save much people alive."

Charles Cowman's lifetime throughout was just one series of providences, and often when asked why he had chosen to become a missionary he would reply, "I did not choose. It was God's choice for me." How can a man "choose" a "calling"? If a man is called *he* does not choose. It is the One who calls who does the choosing. "Ye have not chosen *ME*, but *I* have chosen *you*, and ordained you, that ye should go and bear fruit," says our Lord. Men act as though God threw down before them an assortment of plans from which they might choose what pleases them, even as the shopkeeper tosses out a dozen skeins of silk to a lady purchaser, from which she might select that which strikes her fancy. But this is not true. It is God's right to choose. It is simply ours to ascertain and obey. For next in its eternal moment to the salvation of a soul is the guidance of the life of a child of God. And God claims both as His supreme prerogative.

"Jesus said unto him,—go sell that thou hast—and come follow Me." Matthew 19:21.

"After all what would he have had to sacrifice had he followed Jesus? He would have had to give up his house in Jerusalem. He would have had to renounce society; but society would soon have forgotten him, for society has a short memory for people who for any reason have fallen out of it. That is what he would have lost, and what would he have gained? He would have had those walks with Jesus across the fields, and he would have heard Him say: 'Consider the lilies.'"

—Mark Rutherford.

"He is a great man who has a great plan for his life— the greatest who has the greatest plan and keeps it."
—Prof. Drummond.

CHAPTER VIII

THE CALL

There are three great epochs in the life of every man of God; the revelation of God, the collapse of self, and the commission for service. Charles Cowman had passed through the first two and we find on a blank page in his Bible, this brief sentence:

"Called to Japan. August 11, 1900. 10:30 A. M."

"There was no day like that" (Joshua 10:14). It stood alone in the history of his life. There had been memorable days in his life before this—the day when God for Christ's sake had forgiven him his sins, the day when the Holy Spirit came in to abide forever—but this day stood alone, and from then all his life was altered. The supreme hour had come for which all previous years had been the preparation, and from which all future ones would date. He had arranged his own program, but Christ, the unescapable Christ, crossed his path, and he yielded—yielded life, yielded will, yielded all, and then in a quiet place he wrote, "I met the Master face to face."

The pilgrim path will be divinely illuminated when we purpose in our hearts to follow Him whithersoever He leads us. God is never an instant too late. He may keep us from the knowledge of what He is going to do; but He always has His perfect plans successfully made. All we need to do is to put ourselves wholly in His hands, ask His guidance, follow His leadings, and count confidently upon His blessings.

It was not in a crowded gathering where there was a great wave of missionary enthusiasm, when touching tales of heathen lands were told, exciting heart sympathy, but in the hush of the Sabbath morning, away from his busy office, with a heart stilled to hear the smallest whisper of His Voice, that he received his call, the call which bore him through all kinds of testings and disappointments in the years which followed. A picture will ever remain in memory of that Sabbath morning, when on my return from the service, he met me with tear-stained face, took my hand in his and led me into the study where be broke the wonderful news. He read the verse that clinched his faith for the difficult emergency: "Go ye also into the vineyard and whatsoever is right I will give you" (Matt. 20:6). The text itself was a treasure-trove. In all the Book was no more apt nor more inspiring missionary message; yet it had lain in the grave of the unrealized and forgotten till it woke for Charles Cowman and held him in its risen power. To him it meant everything, a Divine commission, a Divine supply. The vision was almost blinding.

He had earnestly prayed that his life companion might be willing to accompany him, and on this occasion the answer was not long delayed. It was almost as in the days of Daniel, "At the beginning of thy supplications the commandment came forth," for I said to him, "Charles, six weeks ago while all alone, God spoke to me about going to Japan, and I have kept it hidden away within my heart, waiting for the right moment to tell you."

In the feudal days the vassal did homage to his lord by putting his hands together and placing them in the hands of his master as a token of entire submission and an absolute surrender of all his active powers to his service. Obedience to God is one condition of blessing from God. When He says, "Go," we stay at our peril; when He says, "Speak," we keep silent at our cost. The Master does not waste His special orders upon those who are not ready to obey. Only let a man live, waiting for the Lord's word and near enough to hear Him when He whispers His will, and that man will not lack a plain direction.

There is a splendid crest for the Lord's workers with this motto, "I fly where I am sent." It is a crest and arrow, polished and feathered—content to lie in the quiver until the Master uses it—lying on the string for His unerring fingers to send it forth; then going, strong and sure, smiting through the heart of the King's enemy.

Quoting S. D. Gordon: "There is a tender awe in knowing that there is Someone at your side guiding at every step, restraining here, leading on there. He knows the way better than the oldest Swiss guide knows the mountain trail. He has love's concern that all shall go well with you. When you come to the splitting of the road into two with the third path forking off from the others, there is a peace in just holding steady and very quiet while you put out your hand and say, 'Jesus, Master, guide here.' And then to hear a Voice so soft that only in great quiet is it heard, softer than faintest breath on your cheek, or slightest touch on your arm, telling the way in two words or syllables—that makes the peace unspeakable. If perhaps the chosen road leads to crowds and great service and praise of men, you will be thinking it was His leading that brought you there, not your own wisdom or talent. He has some great purpose for these crowds, and maybe some purpose *through* these crowds farther on. And you will be very careful not to disappoint or mar His plans. And, too, you will keep very quiet and close that the dust the crowd is raising may not bother your eyes and dim your vision of His face."

It was just at the time when the call was ringing in his heart that another splendid promotion was offered him— an almost enviable one. His officials, having an inkling

7

that he was leaving the telegraph service, left no stone unturned in order to keep this valuable worker with them; but the attractive position offered him could not satisfy. God's clear call had come, a Divine Hand was upon him; a Divine Voice was calling him.

"Two crowns were held out to Jesus. The people wanted to take Him and make Him King. They even wanted to take Him by force. They offered Him a crown studded with diamonds and sapphires and rubies, but there was another crown held out to Him. It was the crown of thorns.

"Two thrones were held out to Him. The ivory throne of David, His father; the other throne, a cruelly made cross.

"Two robes were offered Him on that day. One of the crimson purple of his ancestors, the other the crimson of His own blood, as it shall fall across His body on Calvary. Which should He choose? It was His moment of decision. He chose the way of the cross."

Who would not willingly count all things but "loss" for the high honor of fellowship with Him in such a purpose? An Oxford University professor once said to his students, "Beware of having an earthly future." God would have us with our hearts and minds on His heavenly kingdom and not on the perishing things of this transitory world.

The friends of Charles Cowman were really afraid that if he went to the mission field he would be wasting his life, throwing it away, forgetting that the Master said, "Except a corn of wheat fall into the ground and die, it abideth alone, but if it die, it bringeth forth much fruit." However, the blessings which followed far outweighed anything of worldly advantage he was laying down. When he returned after twenty years he said, "I have been overwhelmed at the glorious opportunity God granted me and I have never had one hour of regret right through these wonderful years. I would have gone to the ends of the earth alone for the enjoyment of the unspeakable fellowship with Christ. And as to the fruitage, I say it humbly, I have seen thousands seeking Christ and the work has gone forward with results such as I have never dared to even dream."

It was not merely enthusiasm for humanity that touched the heart of Charles Cowman and made him willing to give up life and all for the benefit of the millions in heathendom. Men have done noble deeds under the stimulus of philanthropy, but a higher motive than this was the mainspring of his life, and that was the consuming love for the Divine Master. Like Saint Paul, he was willing to become a fool for Christ's sake, and not a few of his business associates so regarded him. They saw but an opportunity before him of enriching his own life. His singleness of purpose and consecration are only too rare. How very much his great crisis-choice has meant to thousands of lives!

He passed through the allurement of a lucrative position and maintained untarnished his devotion to his calling, his love for the souls of men. A true vision from God will save one from shortsightedness and deliver him from this present evil world. He could not ignore the fact that he had been signally useful in his present vocation, nor could he be insensible to the reasons why his officials urged him to remain. In the after years when reviewing it he said, "I am sure that God planned it all and caused me to understand the way in which He wished me to walk. At the time the call came there were a number of definite conversions among my men, but I had a feeling that the hand of God was upon me for something which I could scarcely discern. My barque seemed to be sailing into new seas. The breath of Jehovah was carrying me into realms of thought and feeling in His kingdom which I had never voyaged before. It seemed like a mystery. I sought the Lord for counsel, and this passage of Scripture was given me: 'There stood a man of Macedonia, and prayed him, saying, Come over into Macedonia and help us. And after he had seen the vision, immediately we endeavored to go . . . assuredly gathering that the Lord had called us for to preach the Gospel unto them.' When looking to God in an hour of perplexity, these words seemed wafted down, 'I will instruct thee and teach thee in the way which thou shalt go. I will guide thee with mine eye.' These were the two angels who met me in the way as Abraham and Jacob were met."

"By faith Moses had respect unto the recompense of the reward." He yielded that which was immediate for the winning of the distant. He had the treasures of Egypt and even the crown itself at his disposal, but no immediate and temporary gain allured him. To a man of faith the ignoble and fleeting pleasures of the present pale into utter insignificance beside the glories of the great and divine reward of the future. Earthly delights shrivel, dwindle, and disappear when the light of the recompense God gives shines upon them. The paltry toys of childhood are nothing beside the achievements of a great life.

The power to choose the spiritual rather than the material; the vision which sees Him who is invisible, rather than that which only the eyes of the flesh behold; the ability to strive for the eternal reward rather than the temporal—are the forces which lift man to the highest heights and present him to God and the world as the chief asset of all time, namely, a purposeful, highly resolved, nobly consecrated personality.

REV. JUJI NAKADA AND FAMILY.
HIS MOTHER WAS ONE OF JAPAN'S EARLIEST CHRISTIANS.

There are positions of distinction and honor, such as military renown, on which poets and historians converge the rays of glory until they dazzle, fascinate, inflame, but, "How different," says a well-known writer, "is his lot who toils under the same sun to turn men unto God. His deeds rejoice the hosts who little reck of the battle's issue, but sing when a soul is saved. His name is written in letters bright as Heaven's crystals, incorruptible as its light. His earthly reward is God's approval; and when earth is burned up, a crown flashing with the glories that beam from the Deity unshrouded; a throne that even eternity cannot crumble, and which immortals whom his toil was the means of saving will joyfully surround. Let the merchant tell his gold, the statesman sway his realm, the warrior trample on his foe; let the philosopher expound creation, the scholar elaborate his theme, the poet attune his lay, but let him that would have bliss forever unshorn, go and win souls!"

The wonder of it all is that thousands more do not eagerly go to do this blessed and Christlike work. What a field there is in the missionary cause for Christian heroism! What a place for the development of more Pauls! But how very few care to enter the arena. Alas! The desire to shine at home eclipses the greater vision.

The Holy Spirit always has a definite purpose in His directions and He does not waste the time or strength of those who follow His leading. His errands are not aimless. "The chariot of God's providence runneth not on broken wheels." God still calls and sends forth His messengers and the modern missionary should of all men be sent of God. He should go to his far distant field with a clear and settled conviction that he is a messenger of God, an ambassador of Christ, and that he has no more right to disobey his calling than he has to wreck his soul by abandoning the service of God and going into the ways of sin and death.

Know when your work is ended, or you will do something besides your work and miss that which will fit you for the next work that is to be done.

Charles Cowman's work in the telegraph office was finished. The years spent there were years of training meant to perfect his powers ere he was thrust forward to realize the vision given him from above. The time had come, yea, the set time. To tarry longer would have been disobedience to the heavenly vision. Well it was that when the call came he did not confer with flesh and blood, for how often men and circumstances would fain defer our starting on our pilgrimage! God demands instant obedience with no dallying or delays. When He asks of us the question, "Wilt thou go with this man?", we should quickly and promptly answer, "I will go."

God had planned for Charles Cowman a different field from India with a fuller ministry than to heathen people only, but the time had not come for it to be revealed. Had He told him that He planned for him to establish Bible Training Institutes in three countries, to put the Word into every home in Japan, to tour the world time and time again in the interest of His kingdom with no financial backing whatever, but with simple trust in His promises, it would have staggered him, and he might have been compelled to draw back. So He guided him step by step, first calling him out in a small way into the life of faith, then in a little larger way, until trust was easy. He dared to go where the Holy Spirit led him and to leave the consequences with Him. He did not blaze his own path through life. God made it for him.

"Every man has his own vocation. There is one direction in which all space is open to him. He is like a ship in a river; he runs against obstructions on every side but one; on that side all obstruction is taken away and he sweeps serenely over a deepening channel into an infinite sea."—Emerson.

"God is building history by means of men and women whom He can trust, men and women of faith, men and women of vision, who apprehend the Divine revelation and say, 'Here am I, Lord, take me, equip me, send me, use me.'

"Even God cannot work without man. We are called to cooperate. History is the story of the race, of the nation, of the individual; and so while God has been making His revelation, He has been making it to men and He has been looking for men who will apprehend the revelation and carry forward His purpose here in time. God never wrought anything by means of masses and crowds in human history. He has wrought His wonders through the ages by individuals—people whom He could trust, people who exercise faith. What is faith? 'Faith is the substance of things hoped for, the evidence of things not seen.' The objects, therefore, of faith are the future and the unseen; and the office of faith is to give present existence to future things and vital reality to unseen things. And wherever such faith has been exercised, wherever men have laid hold of the Divine revelation, God has built a new era in human history. It is the advent of personality which alters the current of history. The sharp turning points of history are due to the rise of great personalities. It is not so much by ideas as by personalities that God sets this world forward. The mightiest civilizing powers are personalities, and the mightiest civilizing personalities are Christian men."—W. Graham Scroggie.

"A man who walks with God always gets to his destination."

"God's path is on the sea—just where we would not expect it to be! So when He leads us by unexpected ways, off the strong, solid land out upon the changing sea, *then* we may expect to see His ways. We are with One who finds a path as He goes. That is better than having a path ready tracked out, for it makes us perfectly independent of circumstances."
—C. A. Fox.

CHAPTER IX

THE FIRST VENTURINGS

"For ye shall not go forth with tumult, neither go by flight; for the Lord shall go forth in advance of you, and the God of Israel shall be He that brings up your rear" (Isa. 52:12—Septuagint).

It is "the steps" of a good man and not merely the journeys as a whole, that are ordered of the Lord. These were days of very much prayer and waiting upon God for definite direction, and He did not keep His trusting child waiting very long until He spoke to him. The home and furniture had to be disposed of. An advertisement was printed in the daily newspaper, also a large sign was placed in the window, but not a person came near. Remembering Gideon's fleece, he asked that he might have some sign from the Lord. The "For Sale" card was taken from the window while he prayed definitely, asking the Lord to direct someone to the house. He did not have long to wait, for almost immediately Robert Fisher, his second convert, called and asked what he was going to do with his apartment and the furnishings. In less than one hour everything was in Robert Fisher's possession. This was indeed a "confirming of the Word with signs following."

When God thrusts forth into service, we can reckon absolutely on His co-operation with us, for are we not called into partnership with His Son? Like the priests of old, at the command of the Lord to "go forward" he put his foot into the cold waters. Then they divided, and he walked through the river on dry ground. He was now ready for the fulfillment of the promise, "and every one that hath forsaken houses or brethren, or sisters, or father, or mother for my name's sake and the Gospel's, shall receive an hundredfold,"—and no sooner had the Master's command to leave all for His sake been obeyed than blessed *manifestations* were in evidence, which have ever been flowing and widening unto the present time. The providences were threaded together like pearls on a string. When God calls us to leave all and follow Him, He also gives the assurance that *with Himself He freely giveth all things*. God is prepared to co-operate with any who will faithfully fulfil His conditions.

Robert Fisher wished immediate possession of the apartment and it was necessary to vacate. Into our home some months before a small eight-page religious paper had found its way. The name of the paper was "The Revivalist" and its editor was Rev. Martin Wells Knapp, of Cincinnati, Ohio. The paper had such a deeply spiritual tone that Charles Cowman had a great longing to meet its editor ere he sailed to Japan, so the journey was taken to Cincinnati for that purpose.

"How homeless we felt as we walked out of our apartment," he said to a friend, "but I look forward to the time when on the mission field I shall be literally homeless indeed as was my Master, for doubtless much of my life will be spent in itinerary and pioneer work, away from the little spot I shall call home."

A Bible Training School was in embryo at Cincinnati under the direction of Rev. Martin Wells Knapp. Charles Cowman had spent six years in the Moody Bible Training Institute, and consequently had some experience in conducting Bible Schools, and in training young people for the Master's service. A warm friendship sprang up between the two men whose interests were in the same line of work, and six happy weeks were spent in this new school while waiting for further orders to leave for Japan.

He was on his way to the mission field under his own church Missionary Board, a cable having been sent stating the date of sailing. There had been a vacancy in one of the Mission schools and Charles Cowman was to fill the position as a teacher of English, his wife a teacher of music.

During these days a strange burden possessed his heart, the glow of going turned to gloom, which he could not interpret. It is well at such times to be quite still and inquire of the Lord as to its meaning, so for three days he scarcely ate or slept. God was ordering a halt. Rev. Martin Wells Knapp was carrying a similar burden. Of his definite call there was not the slightest doubt, the enemy never touched that, and light soon was given revealing God and His plan for his future work. It came in the stillness of the morning, long ere the sun had risen, and that particular meeting with God was the turning point of all his future life. Had a mistake been made at this crisis, the work which the future held would not have been accomplished. Doubtless he would have left the mission field and returned to the telegraph office.

"Step by step as thou goest, thy way shall open up before thee." The *steps* are ordered and the *stops* as well. If we take the first step, our obedience will give God a chance to show us the next.

Alexander McLaren writes: "Is it not a thing worth having, to have this settled conviction of your hearts, that Christ is moving all the impulses of your life, and that nothing falls out without the intervention of His presence and the power of His will working through it? Do you not think that such belief would nerve you for difficulty, and would lift you buoyantly over trials and depressions, and would set you upon a vantage ground high above all the petty annoyances of life? Tell me, is there any other place where a man can plant his foot and say, Now I am on a rock and I care not what comes!"

All have gifts just a little different from another. Emerson said, "Nature arms each man with some faculty which enables him to do easily some feat impossible." This brings to each one a tremendous responsibility, and if we fail in doing the thing assigned to us, it will be forever undone. Some sheaves will never be gathered, but will be eternally lost and destroyed; some reward forever unbestowed. Finding God's plan and taking one's place in God's work is to mount His chariot, and with Him, ride on to the final goal of the ages, conquering and to conquer.

"If any man willeth to do His will, he shall know of the teaching." The Apostle Paul tried to find the way of God's will. He tried to go into Asia and was forbidden; he attempted to go into Bithynia, but the Spirit suffered him not. But he went down into Troas and there the vision came. The guided life is possible, gloriously possible, but the guided life is the sacrificial life, it costs. We recall the words of the Master to the young man, "and renounceth his own life also." If we but yield, follow, and obey, then we shall be like David, who was "the man after God's own heart, who shall fulfil all my will." When yielding ourselves unreservedly to Him, we little know to what lines of service His unfolding will eventually point.

It was on a December morning and he was up early for his "quiet hour tryst." He wanted to talk the matter over with the Lord and be assured of the will of God beyond a question of a doubt. One of the beautiful

CHAS. E. COWMAN AT HIS DESK IN TOKYO.
INSERT—THE CHICAGO BUSINESS MAN AT TWENTY-EIGHT.

pictures hanging on memory's wall is that of a glorious sunrise stealing over the Kentucky hills; a young man standing in the doorway of the new Bible school, his face toward the dawn; in his hand, a New Testament, his eyes aglow with a holy light, as if he had seen the King in His beauty, as indeed he had. As he looked into the face of her who had promised to accompany him to the ends of the earth, what was it that he was hesitating to tell her? What secret did he hold that had no words for expression? Handing her the New Testament he simply pointed to Matt. 20:6, saying, "God has again spoken to me through these words, 'Go ye also into the vineyard and whatsoever is right, I will give you,'" and further added, "I am sure that God means us to launch forth into His work quite apart from any Missionary Society and trust Him for all. It is His will for us, we must obey."

A note in his diary on that date reads, "I made an unreserved, an unconditional, cheerful, and eternal surrender of myself to God. I do not feel the least bit of anxiety about my future path. I want only to be holy."

It was no mere child's play to which God called His servant, foregoing all methods of self-help, cutting loose from the old moorings and launching forth upon the bare word, "Go ye . . . . and whatsoever is right, I will give thee." A dear old saint once wrote: "If any will dare to venture forth on a path of separation, cutting himself from all future aid and from all self-originated effort; content to walk alone with God, with no help from any but Him—such will find that all the resources of the divine Almightiness will be placed at his disposal, and that the resources of Omnipotence must be exhausted ere his cause can fail for want of help."

This seemed to Charles Cowman to be the Apostolic plan: to go forward at God's call, letting Him supply the need. He plunged gladly into a life of trusting the Lord alone, and he found that the resources of God are promised to those who undertake the program of God. He simply fell into his place in the divine plan.

The next Sabbath morning after this definite dealing with God, he went to a little church in the suburbs of Cincinnati to conduct the service. At the close, a good sister in the congregation came to the pulpit and slipped a dollar bill into his hand. It was wholly unsolicited, and this first dollar, of more than one million and a half which was later entrusted to him for the work in the fields, was received with perhaps the greatest joy of all; for it came as a token that God was indeed in the voice that had spoken to his soul the previous week.

Too many of us want to *see* our way through before starting new enterprises. If we could and did, from whence would come the development of our Christian graces? Faith cannot be plucked from our trees like ripe apples. After the words, "In the beginning," comes the Word, "God." The first step turns the key into God's power-house, and it is not only true that God helps those who help themselves, but He also helps those who cannot help themselves. He can be depended on at all times.

It is very blessed to learn obedience experimentally. Whether the command be "Give ye them to eat," or "Fill the water pots with water," in any case all we have to do is to obey. The miracle can be left absolutely with Him, the promise is sure and bound to be fulfilled. Yes, whether the command seems to be unreasonable; whether it appears impossible; or whether it appears dangerous to a degree, obedience is *our* privilege, manifestation His, whose we are and whom we serve. Let us, when once persuaded of His call, however full our hands may be, however great our weakness and natural inaptitude for the task in question, rest on His infallible guidance, while claiming an accession of strength and needed capacity for every emergency for which the Master says, "Go forward." Hesitancy is not characteristic of heroes.

It is a glorious thing to see a faith which, with no outward appearance to warrant it, will yet step out on a path of literal obedience though there seems nothing but thin air to tread upon. Not arguing or questioning, or reasoning; but believing that "all the promises of God are yea and in Him Amen"!

It took a God-given conviction to step out unheralded and alone without a Home Board to back him, and with few friends who could stand behind him and launch a work for God, but he took the step in the divine program and every detail in this program is vastly important.

A Christmas Convention was being held at the new Bible School and Charles Cowman was given an opportunity in an afternoon service to tell of his call to Japan. A man sat in the audience under deep conviction. He had traveled a long way to this special convention to seek the blessing of a clean heart, and when the opportunity was presented, he, with a number of seekers, came to the altar. Here was a chance for some special personal work and Charles Cowman was quickly down by his side. The dear brother told him that he had been an elder in a Presbyterian Church for twenty years, but during the address of the afternoon he made the discovery that he had never had a change of heart, had never been "born again." Soon he was rejoicing in the witness to sins forgiven. The next day he was at the altar seeking the blessing of a clean heart, and Charles Cowman again was used of the Lord to lead a soul over into Canaan.

This brother left the convention as did others who had come from outside towns and country places. A week later a letter was received from him and in it was a cheque for $300.00 (£60.0.0). It read, "Please accept this gift for your steamer fares to Japan." After he had received the blessing of full salvation, he went to Iowa, sold a farm, and sent a tenth of the amount received, which was just sufficient for the steamer fares. Could anything have been more directly from God's own hand?

How marvelously everything opened when God's hour had arrived! A Christian soldier is not required to go to warfare at his own charges, but is led on step by step and every emergency is anticipated and provided for by the great Captain of his salvation.

How shall I know that . . . . ? "Is it not that thou goest with us?" Farewells were said to new-found friends, and Charles Cowman and wife were off again to their home city, Chicago, for final farewell meetings. In the meanwhile his friends had learned of his going out to the mission field trusting in Jesus alone, and many were alarmed because he was starting off with "nothing behind him *but God.*" But at that moment he could hardly know alarm. The strange interaction of body, mind, and spirit were producing in him something more like exaltation, hope was flooding his heart, and the disciple saw only before him the longed-for task allotted by the Master's hand.

The dear people of his home church remonstrated long with him over such a daring step. Failure was prophesied on the right hand and on the left. The more conservative minds waited to see how the glow of his enthusiasm endured the strain and toil in learning the native language, and living by faith. Had he waited for the opinion of every one, he would have met death ere the occasion could have been improved. "If you are willing to run risks for God, He will never fail you. Be sure that you are doing His will, then forward march, come what will, and those who waited to see you fail will come and help you after you have made the venture," were lines in a letter written after he reached the field.

"We boast," said the inimitable Dan Crawford, "of being so practical a people that we want a surer thing than faith, but did not Paul say that the promise is by FAITH that it might be SURE?" (Romans 4:16).

> "Nothing before, nothing behind;
> The steps of faith
> Fall on the seeming void, and find
> The Rock beneath."

In one of the farewell services a brother slipped a cheque into Mr. Cowman's hand saying, "Please accept this for the first year's rent of your proposed Bible Training School. It does not represent any abundance of wealth, but if you for Christ's sake can separate from your business and all, and go without purse or scrip, I cannot give less than this." The cheque read $240.00 (£48).

His career seemed marked by signal providences at every step, and it is full of the most beautiful examples of the way God loves to take full charge of the most incidental occurrences to work out His great designs and manifest His presence and power.

It was clearly manifest that the cloud was moving on and that the Shepherd had gone before. He went forth confident of victory, and what can endue one with greater strength than to have "gathered assuredly" that the Lord had sent him! He went out much as Abraham, feeling that he could stake his all on the faithfulness of God who had bidden him go forth trusting. He put his hand of faith into God's hand of love and we believe that the secret of the marvelous growth of the work, and God's

8

abundant blessing upon it, has been because he caught the divine thought for it and through obedience entered His plan. For surely it was not a man-planned work, or years ago it would have come to naught.

William Jennings Bryan once said in the midst of an address: "The great things of the world have been accomplished by men and women who had faith enough to attempt the seemingly impossible and to trust God to open the way."

A simple ordination service was held ere he left for his far-away field. Rev. Martin Wells Knapp, who had accompanied him to Chicago and who felt that Charles Cowman was answering his own call (as he had felt called some years before), Rev. Seth C. Rees, his gifted son Byron, and Rev. Charles Stalker laid their hands upon him and his wife, separating them unto the ministry. They took upon them the consecration vow, being "allowed of God to be put in trust with the Gospel" (1 Thess. 2:4).

Many old friends attended that simple service. Among them was his best friend, Ernest A. Kilbourne. How greatly he disliked leaving him, but Ernest Kilbourne pledged him his prayers, promising also to stand back of the Telegraphers' Mission Band, which was as dear to Charles Cowman as his right hand.

His going to the mission field not only stirred a lively missionary interest among telegraph circles, but it taught them what it really meant to give themselves wholly to Christ. It taught them the meaning of literally leaving all to follow the Lamb whithersoever He leadeth. Late in December came the final parting from friends and colleagues, the real venture of faith was made as he turned his face westward.

In his brief farewell address he spoke of his prospective work with something of enthusiasm, something of glee. It was the prospect that thrilled and fired him. His face was fairly glowing with delight. The following are a few excerpts from his message:

"Some years ago I read a book entitled 'Dawn on the Hills of Tang.' In it was this statement: 'The investment of life is the most momentous of all human decisions. As Jesus, before entering upon His active ministry, went up on a mountain-top and beheld the kingdoms of this world and the glory of them, so should every Christian examine the opportunities for a life investment presented by the nations of a weary world.' This statement impressed me with its deep significance.

"Later, I read Hillis's 'Investment of Influence' and this gave me larger vision of the fact that it is not a light thing to live out a whole human life and not live it in such a way as to bring large returns. Added force and beauty come to that statement of the Master, 'Work not for the food which perisheth, but for the food which abideth unto eternal life.'

"As I have pondered over these facts, there has come to me a great longing to give to our young people this true conception of a life investment, and not to these only, but to hundreds of Christian men and women with wrong views of true success. In this commercial age even the preacher is tempted to leave the pulpit and engage in some work that will bring larger returns in dollars and cents. The paramount question that towers above every other, not only in youth, but at whatever point we may have reached, is this: 'How can I now invest the rest of my life so that it will bring the largest return?'

"We cannot blame our young people for turning away from the ministry at home or in other lands, when in the home we talk as if money and ease were the ultimate goal to be sought. Many of our leading periodicals hold up the rich man as the successful man, and one would almost conclude that the title to happiness is written only on the back of bank bills. From the pulpit we condemn the love of money for mere selfish uses, but nothing practically better is offered as a greater inducement.

"Oh, young people, lift your eyes and look on a world to be won for Christ before you choose your life work. See the millions of men and women living out a whole lifetime with nothing to comfort, elevate, or inspire— nothing beyond the sensual tragic life which they are now living, but a great black abyss; no one to touch their fevered, sin-sick lives with the sweet old story of the Great Physician.

"It is a matter of serious concern when we contemplate what Christians of today are doing as compared with what we could and ought to be doing, at home and abroad. Joseph Parker said, 'As long as the church is simply one of many institutions, she will have her little day, she will die and that will be all, but as soon as she gets the spirit of Christ, until the world says she has gone stark mad, then she will be on the high road to capturing this planet for Jesus Christ.'

"When Henry Martyn, that splendid young hero of the cross, lay dying with a fever in Persia, he received a letter asking how the missionary interest of the church at home could be increased. The dying saint said, 'Tell them to live more with Christ, to catch more of His Spirit; for the spirit of Christ is the spirit of Missions, and the nearer we get to Him, the more intensely missionary we become.'

"The Christian must literally burn himself out to the world. Too many of us want to shine, but not to burn out. 'If any man shrink back, my soul shall have no pleasure in him' (Heb. 10:38). 'The field is the world,' and God has given His Son the heathen for His inheritance and the uttermost part of the earth for His possession. If we draw back, God will raise up other laborers to reap the glorious harvest. Draw back! In a cause for which God gave His Son and Jesus spilt His precious blood, in which the Apostles agonized and martyrs burned at the stake, and holy angels watched with breathless anxiety? Draw back! In a cause which binds the human family in the golden bonds of love,—which communicates living hope and dying consolation and everlasting happiness to thousands of our heathen neighbors? Draw back! And leave our heathen brother to perish on the highway of perdition, in his sin, and in his blood, while we, like the cold-blooded Levite, pass by on the other side? No, so long as the life-blood ebbs and flows in these veins, so long as our hearts beat true with the love of God and man, I solemnly pledge myself to God with every gift and talent I possess to do my utmost in bringing the heathen home.

"Let us beware of doing any part of life-work or soul-work in a half-hearted manner. If a man has such a vision, then difficulties and even death itself are but mere details in themselves. There are hundreds competing for the one jewel that you are striving for at home, and when you grasp it you will have to share it with others. There are treasures in dark mines abroad that none can claim with you, but which you and your precious Lord may share together through the ages of glory, as a recompense for your labors.

"William Carey might have been the pastor of a little English village, but now he is the Apostle of India. Judson might have had a very prominent place in New

England, but he is the father of the Karens of Burmah. Oh, let us realize the honors and opportunities of our life, and despise the sacrifice and trials through which they must be won."

If we could ask Charles Cowman today if he wasted his life by going to the mission field, if he made a mistake in investing his life there, I believe the words would come back from those lips now so still, in one glad enthusiastic response, "I made the greatest investment—for the dividends are the greatest—the salvation of the heathen." He lived for the inheritance incorruptible.

"Blessed is the man who has found his work; let him ask for no other blessedness; he has a life purpose," wrote Carlyle.

There are those who say that Charles Cowman buried his life. There are others who say that if buried, there will one day be a glorious resurrection.

Upon whom shall his mantle fall? Where are the others who stand in full view of earthly honor and emoluments, and rejoice to make them a sacrifice for Christ for the extension of His kingdom?

These lines were found penned on a blank leaf in Charles Cowman's Bible:

"God is looking for a man, or woman, whose heart will be always set on Him, and who will trust Him for all He desires to do. God is eager to work more mightily now than He ever has through any soul. The clock of the centuries points to the eleventh hour.

"The world is waiting yet to see what God can do through a consecrated soul. Not the world alone, but God Himself is waiting for one, who will be more fully devoted to Him than any who have ever lived; who will be willing to be nothing that Christ may be all; who will grasp God's own purposes; and taking His humility and His faith, His love and His power, will, without hindering, continue to let God do exploits.

"There is no limit to what God can do with a man, providing he does not touch the glory."

> "How sweet to know that I am Thine,
>   All Thine!
> How sweet to know that Thou art mine,
>   Yes, mine!
> Not tremblingly I go, afraid,
> Not fearful, hesitant, dismayed,
> But firmly on my refuge stayed,
>   I go.
>
> "How sweet to give this life to Thee,
>   To Thee,
> Remembering One Who died for me,
>   Yes, me!
> I know the Rock whereon I stand,
> I know a strong, unfailing Hand,
> I know a Heart that my life planned,
>   I know!"

"Behold, this dreamer cometh!"—Gen. 37:19.

"There is nothing so striking as a dreamer in action."
—*Victor Hugo.*

"Thanks be to the dreamers for waking a sleeping world! There are souls who are visional, but not visionary. No pessimist breaks new trails,—it is not worth while. Men must always dream dreams before they blaze new trails; see visions before they do exploits."

"The arrival upon the planet of an original thinker, is like the outburst of a fire in a great city. Nobody knows where it will end."—*Emerson.*

CHAPTER X

LAUNCHING FORTH

"Go in this thy might. Have not I called thee?" (*Judges 6:14*).

"The tender light of home behind, dark heathen gloom before,
The servants of the Lord go forth to many a foreign shore.
But the True Light that cannot pale, streams on them from
    above,
A Light Divine that shall not fail, the smile of Him they love."

On the morning of February 1, 1901, a little group of friends, among them a number of telegraph operators, stood on the pier at San Francisco to wave farewell to their friends, Charles Cowman and his wife. At twelve o'clock noon, the gang plank was lifted, the steamer slowly moved away from the dock, and the "China" began ploughing her way across the Pacific. It was an hour, not of sadness, but triumph. Charles Cowman sang to the group of friends on shore the lines that since his venture of faith God had made a blessing to him:

"I do not ask to see the way,
  My feet shall have to tread,
But only that my soul may feast
  Upon the Living Bread.
'Tis better far to walk with Him
  By faith close to His side,
I may not know the way I go,
  But Oh, I know my Guide.

"His love can never fail!
His love can never fail!
My soul is satisfied to know
His love can never fail!"

And right down through the twenty-three years of missionary service, when at times everything seemed to fail, when funds often went down to the last limit and health finally failed, he still could sing, "His Love Can Never Fail!" His fellow-travelers, who saw him walking the deck day after day, dressed in his suit of dark gray, doubtless mistook him for a business man who was going abroad in the interest of his firm. On board the steamer he kept much to himself and spent a great deal of time in prayer in his cabin. One of the travelers said of him, "There seems to be something on that man's mind." Yes, there was something, and that something was lost souls, and his responsibility to his Master.

A storm at sea was a thrilling experience and a letter written to a friend gave a brief description of it. "The waves are in their heroic mood and are engaged in a pitched battle. A lashing, tossing, heaving, foaming, falling, glancing, rise and fall of liquid mountains and valleys, awful but ravishing to look upon! 'It is the Lord that commandeth the waters; it is the glorious Lord that ruleth the sea!'

> "No water can swallow the ship where lies,
> The Master of ocean and earth and skies!"

"We stand for hours together, listening to the music of the waves and gazing at their inimitable beauty. Many a night we reluctantly say goodnight to the sea and sky and step into our cabin, to be rocked in the cradle of the deep. We do not feel alone. One is walking by our side whose smile is as gentle as the breath of evening, but Whose Hand holds the vault of Heaven and controls all the forces of the earth. Unseen hosts are marching by our side. Invisible armies are filling the air. We expect great and mighty things to come to pass." A delay of three days was caused by the storm.

On February 21, the dim outline of a shoreline was sighted. It was an hour of thrilling happiness as it was his first glimpse of a foreign land. There was a triumphant glow about him, for this was a great day and Charles Cowman, with his wife on his arm, amid a chattering crowd, went ashore to the land of his dreams. Rev. Juji Nakada was there to greet him. It seemed like a homecoming. Throughout the years that followed he often said that there was no spot in all the world so dear to him as the Isle of the Morning, beautiful Japan. He was now face to face with the teeming multitude, and here began that unbroken record of usefulness which extended for nearly a quarter of a century, until he was called to his great reward.

He had gone to the mission field by Divine appointment and saw naught before him but the task allotted to him by the Master's Hand. Writing home he said, "How glorious it will be to live for Jesus here! How glorious if I could even die for Him!" He felt a great aloneness during this first time in the Far East; felt now the power of the spiritual force which against his life was hurled. It was no untrained soul that felt there the "prince of the power of the air," and shuddered as if in the dominion of the prince of darkness. The fiends of darkness seemed to sit in sullen repose in that land. The battle was set, the hour had come, and the man was at hand. "To every man his work."

It may be said that the work was made for the man and the man for the work. He found his kingdom waiting for him and he entered into it, the work for which God had set him apart and for which he had been preparing throughout his thirty years. Paul writes to the Ephesians, "We are his workmanship"—product of skilled labor— "created in Christ Jesus unto good works which God has before ordained that we should walk in them." The man and the works were fore-ordained and pre-adapted for each other, and when they came together they fitted mutually and perfectly. Not always can the man prepare himself for the service, for he knows not his predestined sphere. The problem is solved at once when we admit a Divine purpose, forming and fitting each man for his work, so that, without any previous intimations what the demands on him would be, he finds himself already trained for that special form of service. Oftentimes faculties and powers, acquisitions and discipline, education and experience, earliest occupations and trades, all prove to be just what are needed, though the need could not be foreseen. When the Temple was being built, the stones were so completely hewn in the quarry, and the timbers in the shops, that there was heard no axe or any tool of iron while the great building was going forward.

The first entry in his notebook upon arrival was, "Tokyo, Japan, February 22nd. A new era in our lives. New responsibilities, new hopes, new avenues of thought, new subjects for prayer. Oh, for faith, unyielding faith! My soul yearns for a close alliance with God."

The story of the Oriental Missionary Society was the answer to his fervent outburst.

"February 23rd. Promises claimed this morning: 'I will sanctify my great Name which was profaned among the heathen . . . and the heathen shall know that I am the Lord, when I shall be sanctified in you before their eyes.' 'I will give thee the treasures of darkness and the hidden riches of secret places, that thou mayest know that I, the Lord, which call thee by name, am the God of Israel.' What are we here for but to make known that God is the Lord? Gracious promises. What have we to fear, for God is with us and God has sent us!"

Charles Cowman believed that God had sent him to the Orient for just one thing, and he kept in that plan

HIS AND YOURS FOR THE SPEEDY EVANGELIZATION OF THE ORIENT.
CHARLES AND LETTIE COWMAN.

until the close of his day. No life can be great unless it has some mastering objective. Jesus was the greatest Man because He had the greatest purpose, namely, to accomplish the work God gave Him to do. At twelve years of age He says "Wist ye not that I must be about my Father's business?" His life throughout was an expression of the thought. In the Garden of Gethsemane He cries, "Not my will, but thine be done;" and on the cross, "It is finished!"

In simple faith Charles Cowman gave himself to the great work with all his ransomed powers. He was a born leader of men, with a genius for organization. He was a practical business man, throwing his capacities into the work for the evangelization of the Orient. This talent was laid at the Master's feet, and without this consecration, he would have remained nothing but a successful business man, or a high-priced permanent official. His one talent was put to the exchangers and multiplied to ten because of its use. Marvelous works come out of nothing, seemingly, and he began a work which may change the history of millions.

The closer we study his career, the more obvious it becomes that for this purpose God raised him up, fitted him in advance with a strange exactness for the precise work for which he was destined. We see the aptitude, not only in his experience, but also in his whole history and character and training. His organizing faculty, his singular tact, his readiness of resource, his spirituality—such elements of fitness could only be secured by One who, aforehand, makes His instruments ready for His work.

Charles Cowman ever felt himself a humble instrument of an unseen Hand, fulfilling a purpose deeper and higher than he knew.

Charles Cowman and Juji Nakada dreamed of a great Bible Training Institute where hundreds of native preachers might receive the training for their life's work; but, with no denominational missionary board to back them, no human resources in sight, it looked like a dream indeed. They could well understand the feelings of the people of Nehemiah's day when the little company made an attempt to rebuild the walls. Little wonder that they mocked and jeered, saying one to the other, "What do these feeble Jews?" God who prepared His work through the ages, accomplishes it, when the hour is come, with the feeblest instruments.

Had the work been of human origin, it would have failed, but it began aright—with God—and God never launched a failure since the world began, therefore they were confident that it would end aright.

Charles Cowman believed with all his heart that he was called of God to go to the Orient and in simple, child-like faith to depend on Him for the supply of all the needs. He further believed that the provision would always be found right beside His plan. He did not start to build upon another man's foundation or pattern by other societies, but held firmly to the conviction that God had given to him the "pattern in the Mount" as much as He did to Moses. The work was outlined by the Spirit of God. There were no distinctive Bible Training Institutes in Japan and no Holiness movement, and it was no light undertaking which faced these two pioneers and a few kindred spirits of that early day.

It meant the blazing of a new missionary trail in the Orient. Only God knew what was bound up in the issue of the next few years and it was none other than God Himself who made such a little spring the fountain-head of a mighty majestic river that now sweeps on, fertilizing the deserts of the East.

The aim of the Bible Training Institute was not to produce classical scholars, but young men and women who could handle their mother tongue with effect, who were steeped in the Bible, and who could so proclaim that Word as to arrest and influence all classes of people.

Many have heard of the Bible Training Institutes in Japan, Korea and China, who would like to know more of their history.

No sooner had Charles Cowman reached the field, than a diligent search was made for a suitable building in which to begin the work, and in his notebook among the first entries, we find these brief lines:

"April 2, 1901.

"Today we have been taught a lesson on *exactly-timed* guidance. Brother Nakada and I called upon the landlord of the Jimbo-cho mission property. We were delayed in getting through the crowded streets, but reached the house around 9:30, and found a pleasant Japanese, about fifty years of age. We made known to him our errand, and he smilingly said to us. 'I have wished that I might rent my buildings to Christians as I have found them to be so reliable and prompt in paying their bills.' It was not long until we had in our possession the lease for the Mission building. The rental was but a trifle more than $240.00 (£48.0.0.) a year.

"As we were leaving his house a gentleman rode up in a jinricksha with the express purpose of renting the building, but he was just ten minutes too late. I could only stand in awe before the King of kings, who hears and answers prayer. There can be but one solution to this, *God* is in it. What a blessed thing to have God as your partner!"

How wonderfully God led even in the smallest details. The building was singularly suited to the need and soon became one of Tokyo's greatest salvation light-houses. It was right in the very heart of that heathen city of three million souls. There was room on the first floor for a good-sized mission hall, also an apartment for Brother Nakada. On the second floor were rooms for prospective students, and Charles Cowman and his wife. It was quickly put in order and a large sign swung over the entrance which read:

"Jesus Doctrine Mission Hall.
Services Every Night, Everybody Welcome."

Scarcely had the signboard been placed, when a scholarly-looking gentleman called, inquiring into the meaning of it. He belonged to the *literari* class and was ever searching, like the Athenians, for something new. It was the first time he had come into direct contact with Christians and missionaries. A New Testament was given to him, he was asked to read it, and every evening for a week he was a faithful attendant at the services. He became a most earnest seeker and before the close of the week he was rejoicing in the Lord. His name was M. Takemaye and he continues to serve the Lord faithfully unto this day.

One night while passing through a very narrow street, returning from an open-air service, one of our number shouted out through a megaphone, "A Jesus doctrine meeting will be held tonight at the Mission hall in Jimbo-cho. Anyone desiring peace, come and hear about the true God."

In a little home in an out-of-the-way narrow street, sat an aged couple, and the sound reached their ears, "Anyone desiring peace." It was like sweet music floating across the waves, and the aged grandmother thought within herself, "Peace, what a lovely word, but *where* can it be found? Can it be possible that, after all our weary years of searching, at last we shall find peace? Perhaps these foreigners can tell us. At any rate, I will venture to go and hear what they have to say."

Scarcely had we returned when a little woman entered the hall, the first arrival of the evening. She was bent with age and hobbled along with the aid of a cane. She sat on the front seat and listened with all of her heart to the wonderful story of peace, and at the close of the service we learned something of her life-story. Sixty years before, she was married to a fine young man, and when they started life together, they decided that, just as far as possible, they would live righteous lives. As the heathen priests were their religious leaders, they naturally consulted them, becoming faithful attendants at the temple. Every heathen festival was faithfully observed and each idol devoutly worshipped, but as the years wore on, they still had the same heart yearnings which were never satisfied.

The priest told them if they would visit the various temples of the land, there was a possibility that they might find peace, and as they had considerable money, and were not obliged to work for their living, they started out on their quest. They became pilgrims, devoting their lives to religion. Year after year they visited heathen temples, tramping hundreds of miles, now far up the mountain where stood a dumb idol, again into the heart of a chain of mountains, which necessitated hours of hard climbing to reach a shrine at the summit and to receive written prayers from the priest in charge. But they always returned with the same dull ache in their hearts. Still they continued their search for sixty long years.

Their money was now all spent, they were too old to continue traveling, so they came to Tokyo and settled down in a tiny room to wait until the end.

9

The second evening, long ere the doors of the Mission hall opened, came this aged grandmother. She found the same seat and listened again to the wonderful story. Every night for two weeks she occupied the same place, but one night the old despairing look had vanished and in her face was a light, not of this earth, as she said with rapture, "I have found peace. I have found Jesus." She brought her aged companion with her and together they sat side by side listening to the sweet story of Jesus and His love. Over the pulpit hung a banner on which Matt. 11:28 was written, "Come unto Me, all ye that bear burdens and are heavy laden, and I will give you peace." The aged man was fairly entranced by these words. Tears, unbidden, began to trickle over the wrinkled cheeks; the heart's door which had been closed for eighty years was being gently opened by an unseen Hand. The long, long night was passing, the new day dawning. Pointing to the banner he said, "I never heard such gracious words as these." He, too, entered into the joy of the Lord and this aged couple, whom we named "Grown Old Waiting," became a continual inspiration to us. They were just two of the many who groped about in the darkness earnestly yearning for something that would satisfy the needs of their hearts.

Nor was this blessed, self-denying work in vain, for ninety souls knelt at the humble altar during this first month, and the Sabbath afternoon Holiness meetings were richly owned of God. A Vi-countess was among the first to "enter into the blessing," and a work among the royalty and upper classes began through her efforts, which has been a stream of blessing from then until now. A number of "elect ladies" from the Women's College came with hungry hearts seeking a deeper work of grace, and found Full Salvation. A student from the Imperial University was soundly converted. At the opening service they had prayed for a great ingathering of souls. That prayer was answered to the full. God alone has the record of the many thousands who have been converted on that spot.

A number of young men and women had already heard the call of God to preach the Gospel to their own people, and scarcely had the doors of the Bible School opened when numbers of applicants were received and Charles Cowman was overwhelmed with the great need. As many students were received as could be accommodated. These earnest, diligent young men and women studied during the morning, held street meetings in the afternoon, and attended the Mission hall in the evening. The object of the school was to make *experimental* preachers. These became great soul-winners.

Not many weeks went by until a larger building was required. This meant another new venture of faith, and much prayer was made for funds with which to purchase a location, and God answered. An answer to prayer is the grandest thing in the universe, for it is the soul in direct communication with God. The work grew and so did faith. A brother in the homeland felt the Lord leading him to make a gift to missions and it came just in time to purchase a splendid mission hall, on Awaji-cho. It was also suitable for a Bible School. It was one of the most strategic centers in all Tokyo at that day. Thus the second Mission hall was opened; services in this Hall continued every night for ten years, an unbroken record. There was an average of one thousand seekers a year and a volume could be written about these wonderful years which would read like the Acts of the Apostles.

God's providential care in times when great fires swept the city was very marked. Several times entire districts were literally in ashes. At one time a fire swept along one of the streets for more than a mile, until it reached the corner where Central Mission was located. People watched it creeping along, and the heathen said one to another, "The next place to burn will be the Jesus doctrine building"; however, a sudden gust of wind came up which turned the course of the fire, and the flames were not allowed so much as to touch that spot. There it stood, a lone building in the midst of the debris, a silent witness to the protecting care of God.

The portions of Scripture which were made a blessing during those days were:

"Under His shadow we shall live among the heathen."
Lam. 4:20.

"In the wilderness shall waters break out and streams in the desert. And the parched ground shall become a pool and the thirsty land springs of water." Isa. 35:6, 7.

"Behold I will do a new thing; now it shall spring forth." Isa. 43:19.

"And they went forth, and preached everywhere, the Lord working with them, and confirming the word with signs following." Mark 16:20.

"Take root downward and bear fruit upward."
Isa. 37:31.

"From this day I will bless you." Haggai 2:19.

"The Almighty shall be thy defence, and thou shalt have plenty of silver. Thou shalt also decree a thing and it shall be established unto thee, and light shall shine upon thy ways."—Job 22:25, 28.

"For all things are yours . . . . and ye are Christ's; and Christ is God's."—1 Cor. 3 :21-23.

"I would have you without carefulness."—1 Cor. 7 :32.

"Be careful for nothing; but in everything by prayer and supplication with thanksgiving, let your requests be made known unto God."—Phil. 4 :6.

"The Lord went before them by day in a pillar of a cloud, to lead them the way; and by night in a pillar of fire, to give them light; to go by day and night; he took not away the pillar of the cloud by day, nor the pillar of fire by night, from before the people."—Ex. 13 : 21, 22.

"Jesus Christ, the same yesterday, and today, and forever."—Heb. 13 :8.

"Fruit springs out of death. Selfishness **is always** solitary. It is the lives poured out in sacrifice that abound in blessing. The way of conquest is the way of the Cross. The names that are honored in history are the names that stand over graves where self was buried, long before the body died."

CHAPTER XI

THE FIRST HOME

Jimbo-cho is the name of a district in the very heart of the city of Tokyo, where our first missionary home was established. The street on which the building faced was about eight feet in width. There were markets of every description. European houses in more healthful districts were available, but the rents were so high that the very thought of occupying one of them was an impossibility; so rooms on the upper floor of the school building were used as the first home in Japan. Few Europeans would have considered living there at all, but to Charles Cowman, this was just as he had pictured missionary life. It was during this time that he wrote home, "You have no idea what joys we missionaries have"! He was as happy as if he had been in a palace, for he had no ease-loving spirit.

No mere human compassion, or enthusiasm of a missionary meeting, would have proved sufficient to have carried him through the stress and strain of actual life and work among the heathen. A sincere and prayerful conviction that God had called to the service, and every step was according to His will and by His guidance, was necessary to produce the steadfastness and full purpose of heart that were absolutely needed.

Deep peace can make us independent of our surroundings and conditions. A letter written to a relative gives some impression of the spirit he brought to bear upon the past. "I wish you could see us in our new home in the Orient! The building which we rented had been used as a children's school and the tots had taken their 'fude' (brushes used for pens) and painted Chinese characters all over the walls. It was a sight to behold and would have made an interesting study for some interior decorator. There was nothing left for us to do but to paint it. I searched through every shop in the neighborhood for some paint but could find nothing but red—a bright red. Now imagine your sitting room, your bedroom, and kitchen walls in flaming red! But it is cozy and clean and that means much out here.

"We were able to furnish our home for about $20.00 (£4). Extravagance! I used the $10.00 gold piece which you gave me for that purpose. In our front room we have straw matting on the floor, a plain couch without springs, two straight-back chairs and a bamboo center-table. The Bilhorn organ given to us by our Grace Church friends fills a space in one corner.

"This way, please, to the bedroom, and look out that you do not fall on the newly painted floor. Where is the bed? In the corner on the floor. We searched through every second-hand store for a bed, but we could find none, so we did the next best thing, made a mattress of bamboo leaves, and there we sleep from midnight until dawn. No dozing after that, as the people are up bright and early in this wide-awake land, and the daybreak sounds are not the singing of birds, but the clank of wooden doors opening and closing. It is the best hour for prayer, study of the Word, and the language.

"And what about the kitchen? I must not forget to tell you, as that is the part of the home you will be interested in. We found a small second-hand cook stove which cost the sum of $4.00 (16/). The cooking utensils cost a trifle over $2.00 (8/). In one corner closed off by a tall screen, is our dining room. For fifty cents (2/)

we bought some of the quaintest dishes on which were painted pictures of Mt. Fuji. Drop in for a day, and such fare as we have we shall give thee. It is usually rice for breakfast, rice for dinner, rice for supper, with no trimmings of milk and sugar.

"I do not fancy you would enjoy spending the night with us, as rats, small rats and large rats, turn handsprings over our bed. For a change they hold high carnival, racing around the room and over the ceiling until frightened away.

"We feel rich, and thank God every day for permitting us to be here. The center of God's will is our home. Why should we want any other? After all, the words of Jesus are true, 'A man's life consisteth not in the abundance of things which he possesseth.' We are just as poor as the Lord and His apostles. We cannot say as He did—that He had no place to lay His head."

It was under just such conditions that mission work was begun in the city of Tokyo which is now one of the strongest centers of the Christian Church in the Orient.

That was the spirit which ever characterized Charles Cowman. The will of God, whatever it might be, was always precious. He never shrank back from trials or hardships, and was early developing the graces and gifts of a real pioneer.

How friendly the people of this neighborhood were! It was a new innovation for them to have missionaries living in their small, narrow streets. While at first they looked on in a sort of wonderment, the strangeness melted away and soon they were smiling at us, and even bringing us dainties from their homes. They made us welcome in their midst. They understood we had come to do them good. Light and love radiated from the center to the hundreds of homes throughout that vast district, even throughout the city, yea, throughout the Empire. Today after twenty-eight years, when traveling through the land, we meet numbers of people who tell us that it was there that they received their first light.

"I think it probable," said John Newton to a friend who was admiring sculpture in Rome, "I think it probable from passages in the Apostle Paul's writings, that he had a taste capable of admiring and relishing the beauties of painting, sculpture, and architecture, but then he had a higher, a spiritual, a divine taste, which was greatly shocked and grieved by the ignorance, idolatry and wickedness which surrounded him, insomuch that he could attend to nothing else."

Charles Cowman was a disciple who had literally "left all to follow his Master" and whose consistent walk had through many years illustrated the practical meaning of that little understood phrase. His whole soul was engrossed in his work. No sacrifice, however great, could have turned him aside from his delightful task. It was an enthusiasm with him.

A small volume of the "Life of David Brainerd" was often carried about in his pocket and these words were found heavily underscored: "I cared not where or how I lived, or what hardship I went through so that I could gain souls for Christ. While I was asleep I dreamed of these things, and when I wakened the first thing I thought of was this great work. All desire for the conversion of the heathen, and all my hope was in God."

There is very little romance about the *practical* work of missions, however during those early pioneer days some rather amusing incidents occurred. The end of the month had come, the bills had all been paid. He strictly adhered to the rule of his life never to incur debts. After the actual need of the Society had been supplied, there was just ten cents (5d) left in Charles Cowman's purse. It had been his custom to provide first of all for the others. Little did the students guess what a test of faith their missionary was often called to pass through! The last bit of flour had been used the day before, the last bit of butter, and the larder was absolutely empty with the exception of half a loaf of bread and a small amount of tea.

A fastidious guest called unexpectedly and remained for supper. Can the reader imagine the predicament? The table was covered as usual with a dainty white cloth, and on it was placed the bread and cups of tea. With as much dignity as if he had been presiding at a banquet, sat Charles Cowman at the head of the table, the guest seated at his right. He bowed his head and thanked God for the food, making no apology whatever for the meager serving. We are wondering what ran through the mind of our fellow-missionary, a well-known author from the British Isles. Poverty seemes to be a necessary part of the training of God's children.

In relating this incident some years later to a close friend whose eyes filled with tears as he listened, the question was asked, "What did you do?" Charles Cowman replied, "There was nothing left for us to do, but to pray, 'Give us this day our daily bread.' This my good wife and I did with all the earnestness we could command."

The founding of institutions and mission stations very often costs more in the way of personal sacrifice than can be expressed in money values, even though the figures mount up to the million point. To say this, however, is to speak after the manner of men. To the faithful missionary who rendered the service, there was no sacrifice in the case. It was merely an incident in the pathway of duty, and as such was accepted without remonstrance and without remark. Mere romantic feelings will soon die out amidst constant discomforts and will amount to but little when the testing time comes, when money fails, and when illness stalks into the home. May we have a fellowship in poverty with Him and rejoice and be glad!

When Christianity is genuine, it demands unconditional sacrifices, but it also promises perpetual miracles. "The month has been full of testings," wrote Charles Cowman to a close friend, "of every conceivable kind, more than 'fifty-seven varieties,' but I have had some of the nearest approaches to God that I have ever experienced in my lifetime. The Word of God seemed to live and the letters were aflame. We are in a land and among a people that need wonder-working power and we can obtain it only in the self-same manner as did those in the eleventh chapter of Hebrews."

A visitor from America wrote to his friends, "Contact with the missionaries has given me a clearer conception of Christian work than forty years of study at home. We find here enterprises of the triumphantly successful sort, where a gift of $500.00 (£100) would double or treble the efficiency and the results. If some generous givers from home could only get a glimpse of the work and its needs, they would not withhold their money.

On one occasion there came to this first home in the Orient several interesting visitors, who had heard at their station in the far North, that a very aggressive missionary was at work in the heart of Tokyo, and their curiosity brought them to investigate. They were shown the school rooms, then the humble quarters where the new missionary lived. The motto on the wall, "That in all things He might have the preeminence," attracted their attention. One of them, a young woman from a well-known American college, made bold to ask the question, "Where are your diplomas, your credentials, Mr. Cowman?"

He told her that his college of Missions had been the telegraph office in Chicago, and his credentials, all that he possessed, were found in 2 Cor. 6:4-10. In her face was a look of amazement, but how little did she realize that a new force had appeared, who, like every leader, was a decade or two ahead of his time, one who was definitely laid hold of by God to do a marvelous work.

The world's great men have not commonly been great scholars, nor its scholars great men. God's and man's ideas of greatness, are vastly opposite. God's standard is not as man's, and His verdict rests upon an order or rank of merit not known by human insignia.

Charles Cowman's life verified the saying that "If your eye is on the Eternal, your opinions and actions will have a beauty which no combined advantages of learning or accomplishments can rival."

It is better to be a saint than a scholar; indeed, the only way to be a true scholar is to strive to be a true saint.

In the later years, after the toil of battle, after the tears, the heartaches, the hardship, the weariness, the loneliness, came the glow and the glory, but with the author he would say, "Forbid it, Lord, that I should boast save in the cross of Christ my Lord." A college conferred upon him an honorary degree, but he never permitted it to become known. The parchment was tucked away in a drawer of his desk as he preferred his own title, Charles E. Cowman, missionary.

"If no supernatural power is expected to attend the Gospel, its promulgation is both insincere and futile."
—*Arthur. Tongue of Fire.*

"Your greatest trial may be your fellow-missionary," said a wise old Chinese to a missionary, "but he may be also your greatest joy."

A dying Buddhist priest said to a missionary: "Christianity is like the sun rising in the morning. Already the light is seen above the tops of the mountains, and it will rise higher and higher until its light is everywhere. Buddhism and other religions are like the setting sun; they are sinking lower and lower, as the sun is in the west."

CHAPTER XII

FIRST THINGS

First Meetings

The mission hall in Tokyo had been opened less than a week, when one evening after a rousing evangelistic service, a sufficient number of personal workers could not be found to deal with the many seekers. Brother Nakada seemed perplexed and beckoned for Charles Cowman to come to the front as he had found among the number a young man who could speak a limited amount of English.

One of the greatest trials of a new missionary is his inability to speak the language. Although his heart may be fairly bursting with a desire to tell the sweet tidings, he must sit as did Ezekiel, dumb, "in silence." To a worker as eager to win souls as was Charles Cowman, this was a tremendous test, and more than once did the Lord take pity upon him and allow a "handful of purpose" to fall in his pathway.

He went quickly to the altar-rail where the seekers were kneeling and took the young man quietly aside. For more than an hour they had what the young man afterward termed "the most delightful conversation of his lifetime" for he learned that there was a God of love, —a God who loved him.

It was customary for the mission leaders to take the name and address of each seeker in order that he might be called upon and dealt with further. This young man gave his address, S. Taniguchi, Central Telegraph Office, Tokyo, Japan. When Charles Cowman's eye fell upon this address his joy was unbounded. *For this was the first soul* which God had permitted him to lead to Himself in Japan, and besides, he was a telegraph operator!

The next evening S. Taniguchi was again in attendance. Accompanying him were two young men whom he introduced as telegraph operators. They, too, could converse in English, and before the week ended seven young telegraph operators had been gloriously converted. In the Central Telegraph office in Tokyo, the greatest office of the far East, was an evangelizing force that must have made the adversary tremble. These young converts were immediately set to reading the Word of God and a Telegraphers' Mission Band was formed for the purpose of reaching their profession, an exact replica of the Chicago Band. Its leader was S. Taniguchi, a raw heathen who had been saved by grace. Was it too early to put upon a young convert such a heavy responsibility? Let us see. Charles Cowman promised to teach the Scriptures to this new convert. Every evening he was promptly on hand carrying his Bible and notebook wrapped in a large blue handkerchief. His lodgings were five miles from the mission hall and he walked this distance after working all day in the office. It was pouring rain one night and S. Taniguchi was not expected to venture out in the storm, but a rap at the door was heard and there stood the student, his clothing dripping wet. He had walked the entire distance in the rain. When questioned as to why he did not take a jinrikisha, he hung his head and made no reply. Several nights later a telegraph operator attended the service and said to Charles Cowman, "S. Taniguchi is giving away a large number of New Testaments in the office." Then it was understood why he walked in the rain. His monthly salary was only $7.00 (£1.10). His few spare pence, after paying for his lodging, were spent for Testaments. He became one of the most zealous soul-winners. After a few weeks God loosed his hands from the telegraph key and sent him out throughout the length and breadth of the Empire as an evangelist. He was possessed with a consuming passion for winning souls and saw men seeking God by the roadway, in trains, on street corners, and in mission halls. Many bright gems will be his in that glorious day when His praises like sea billows roll. He lived but three years and burned out for God.

It seemed to please the Lord to single out some of the most difficult cases, send them to the Mission Hall where they were gloriously converted, then to send them back to their former associates with a glowing testimony of the power of the Cross of Christ. There were noted idolaters, drunkards, gamblers, the lowest of the low, as well as the upper classes, who prayed through at the altars, and the transformation was a blessing to witnesses.

To a close friend at home, Charles Cowman sent these few lines: "We are absolutely free out here to pour out our lives to the very last drop. We meet hundreds daily who have never heard the precious Name. It is our great joy to see from among these heathen souls, large numbers genuinely born again. Would that you might have been with us in our service last night. The altar was crowded with earnest seekers. Every seat in the hall was occupied —even the window spaces were filled. Nakada San was the preacher and he is a master of crowds. I was never so impressed in my life as I was with one of the seekers right here among these stoical undemonstrative people. This man prayed until the perspiration dropped from his face like rain. He struggled toward the light and we just left him to wrestle it out alone. Finally someone began to sing, 'In my hand no price I bring, simply to Thy Cross

10

I cling.' The light broke through, and he leaped to his feet praising God with a loud voice. The haunting fear, the self-torture was gone and he was jubilant in the peace and comfort of a simple faith in Jesus Christ. All we need to do is to preach the Gospel of the Cross which brings down heathen hearts." To another friend he wrote: "A mumber of our students accompanied me yesterday and I had the privilege of preaching through an interpreter at a great open-air meeting held in Uyeno Park. It was not a congregation, nor an assembly, nor a crowd, but a tremendous torrent of human beings, produced by the conflux from twenty points of the compass of this great city and vicinity. It seemed as if preaching would be impossible, and indeed it would have been had not some of our students carried off part of the crowd to another place in the park.

"We began at 2:30 P. M. and kept right on for hours. I spoke until my soul and body were nearly bidding each other a final farewell. The spirit of glory rested upon all; I felt there were multitudes who will never, never worship idols again. Next Tuesday we go again to this same place, but I almost dread the human billows, the mountain-swells of thousands who will be there. This work is altogether new and we are not building upon another man's foundation."

To a former telegrapher, a member of the Chicago Band, he wrote:

"We are in the midst of an old-fashioned revival and that right here in Japan. Our own small halls would not hold the crowds. We took a step of faith and rented one of Tokyo's largest halls, right down in the very heart of the teeming populace. The doors had scarcely opened when fifteen hundred people rushed in. Never before have I witnessed such meetings. Great conviction for sin is upon the people, poor heathen are seeking forgiveness, lukewarm professors are being revived. It is a time of great revival and Tokyo is being moved by the power of the Holy Ghost.

"It is a solemn work to stand here between the living and the dead. I have never been sorry that God called me to be a missionary to the heathen, but what an account I shall have to render! The work is glorious and far exceeds anything I have ever witnessed in America. This fruit among the Gentiles, these sheaves, these crowns of rejoicing, how they swell the heart with gratitude, hope and joy!

"God has given us some rare opportunities for witnessing for Him. Every Sabbath evening we hold a service right under the very dome of an old pagoda. It is in the court yard of one of the largest heathen temples in Tokyo and tens of thousands of worshippers from every corner of the Empire assemble here. Just imagine the hour of sunset, the old priests in their temples burning incense to the idols, their doleful chants, the tolling of bells, all of which are in the minor tone, and contrast it with a Gospel service just at the entrance way! One of our students played the cornet and last night we were given a real heart-thrill when we heard the clear notes of 'Precious Name, Oh, how sweet.' The native Christians of our party took it up, sang a verse through, then we sang it in English and the echo seemed to ring throughout the city and over the hills and vales. Somehow it seemed to echo all over the Orient. There is a time coming, thank God, if we do our utmost, when His Name shall be made known.

"I know of a land that is sunk in shame,
  And of hearts that faint and tire,
But I know of a Name— a Name— a Name,
  That can set that land on fire.
Its sound is a brand, its letters flame—
  I know of a Name— a Name a Name,
The precious Name of Jesus."

The teacher of a Mission study class wrote to Charles Cowman asking him some pointed questions and the following are excerpts of his reply:

"If we get the idea that the heathen are going to be converted by some educational process instead of the regenerative, it will be a profound mistake. In these lands there are hoary systems of philosophy, religion and culture; we do not seek to add to these. One thing supremely is lacking; one blessing we wish to bring—the knowledge of Christ and His salvation. Christ, and Christ alone is her paramount need.

"It is simply wonderful the way God uses the simple messages to the salvation of souls. The early missionaries in Greenland supposed that they must spend a long time in preliminary teaching, *preparing* the natives to understand the Gospel; and so they taught them the principles of the Old Testament, the law of God, etc., without spiritual fruit. One day when the missionary read the story of the third chapter of John, an old chief was overwhelmed with wonder and joy and immediately spiritual fruit appeared, and he and many of his people gladly accepted the Saviour of sinners.

"Talk theory to the heathen, and they are generally unmoved; tell them merely of blessings in store for their future, and they are often too skeptical or too occupied with the pressure of present necessity to hear what you have to say. But, as experience proves, tell your audience that you have an infallible help for every gambler, every drunkard, that you proclaim a Saviour Who has never

ABOVE—CENTRAL GOSPEL MISSION, IN THE HEART OF TOKYO.
CENTER—THE MISSION HALL ON AWAJI-CHO WHERE 15,000 SOULS SOUGHT THE CHRIST DURING TEN YEARS.
BELOW—O. M. S. MISSION HALL, NEAR ONE OF TOKYO'S FAMOUS HEATHEN TEMPLES.

once failed to save immediately every soul that trusted Him, both from the power of sin and its eternal consequences, and you will soon see that the Gospel is good news to your hearers, that it can command attention and will accomplish the mightiest change the mind can conceive or the heart desire.

"The heathen are fast losing faith in the ashes of their fathers and the temples of their gods. The call to grand achievements still increases. Alas! How many are putting their best energies in superficial "reform," instead of grasping the will of God concerning immortalized humanity as revealed in the Word and illustrated in the career of Jesus. Have you ever heard the story of a curious race?

"Several scientists to settle a dispute, conducted a *race* between four bees and four pigeons.

"The course was three miles from starting-point to goal where *hive* and *loft* were placed together.

"The *bees* were dipped in *flour* for *identification.*

"Bee No. 1 arrived twenty seconds before Pigeon No. 1.

"Bees Nos. 2, 3, and 4 arrived several seconds before pigeon No. 2 put in appearance.

"Now a pigeon's *wings* are hundreds of times *larger* and *stronger* than a bee's *wings* and the pigeons logically should have won, but they did *not.* And WHY? BECAUSE THEY DID NOT FOLLOW A 'BEELINE.'

"I would not have come here to engage in teaching school," said Charles Cowman, "there are others who would; nor in a profession, there are those who would; nor in business, there are others who would. But I would come here among these hungry multitudes, and live, and labor, and endure, and die if need be, to declare that

" 'There is a fountain filled with blood
    Drawn from Immanuel's veins;
    And sinners plunged beneath that flood
    Lose all their guilty stains.' "

What is sublimer than the thought of walking under
the sky bearing the commission from the living God—
sustained by Him in doing work that shall last through
and be seen most in eternity? How often during his last
illness did he say, "I would give the world to be back again
in the old Mission Halls. It would be the greatest joy to
live right there again and to spend the last of my days
pointing sinners to the Cross."

MEETINGS FOR THE PROMOTION OF
SCRIPTURAL HOLINESS

There is no feature of the work that is more familiar
to the native Christians of Japan than the meetings which
are held for the promotion of Scriptural Holiness, the
blessed truth which made early Methodism. These meetings began soon after Charles Cowman's arrival in Japan
and have continued with added blessing throughout the
twenty-seven years. It became manifest as time went
on as he became acquainted with the Christians of every
name, denomination and creed, that what they needed
more than anything else was a measure of spiritual power
beyond what they had already realized. Everywhere
among the believers the stir of life was being felt.

Old foundation truths were being exclusively rested
upon, and in consequence, there arose in the hearts of
the native Christians a desire for further edifying. The
rooting downward was being followed by a shooting up-
wards with a fervent desire for blossoming and fruiting.
Into all this active longing there came a sound of a further
breath of life. Tidings were heard of a life of joyous
liberty being unfolded; of a life that might please Him,

of possibilities of victory and deliverance from sin, of a life of unbroken service. People longed to hear more, they yearned that their lives might not be a weary existence, but an overflow, and they began to "ask the way to Zion with their faces thitherward." Jer. 50:8.

Charles Cowman had faith in God and saw a little cloud rising out of a distant sea. He believed that even in the Orient, God would raise up Spirit-filled preachers after the old pattern and plant them down in the very midst of the deadness, idolatry, and darkness.

Hudson Taylor, a prince among missionaries, once said in the course of an address:

"The supreme want of all missions in the present day is the manifested presence of the Holy Ghost. Hundreds of Gospel addresses have been given. Tens of thousands of miles have been traversed in missionary journeys, but how small has been the issue in the way of definite conversions. Human efforts can never meet heathendom on its own ground. There must be Divine power."

The one reason the church has failed to penetrate the mist, the fog, and the blackness of heathendom in two thousand years lies in the fact that so many are afraid, yes, afraid of the blessed Holy Ghost, of His program and His power. "It is safe to say," were the lines Charles Cowman wrote to a missionary, "that if the Holy Ghost had been given right of way in the church, there would have been no unevangelized part in the earth, no great heathen lands with millions going to the grave yearly without a knowledge of the Lord Jesus Christ. The great secret of missions is the Holy Ghost. The great failure of missions is His absence.

"The Orient is Satan's battleground. Here he has entrenched himself behind ancient philosophies and superstitions. Until the church is full of the power of the Spirit, we shall never win an inch of ground. A feeble, trickling stream of water will never carry fertility to so vast a continent. Floods of water are needed to flow over the barren ground."

In this day of decaying faith when people are becoming more and more materialistic, we had a blessed example in the life and work of Charles Cowman, of what God can do with one man filled with the Holy Ghost and faith. All that he accomplished in the Orient was due to the indwelling, infilling of the Holy Spirit, whose plans were worked out through His humble servant.

After he had been in Japan less than a year he wrote to homeland friends:

"The Holiness meetings have increased in attendance until there is not standing room in the hall. The meetings are being more and more owned of God. Young and also old converts are hungering and thirsting for the blessing of Full-Salvation, and, realizing their need, flock to these services like doves to their windows. Today we again witnessed a marvelous scene when the altars were crowded with young women from the Women's College, kneeling in prayer. Groups of young men from Aoyama College and the Imperial University were kneeling in prayer all over the entire hall. Some were praying to be sanctified wholly, others were waiting in silence, utterly oblivious to their surroundings, but all in an attitude of expectancy. Some were softly singing,

> "Let it come, Oh, Lord, we pray thee
> Let the showers from Heaven fall.
> We are waiting, we are waiting,
> Oh revive the hearts of all!"

"The power of the Lord was present to heal sin-sick souls, to bind up the broken and contrite hearts. We all seemed to be carried right away to a high mountain apart with our Lord. Tomorrow we must be down in the valleys with the enemy-bound heathen and how can we fight successfully if we are not clothed with God's whole armour? More and more I am realizing that we should strongly emphasize the need of being filled with the Holy Ghost. That is the secret of successful soul-winning." A month later another letter followed to the same friend:

"We had a gracious service last night. A gale of the Spirit caught us and sped us out to the high seas where the great tides are running. Nakada San preached for more than an hour and a half and yet the people lingered as if they did not wish to leave. He stressed the blessing of sanctification, numbers came through to victory, and there was a shout in the camp. One young man testified that two weeks ago God had given to him a clean heart and his face was radiant. It rejoices my heart to see the wonderful way in which the Holy Spirit can work in the hearts of these new-babes, giving them the Light. They walk into the blessing heart first, instead of head first. I am so glad that I am here. The only life that counts is that lived for others."

And the times of refreshing continued. A young student in one of the largest colleges in Tokyo, who strolled into the services one evening, was so deeply convicted of his heart's need that before the invitation was given to come forward and seek Christ, he was kneeling at the long altar-rail weeping and praying. God met him; he rose from his knees, with face aglow. He returned to college and began telling what great things the Lord had done for him. In less than one week he had led twenty-five of his fellow-students to Christ. A genuine work began in that college through the testimony of this Spirit-filled student, and in a brief time an old-time revival swept through this institution.

"Is it thought an incredible thing that God can sanctify a native convert?" said Charles Cowman to an enquirer. "What limits we place upon Him! Is His hand shortened, His power limited to the white race? Nay! I believe that right here in the midst of this heathen land, He will raise up, is now raising up a company of sanctified believers who will be as 'clear as the sun, fair as the moon, and terrible as an army with banners.' Who knows but that they shall lead the world?"

Two years later he wrote again to homeland friends: "The Sabbath afternoon Holiness meetings have increased in attendance and our mission hall is filled to its utmost capacity. The native pastors and Bible women from the various denominational churches of the city are among the faithful attendants. Last Sabbath the altar was filled, three rows deep with earnest seekers. I counted sixty-four people kneeling seeking to be cleansed and filled. I never heard such praying! One after another rose to their feet and with faces aglow testified to the fact that 'He had come.' Among the seekers was a Bible woman of a leading church. She had attended our services for five consecutive Sabbaths and her heart was hungry. In her testimony she said, 'I have been a Christian for twenty years, but my heart has not been entirely satisfied. I have realized a need and today I made a full and complete surrender of myself to God for time and eternity. All I have I have placed upon the altar and according to His Word I believe that the 'altar sanctifies the gift.' While she was thus giving her testimony the witness was given to her that her offering had been accepted and she burst forth into praise that sent a thrill into every heart. This encouraged the others who were seeking and one after another rose and testified. This service continued from two thirty until seven o'clock and doubtless would have continued right on, but sinners began to come in and believers had to return home to make room for them."

To the worn missionary, these were times of great refreshing. After more than a quarter of a century these Sabbath afternoon Holiness meetings remain unchanged in the manner of their conduct, and they are still a radiating point for service, a hallowed center of attraction. What they have meant in the lives of thousands of believers will only be known on that great day when One will point to the throng and say, "These are they whose garments have been washed white—therefore are they before the throne."

THE FIRST ANNIVERSARY

April 2, 1902. "My first year on the mission field has come to a close. My heart is too full for words," was a sentence in his diary. "This is the first anniversary of our Gospel Mission and the report which was handed me reads: During the year 1901, every night without exception, we have seen souls coming to Christ; sometimes one, often five and ten, and not infrequently on Sabbath evenings there have been twenty or more seekers. What a glorious record for one year! Well may our hearts bow down before Him in praise for the past and in glad expectancy for the future. God has given us a thousand tokens of the reality of His presence. The response of these blinded minds to the Gospel message has been so profound, so striking. What marvelous results from our slightest efforts! What a privilege God has granted to me in dropping me right down into the very heart of heathendom, but opportunity spells responsibility."

> "Lord, give me this year, a burning zeal
> For souls immortal; make me plead with such
> With earnestness intense, love strong as death
> And faith God-given. Will the world cry 'Mad?'
> Such madness be my joy."

Although the work grew rapidly it was not a mushroom growth. Each seeker was personally dealt with, he was led to give up idolatry, and hundreds were genuinely born again. Not quantity, but quality was the object, yet God gave both. "Much more" is the Lord's way. His work always grows and growth is the sign of life.

The following extracts from the Yearly Report for 1902 show the progress made in the work.

"Jan. 14. Crowds attended the Holiness meeting today. No standing room left. The sense of the Spirit's presence was so vivid as to be almost visible.

"Feb. 12. A packed hall this afternoon. Many went away to get in. I am daily asking God to give us a larger hall for meetings.

"April 21. Received a letter today from a poor woman who said that the Lord had impressed her to send $5.00 (£1). She quoted the word in Isa. 54:2. 'Enlarge the place of thy tent.' It sent me to my knees and I claimed from God a larger building.

"May 30. A gift of one thousand dollars was received today. It will be used for purchasing a larger hall. The gift came from an entire stranger. A sentence in his letter read, 'I am sure the Lord will give you all that you need.'

"June 15. Searched for locations, but found nothing suitable. 'Thine ear shall hear a word behind thee saying, This is the way, walk ye in it.'

"July 21. We moved into our new Mission Hall on Awaji-cho. Every dollar needed for its purchase was received. Yesterday held an all-day service and the new hall was crowded. Twenty-seven seekers knelt at the altar. We are a united little band, happy in the Lord, well assured that in His own time 'the little one shall become a thousand.' We know that we are preaching the truth and so we wait upon the Lord."

REV. ERNEST A. KILBOURNE AND FAMILY (1903)
INSERT—REV. KILBOURNE THE YEAR OF HIS HOME-CALL (1928)

The mission hall mentioned above became one of the greatest salvation lighthouses in the city of Tokyo. It was here that services were held every night for ten years, which resulted in 15,000 souls seeking Christ.

On New Year's Day, 1904, Charles Cowman wrote to a friend, "We are just entering upon our New Year's Convention and while reading the Word this morning John 16:8 made a powerful impression upon me. 'When He is come, He will convince the world of sin.' That is the secret of revivals. 'Not by might, nor by power, but by my Spirit, saith the Lord.' I fear that the absolute dependence upon the presence and power of the Holy Spirit in the conversion of sinners and sanctification of the believers is too little felt everywhere. There is too much dependence placed on machinery, learning, eloquence, and popular preaching. God grant us anointed eyes to see our own nothingness, and may the fire burn up every thing human during these days. The voice of agonizing prayer breaks the stillness of the morning. I have but little fear of the noise of praying Christians. The prayers of some of these precious natives are heaven-moving, heaven-opening. What wonderful and striking types of men, what glorious Christians!

"At the opening meeting the spirit of prayer was mightily outpoured and for several hours we heard one stream of continuous intercession. Everybody prayed, quite oblivious to one another, when suddenly there came a hush like the receding of an ocean wave, then a time of intense silence when you verily heard the footfall of the Master and all returned to their rooms in the hush of His presence. The very atmosphere was fragrant and refreshing."

In 1917 he wrote again; "Again we have come up to another convention and our workers are here from every province; from far away Leo Choo Islands, Hokkaido, and other points. Every train brings in great numbers. There is also a fine delegation from Korea. Three full days were spent in waiting upon God before these meetings. Far off in the quiet country, in an abandoned farm house, the native workers waited and prayed until all felt that God had heard them and they returned with faces shining as if they had been on the Mount of Transfiguration. God came in mighty power at the first service.

"The workers were drawn together in tender love; there were no divisions to be found anywhere; and God truly poured out such blessings upon us that our hearts have not found room enough to contain them all and I only wish that you could share with us a fraction of them. I wish you could have heard them singing, 'Crown Him Lord of All!' It was like a great wave of praise surging up against the pillars of the throne of God. Just beyond our compound is a great heathen temple, and the echo must have reached the worshipers there. It made us feel like girding on our armor afresh, for how can they crown Him Lord of all 'of whom they have not heard, and how shall they hear without a preacher?'

"We had a real foretaste of heaven yesterday. There were present at the morning service six hundred who partook of the communion. The majority were our own converts.

"We do not want anything new in revivals; we want always the old factors—the living Spirit of God, the living Word of God, the old Gospel. We want crowds coming to hear—crowds made up of the old elements; perishing men and women finding their way to prayer meeting, Bible reading, and the altar of prayer."

"I cannot go all your lengths," said a prominent missionary who attended the Convention, "but I believe you are on the right lines. Keep on as you are doing."

After the Convention, which was attended by fully one thousand people, Charles Cowman was much impressed with the fact that such meetings should be duplicated in every city in the Orient. We find these lines in a letter to a dear doctor friend in the homeland:

"What hath God wrought? My soul is humbled to the dust. Not unto us, but unto God belongs the glory. The converts in the outstations have multiplied beyond all expectations. Multitudes are calling for us to come and bring them the Living Bread, but, 'Whence are we to buy bread that these may eat?' We are confronted with the same problem that the early disciples were when they saw the multitudes and had nothing.

"I meditated this morning upon John 6:21, and the thing that most impressed me was the lad with five loaves and a few fishes. He was the outstanding figure and no miracle was performed until he placed his *little all* into the hands of Jesus. He literally gave his *all,* not one loaf reserved, nor one half a fish *'for himself'* but, then, after he had done this and 'the all' was in the Master's hand, the miracle was performed.

"I searched my soul to see if there was anything remaining in my possession that had not been given to God, but found nothing. I have no bread or fish to give, but thank God all I have has been given to Him. There are no reserves anywhere, no bank accounts for a rainy day, no houses or lands. I do praise Him for this emptiness. I feel that I can ask my Heavenly Father for bread for this multitude and He will multiply it a thousand-fold. It is not a question of the *supply* in hand, but the Supplier."

To a native leader after a great Convention he wrote: "How full is my heart with praises to God after seeing the 'multitudes, multitudes in the valley of decision.' How mightily the Lord wrought throughout the entire ten days. I doubt much if Japan has ever witnessed anything just like it, or if the Christians have ever seen such a supernatural, Heaven-sent outburst of God's blessing. My own soul was wonderfully refreshed, but this morning long ere daybreak, I felt a burden resting upon my heart and rose early to pray. We dare not rest on our oars, but must watch and pray. The pathway *to* victory is usually a safer one than the vantage ground of success obtained. Never more than in a time of marked blessing is a truly watchful and prayerful spirit needed. Indeed, defeats often arise from *absence of prayer in the hour of success*. Let us look well to our girdles and fasten them on anew. God has given us an example of what He can do through a handful of intercessors who 'give Him no rest.' Great things are ahead if we will keep close to Jesus and give Him every bit of the glory. Let us look out that no human hand touches the glory. It all belongs to Him and to Him alone.

"I cannot think that God's heart can be satisfied with the salvation of just a few when His great heart yearns over the millions. We *must* see the multitudes won. Let us unitedly ask Him to help us to so reach out and take these places for Him that there will not be a valley, a mountain, or a tract unpossessed. Let us not remain on the outskirts of the fray, but plunge into the thick of the fight and possess our possession."

And this was ever the spirit of their beloved missionary—onward, ever onward.

These Conventions have made Tokyo a real Oriental Jerusalem whither the tribes of the Lord go up yearly to the feast. Each year they increase, not only in numbers, but in blessing. In 1927 there were more than two thousand in attendance and the large hall must be enlarged to accommodate the crowds.

Charles Cowman was already feeling the responsibility of leadership in a mission which had grown in less than two years far beyond his fondest expectation. The time had come when he needed a fellow-worker. For the provision of this need he looked to God. While waiting in patience and faith God was raising up an instrument through whom He could fulfil the desire of his servant. Often He is working for us when we least expect it; so when the time of unfolding comes, we receive a sweet surprise that He loves to prepare and bestow upon His waiting children. Luther said: "When God has some great work to accomplish He begins to work through one man, and afterwards gives other help, as with Moses and Aaron." In harmony with this divine plan, Charles Cowman realized his great need of a fellow worker, and the Lord Himself raised up a helper and a true burden-bearer, Ernest A. Kilbourne.

It was a happy day when the message was received that the steamer had arrived in Yokohama bringing Brother Kilbourne and family. Strangely enough, this was the first soul whom he had led to Christ. If the whole world had been searched throughout for one who would be a real fellow-worker, another just like him could not have been found. He indeed became a true yoke-fellow. Their lives were the exact counterparts of each other. They moved together in perfect unison, they pulled together like the finest team. The quality of their friendship was peculiar, but no more remarkable than the manner of its origin. These two men made a lasting impression upon each other. They had the same burning love for

Christ, the same compassion for the perishing, and were "perfectly joined together in one mind." They moved along on the same line for a quarter of a century without a break in their unity of service.

Friends in the homeland were now beginning to take a lively interest in the newly established mission and monthly reports of the work were sent to them. These reports were written without the help of a typist and much time was spent at such work. Out of the pressure a small monthly periodical was born which contained reports of the meetings, and its columns glowed with missionary news. It grew from six to eight pages, then to ten, and afterward to sixteen. It had but one message, the evangelization of the Orient. Neither Charles Cowman nor Ernest Kilbourne had experience as editors but God bestowed gifts upon them, enabling them to "write what they had seen." Were a stranger to have picked up their writings, he would doubtless have come to the conclusion that they were the utterances of one mind. The name of the periodical was Electric Messages which was later changed to The Oriental Missionary Standard. It still continues to stir up a lively interest in the great unreaped fields, white unto harvest. From this small beginning has grown a publishing department which sends out millions of pages of missionary literature.

"Facts are fingers of God," said Arthur T. Pierson. "To know the facts of modern missions is the necessary condition of intelligent interest. Knowledge does not always kindle zeal, but zeal is according to knowledge, and will not exist without it. A fire may be fanned with wind, then kindled by God's Spirit, and then scattered as burning brands, to be as live coals elsewhere."

To make known the fact that the heathen are lost, and that "we are debtors" was the burden upon the heart of

Charles Cowman. It continued to the end of life's little day. Ernest Kilbourne, his partner, shared with him this burden. The people who looked on and noticed their close fellowship in life and purpose named them "Cowman and Kilbourne." The name always flowed together and will probably be connected in Jerusalem the Golden. Side by side they had labored in the telegraph office. Side by side for a quarter of a century they toiled under Oriental suns to bring the heathen home. Side by side they sleep in beautiful Hollywood.

"Every institution is but the lengthened shadow of one man."—*Emerson*

"Where is the man emulous of a distinction which God will approve, and panting after a renown which shall never mock the possessor? Is he called to the high office of a Christian Missionary? He may lay the foundations for Christian Institutions that shall shed around them a healing power, and remain an expression of the Divine beneficence to the end of time."
—*Jeremiah Everatts.*

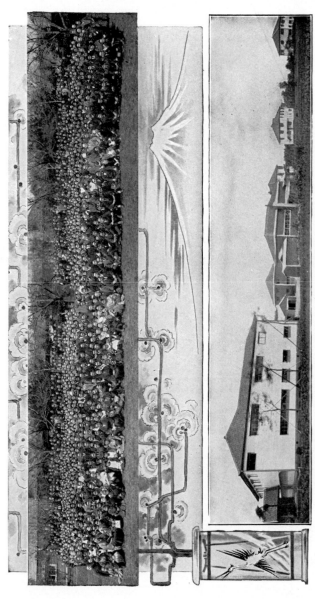

THE ORIENTAL MISSIONARY SOCIETY BIBLE TRAINING INSTITUTE, TOKYO, JAPAN.
VIEW FROM THE SIDE.

ABOVE—NATIVE WORKERS AND STUDENTS OF THE ORIENTAL MISSIONARY SOCIETY
AT THE YEARLY CONVENTION.

CHAPTER XIII

ENLARGED BORDERS

Early in 1903, Charles Cowman wrote to the Telegraphers Band in Chicago, "The Lord is working marvelously and we are seeing a great enlargement in the most important department of the work—the Bible Training Institute. Our rented quarters are cramped and crowded and we simply must have our buildings so we can accommodate the large number who are sending in their applications. Some of the finest fellows I have ever met are here in school. They are red-hot after souls. I only wish that you could drop in and attend some of our meetings. The needs are pressing. The work is expanding. The hall was packed last night to overflowing with eager, earnest listeners and fifteen responded immediately when a call was made for seekers. I am beginning to realize that the day of small things is now passing, that God has sent us to Japan to do business for Him in great waters. He assures us if we will but simply trust Him, we shall see the works of the Lord.'

"Today letters were received from ten young men and four young women seeking admittance to our Bible Training School. What does this all mean? Here are the applicants and no room to receive them. While waiting before God in prayer this morning, I received this promise, 'Enlarge the place of thy tent, lengthen thy cords and strengthen thy stakes.' If we were out under a Mission Board we could write to our Home Council, placing before them our need, but we have no Home Council. 'To whom shall we go?' To the One Who has called us to His work. To the One Who sent us without purse or scrip. We ask Him to look upon this present need and to make room for these students." God marvelously strengthened and developed the faith of His servant, and that far beyond the limits of his thinking.

Two months later another letter was written to the Telegraphers Band. It was dated June 8, and reads as follows:

"Today is our wedding anniversary. We celebrated it by having a special prayer-meeting with our dear Brother Nakada and the students. Prayer was made for the needs of the fast growing work and the new building. The meeting lasted from seven in the morning until late in the afternoon, no one caring to stop for dinner. The students laid hold of the promises, one of them quoting John 10:40, 'Said I not unto thee that if thou wouldest believe, thou shouldest see the glory of God?' Another followed in prayer saying, 'Lord, give us faith to see the dead souls about us resurrected'! My heart responded amen! Into our hearts came fresh assurance that God would give us the needed building. Our mission treasury was drained to the very bottom this morning, but we held out our hands to our Father in Heaven without a shadow of a doubt, or a shiver of fear. We know for certain that He will not fail us, for 'God, who cannot lie, promised.'"

It was a very remarkable prayer-meeting. Each one present had a strong conviction that God was in the lead of this new advance. It had been prayed through, and Charles Cowman suggested that as they had asked according to Mark 11:24, they should *praise* by faith for the answer. A volume of praise ascended to Heaven like a cloud of sweet incense, and from that moment, doubt never entered his mind. It is wonderful to be so sure of the answer that praise can be offered before there is the least visible sign.

"Many an old familiar hymn revealed a new meaning for us then," he said to a friend long afterward, after indulging in a retrospection. How often we sang,

> "In some way or other, the Lord will provide,
> It may not be your way, it may not be my way,
> And yet in His own way, the Lord will provide."

And when standing before some impregnable wall of difficulty a song of praise would lift our faith.

> "Then forward still, 'tis Jehovah's will
> Though the billows dash and spray.
> With a conqueror's tread, we will push ahead.
> He'll roll the sea away."

Difficulties involve conflicts, but they make possible glorious triumphs. There are serious perils and pressing needs, but this means that there are also inexhaustible resources and inspiring victories. When our difficulties and problems are sufficiently grave they drive us to God and make possible a larger manifestation of super-human wisdom and power. Obstacles have always been God's challenge to faith and character.

God is a Divine Planner and Performer. The program is His and the provision is His. When our Lord orders something for the glory of His great name, He is both willing and able to find the needed individuals and the necessary means. Away back in the world when the tabernacle in the wilderness was being erected, not only did He find men fitted for the work of building, but He also touched the hearts of thousands to bring the necessary material, and we read that they brought an abundance of gold and silver. When God calls us to do a definite work for Him and we are fully assured of His leading, then we may confidently depend upon His presence and His power as well as His supply.

An oft-quoted saying of Charles Cowman's was, "Either do not attempt things at all or go through with them," and the Tibetan proverb, "The foot of the ladder is a poor place to sit down." When he was convinced that God was in the lead, nothing in the way of trial or delay was ever able to shake his faith, and he marched on trusting. He began to plan for the erection of a large Bible Training Institute, through the Lord's command, "Arise and build," and at once he committed himself to the project and built an institution that is leaving its impress upon the entire Orient.

Not one dollar was in sight when he began the search for a suitable location. Small tracts of land were available, but every time an attempt was made for the purchase of one, something trivial occurred that would completely block the way. A prayerful search was continued, until one day, Charles Cowman, accompanied by Brother Kilbourne and several others, took a trip to the suburbs of the great city of Tokyo, where they found a field of waving grain. The air was soft and balmy. Mt. Fuji with her snow-crowned summit lay just beyond, and from the slight elevation, miles and miles of country could be seen. It was "beautiful for situation." The choice was made, which later proved without a shadow of a doubt that it was God's own choice. Funds for its purchase came in answer to believing prayer; no great amounts, but small gifts from many saints scattered far and near. Neither of God's chosen instruments for this stupendous work knew how or whence the silver or gold would come, but both were content to trust Him who said, "Shall I bring to the birth, and shall I not cause to come forth?"

Plans were made for plain but substantial frame buildings. Charles Cowman's ideas ran along the line of the early Quakers who believed in plain meeting-houses and not in lavish expenditure of money which might be more wisely used in God's service in other ways. Not without tests of faith were these buildings erected. When God saw that tests were necessary for the development of faith, He lovingly sent them, proving the Word, "He shewed Himself alive," the invisible Head of the work. It required a great step of faith, involving thousands of dollars. God had tenderly led him along through the first three years, giving him faith to step out quite alone for the support of himself and wife, for the opening of the mission, for the support of students and native workers, and now for the new buildings. The wonderful answers to prayer received thus far, nerved him for fresh ventures of faith. God's special help had always come in the hour of deepest need. He was highly privileged in learning these valuable lessons for they brought God into everything pertaining to his life and work, and no detail was ever overlooked by Him.

He related the following incident to a very close friend some months later. It gives the reader a glimpse of a trial and its outcome when the buildings were being erected. "The third payment of the building, $2000.00 (£400), was due in three days and there was but $72.00 (£14) in the Mission treasury. This was barely sufficient to cover the cost of the food supply needed for our large family of workers and students. The day before the payment was due, a steamer arrived from America. The foreign post usually brought a number of letters containing gifts, but this time only one letter was received and in it was a $5.00 bill (£1 note).

"The workmen were busy erecting the building, while the missionaries and native workers were closeted with God. We were at our 'Wits' End' but thank God not at 'Faith's End,' for faith generally begins just at such tight corners. Our last hope of receiving help from America seemed to be gone, but as we continued in prayer, the burden upon our hearts made a hasty exit, as the promises of God rolled in until our mouths were literally filled with laughter. It seemed that God had enabled us to lay hold of His promises. In the course of prayer one of those present was led to remind the Lord that on one occasion He had met the need of one of His own by means of a coin in a fish's mouth. We continued to pray, 'Lord Jesus, Thou hast still fish at Thy disposal. Thou canst supply our need in this way just now, for Thou art still the same.'

"Another quoted Mark 11:24, 'And shall not doubt in his heart, he shall have whatsoever he saith.' Thus for several hours, one after another mounted up in faith until at the end of two hours there was a perfect blend, and prayer ended in praising. All watched, waited, and wondered how God was going to get to us the $2000 (£400) before noon on the following day. Faith burned brightly in every heart. A definite request had been registered in Heaven. Faith claimed the great gift from God, and what was the result? Faith honors God and God honors faith. The clinging hand of His child makes a desperate situation a delight to Him.

"The next morning dawned bright and clear and the army of native workers were on hand early, singing as they worked, for this was their pay day. Nine o'clock came, then ten, still no answer. The noon hour arrived and the simple dinner was served. One quoted the Word in Exodus 6:1, 'Now thou shalt see what I shall do.' Each one present quoted some encouraging promise, and faith held fast. At five o'clock, just about the time for the workmen to quit their work, a messenger boy strolled up the walk shouting out, 'Dempo, dempo,'—'Cablegram,

cablegram.' What did the little band of missionaries do? They stopped their work to listen to the message, which read as follows: 'Two thousand dollars at cable office.' The donor was quite unknown to us.

" 'And Jesus Himself drew near.' Tears were mingled with shouts of victory. God had not forgotten to be gracious. The little company fell upon their knees praising Him from the depths of their hearts for not permitting them to become a reproach among the heathen.

"Who timed this to arrive just at the critical moment? Coincidence? The word is too long and the calculation on the basis of probabilities too difficult. God! This is simple and satisfying. 'How unsearchable are His ways!' The feeling of His hand upon us gave great peace and rest, and such experiences were worth all that they cost.

Our Lord always goes *before* us. Everything is foreseen and taken into account by Him. Nothing takes Him by surprise, and He has made ample provision for the day of our testing.

"Say not, my soul, From whence can God relieve my care?
Remember that Omnipotence hath servants everywhere;
His method is sublime, His thoughts supremely kind,
    God never is before His Time,
    And never is behind."

God's hand was so evident during these days that nothing in the way of Divine interposition excited much surprise. Prayer was made daily, answers were received daily, and marvelous were the answers. We hesitate in telling the public about some answers to prayer lest they be tempted to think these were overdrawn. God has not left Himself without witnesses, but has continued the roll of those who have "wrought righteousness, and obtained promises."

The Bible School buildings were damaged by the great earthquake which visited Tokyo some years later, and had to be rebuilt, but they were untouched by the fire which swept away thousands of homes. They stood out as a monument of His protecting power. The lawns were covered with tents, sheltering hundreds of homeless, helpless, heartbroken, penniless people who had lost all their possessions.

The opening up of this district brought to the neighborhood some of the finest families belonging to business circles. Soon property began to soar in price and today the location is worth more than fifty times the amount that it was at the time of purchase. The city has extended its borders for miles and miles around it, so it is no longer in the suburbs.

The location is so well adapted to the needs of the work that when the great Conventions are held each year there is ample room for the entertainment of the hundreds who come up to the spiritual feast. The Compound consists of three acres of ground, a large dormitory for men, with lecture room for students, a large hall seating two thousand (native fashion), women's dormitory, two missionary homes and three native style bungalows.

The day of the dedication will ever be a memorable one. The students who had been packed into the small, cramped and inadequate quarters down in the heart of the busy city, were now domiciled in new and airy rooms. The faithful teachers who were simply pouring out their lives in the Master's service, moved to the enlarged quarters. The splendid hall which then seated about five hundred, was thrown open and meetings were begun which have turned the tide for thousands of lives.

One old native brother who had watched the work of faith with intense interest through the three years and who had prayed for the buildings to be brought into being, was so filled with joy at their dedication that he arose and with tears streaming down his wrinkled face said, "Let us sing, 'Praise God from whom all blessings flow.' It was heartily sung by the hundreds present at this occasion and he asked that it be repeated twice, then thrice.

"Wherever you ripe fields behold,
Waving to God their sheaves of gold,
Be sure some corn of wheat has died,
Some saintly soul been crucified;
Someone has suffered, wept, and prayed,
And fought hell's legions undismayed."

"God can roll away 'great stones' and make them seats for angels."

"By the thorn road and no other is the mount of vision won."

"Heroes are forged on anvils hot with pain,
And splendid courage comes but with the test.
Some natures ripen and some natures bloom
Only on blood-wet soil, some souls prove great
Only in moments dark with death or doom."

CHAPTER XIV

TRIALS DURING FORMATIVE YEARS

There were many and varied trials during those formative years such as could have bowed down the strongest personality; but those who saw Charles Cowman day after day as he went along under the weight of the heavy burdens, saw only smiles and sunshine. He disguised the secret cross he was compelled to carry. The enemy at times used his utmost skill in shaking the foundations of the work. When it swayed and rocked under hot fire, God held him in a place of perfect calm. To say that he escaped suffering at such times would not be true, for there is no keener pain than spirit pain; but we must draw a veil over the Gethsemanes, the Calvarys, and the crucifixions. They were part of the plan. "When we cease to bleed, we cease to bless."

The torrents which are the melting of stainless snows high up on the mountain, flowing down the mountain-side to carry healing waters afar to dry and desert wastes, leave a scarred and torn mountain-breast behind. How often does the missionary who sets an infinite value on men's souls, understand Paul's heart-aches at Corinth and Christ's sighing over the Twelve. Sleepless nights are not always the result of a hot climate and torments of insects.

A worker with whom he was constantly associated, once remarked, "Nothing impressed me more than Brother Cowman's quiet spirit. I never saw him ruffled or upset, although at times I saw him wounded until the tears silently fell over his cheeks. He was a tender, sensitive spirit, but his secret cross became his crown."

"A fearless ministry," wrote Joseph Parker, "will often be tempestuous, but will bring in its train infinite peace."

Charles Cowman's steadfastness and calmness steadied at times the entire Mission. When a man knows that he has been called of God to a certain work, he is invincible. The testings prove to be of greatest blessing, because faith is more vigorously exercised in the promises of God at such times.

Throughout the book we mention a few facts gathered from practical experience as we have traveled through the twenty-five eventful years. We trust they will serve to confirm the truth that God is the Living One, the Hearer and Answerer of prayer. These experiences have been recorded for the strengthening of the faith of those who from the beginning have been our fellow-helpers by prayer.

Again and again the Lord put the principle on which Charles Cowman stepped out in 1901, to the test.

In many ways the tests grew in intensity. After all, for two people without family, to take a risk of this kind does not seem very striking, but now with a family numbering hundreds, the situation became much more complicated from the human standpoint. We do thank God that when we accept a principle from Him, He accepts a responsibility for us which covers every implication of the original step. Up to this present time He has fully justified our confidence.

"What poor timid heirs we are lying blindly upon our faces, when we should be reveling in the riches of grace," wrote Charles Cowman to a tested missionary. To another he quoted the quaint saying of Samuel Rutherford, "I would be undone if I had not access to the King's chamber of Presence to show Him all the business."

In taking a retrospect of his career, it would appear like one unbroken series of successes; but as memory retraces his steps, we can testify to the exhaustless labors in which he was engaged, the constant self-denial he cheerfully exercised, and the restless activities that ever kept him incessantly calling on the name of the Lord.

The first few months on the mission field were strange in some particulars. They were the beginnings in the primary of faith. Because he went out with no Mission Board to back him he was termed a "Faith Missionary." Many persons looked on, expecting to witness a grand failure and his sudden exit from his post of duty should his supplies be exhausted, but they were disappointed. "What must he possess that possesseth the Possessor of all things," said Savonarola.

"How long do you expect to remain on the field and carry on the work?" was a question frequently asked of Charles Cowman. "Until the Lord forgets to supply the need," was his unfailing answer, but the Lord has never forgotten. "Have you not a reserve fund for the furtherance of the work? Have you not some means somewhere to fall back upon in case of desperate need?" His answer was, "No, we have no reserve fund. When we come to a desperate need, we fall back upon the Lord who has so carefully supplied us and He never fails." We forget that the Great Commission was given to eleven men who had no money, no credit and no social position. The Word of Scripture upon which he ever relied was, "There hath not failed one word of all His good promise which He promised by the hand of Moses His servant." (1 Kings 8:56). Whenever he found himself lacking in faith, he would go alone with the Word and closet himself with God in prayer. A fresh grip was taken upon the promises at such times, until they became a part of his life. In his diary we find such notes:

"Came to the end of the month in great victory, the greatest harvest of souls for many weeks, almost constant revival, but in the midst of this tide of blessing, funds went down to the limit. A few days set apart for prayer and fasting and the Lord was reminded that we were here without purse or scrip, that we had launched forth upon His bare Word, 'Go ye also into the vineyard and what-soever is right, I will give you.' We rested the entire mission right in His hands. It is His and not ours."

Another entry: 'There was a great storm, *but He arose.*' I now understand the meaning of that word. It looked for all the world as if He were asleep in the hinder part of the ship and the disciples were left to battle with the waves that were well nigh overwhelming their small craft, but He never 'oversleeps' and when He does awake, what displays of His power make up for the test-ings!"

Let not the reader imagine that the only difficulties were financial. These were the least of all. Out where the fight is strong and souls are being delivered from the bondage of sin, the enemy often comes in like a mighty flood. Once during a terrible battle with the prince of darkness, a missionary visited us for a few days and thus came in direct touch with some of the inside problems. He remarked, "What a pity it is that upon the top of all these difficulties you have to pray in the funds." Charles Cowman never felt that God's work was divided into sec-tions, and praying for funds was part of his missionary program and the daily trusting for financial needs was one of the greatest blessings.

Now and again we find memorable covenants jotted down in his notebook. Often he consecrated himself

anew to God's service, and implored fresh gifts of divine grace and power, that he might more effectively perform the work which he felt God had called him to do, and witnessed constantly to the grace of God among the Gentiles.

"January 1. I do this day solemnly renew my vows to God to walk closely at His side, to serve and obey Him to the utmost of my ability, to will just what He wills and only what He wills. I desire nothing apart from Him. Reign over me, Lord Jesus!" Every bridge was burned behind him and there was left no road back to yesterday.

In his interleaved Bible, we find the notes of an address he had prepared at this particular time of testing. They were beside the text, "No man having put his hand to the plow and looking back is fit for the kingdom of God." This was heavily underscored and added to it was, "he must not even glance back." "He that chooseth Me must hazard all that he has." Jesus sacrificed six things:

1. Personal comforts.
2. Social enjoyments.
3. Human relationships.
4. Worldly ambitions.
5. Earthly riches.
6. Physical life.

"Jesus had neither lair nor nest. He had not even a secret chamber to call His own. All that He possessed were the clothes that He wore, and those were the poorest. Following Him means losing all you have for Christ; not hoarding for yourself, but allowing Him to control your possessions. Following Him may mean *for me,* even losing the physical life. It may be that He will let me wear out in an effort to save the heathen. Amen! And Amen!

> " 'Here I give myself to thee,
> Friends, and time, and earthly store.
> Soul and body Thine to be,
> Wholly Thine for ever more.'

It was during a time of very great testing that he wrote an article entitled, "Sail on! Sail on!" We quote a few excerpts.

> "What shall we say, great admiral, say,
> If we sight nought but seas at dawn?
> Why, we shall say at break of day,
> Sail on! Sail on, and on and on!"

"So spoke Columbus through the deathless lute of old Joaquin Miller, the poet of the Sierras. So spake the great admiral to his scowling crew when he sailed the unknown water of a trackless deep.

"Columbus was a missionary. If he had not had his dreams, the only Americans there would have been today would have been red skins. On, on he sailed and then, on a sunny morning, he found the new world lying at his feet. So great a faith could not fail a reward! Some one has said, 'Had there been no new world at all, God would have created one for the immortal Genoese.'

"The great Apostle Paul was called of God to carry the Gospel message to the Gentile world; he started, when suddenly he found himself in the midst of a shipwreck in a boiling sea. That is all very well in daylight with plenty of sea-room but at midnight with a starless sky and a rocky coast, it was dangerous to move.

"How the storm raged and billows dashed, days and nights passed by and all hope that they would be saved was taken away. Is Paul confused now, upset, bewildered? Is he 'going over in his mind' his call, wondering if he made a mistake or not? No, thank God, he was sailing under 'sealed orders,' and above the billows' foam he heard a Voice saying, 'Sail on, Paul, sail on!'

"We see him with calm determination exhorting his fellow travelers to 'be of good cheer, the Lord is at hand.'

"We have the inspiring record that Paul came to land with everyone in that old shipwreck, 'some on boards, some on broken pieces of ship,' but not a hair of their heads was harmed.

"We dare not question God's dealings with His children for 'all the ways of the Lord are right.'

"Let any soul attempt to do and dare for God and a thousand blockades will confront him, but a daring faith can surmount them all.

"We as a Mission have just passed our eighteenth milestone and as we take a retrospect, we can but stop for a praise meeting, thanking God for every black trial we have ever met, for every onslaught of the arch-enemy, for through these pressures we have learned to know God, and have gained our greatest victories. Often we have been driven into a corner where it was go under or go through, but God caused the great waves to become ships which launched us further on and on in things divine.

"May we say it for the encouragement of some struggling Christian worker—some one in a hard place today—that we have never undertaken a work for the Lord under His direct guidance for the liberation of precious souls, that Satan has not fought us inch by inch, but in the midst of the battle, as we have gone along with God, our spirits have been hushed and a sweet still voice has whispered to our inmost hearts, 'I am on board, there is no wind wild enough, no wind high enough, no storm fierce enough to wreck the vessel which carries the Lord of the earth and sky. Sail on, Sail on.'"

As to mission Church administration, for the sake of the future of the Church the missionary should train the churches with a view to speedy self-government and self-propagation. Some missionaries possessed of a strong individuality assume in themselves all the functions of the executive; they are in themselves bishop, priest, deacon, and elder; with their stronger personality and fulness of energy they have not the patience to bend to the drudgery of training natives; therefore they take all of the responsibility upon themselves. But this only means disaster in the future, for when the strong man leaves the field, his work falls to pieces. For the sake of the Church and for the future of the Church we must subordinate self and selfish tendencies and bend our energies to get the best we can out of the native Christians.—*Frederick Galpin.*

CHAPTER XV

TRAINING THE NATIVES

The missionary who is called to carry the Gospel to the heathen world, soon learns that this task is not a romantic promenade, but one which could exhaust the resources of the best endowed men and women. Charles Cowman learned this fact during the first month on the mission field. He saw the utter impossibility of the evangelization of the Orient by European agencies alone. God revealed to him part of His great plan in causing him to see that if the heathen nations were to be won for Jesus it would have to be done under the leadership and devoted service of the natives. This solution gripped his mind and heart in such a way that ever after he was an eager and strong advocate of the training of a native ministry. The only way to secure enough workers to meet the demands on the field is to train the native Christians to do missionary work. With his ear pressed closely to the needs of the present, he heard the marching feet of the future. He believed that the present hour called for a truly native church, able by its own spontaneous, Christian initiative to show Jesus Christ to the Oriental. Only a native church, renewed and strengthened by the Divine Spirit, could move the hearts of their own people. He believed that a true church of Christ was to be born in the Orient— a church through which He could speak, a hand with which He could touch, and feet with which He could go.

The native is the best medium through which the message of God can be brought to the native. Charles Cowman recognized this fact as he witnessed the effectiveness of Juji Nakada's preaching to his own people. There is a tone in the foreigner's voice which falls cold and heavy on the ear of the native, whereas there is something in the genuine tone of a countryman's voice which, operating like a charm, falls pleasantly on the ear, touching the heart, and causing the tenderest chords to vibrate.

The natives have many advantages over the foreign missionary in their work among their own people. The contrast is quite in evidence. They can endure torrid heat and unfavorable atmospheres, they can locate themselves amid the hamlets and villages, and they can converse with their country folk with understanding. Having these many advantages, besides knowing the sentiments, traditions, habits, manners, customs, trains of thought, and principles of reasoning among the people, they can strike home with illustrations and imagery, bringing truth and understanding in ways quite unknown to the foreign missionary.

The pattern which God had given Charles Cowman meant an utter effacement of self. Although an efficient soul-winner with a thorough knowledge of the Word of God, he was not seen as a leader, but was rather found hidden away, while the native Christians were brought to the front. He said the plan had been given to him "in the Mount," and he was quite content to risk everything upon the method which was not copied but which was divinely planned. At the root of his plans was faith in the native as well as in the Gospel which was to save him. He toiled on faithfully, looking only for sheaves to be harvested.

He delighted in developing and using to the advancement of Christ's kingdom, the efficient powers of other men. If he could accomplish some desired end, in whole or in part by the help of his brethren, he preferred to do so, rather than take all the work upon himself. Those who intimately knew him, recognized in this concealment of himself behind others, one of his marked characteristics. He always preferred to be in the background, allowing others to appear as the chief actors. For one so intense as he, the power of sinking himself and his own interest and aim was little less than marvelous, and made him both honored and loved. "Blessed is the man or woman," wrote Mary Slessor of Calabar, "who is able to serve cheerfully in the second rank."

Morrison of China wrote: "The great fault, I think, in our Missions is that no one likes to be second. Perhaps the advantages predominate, but I have not been able to perceive them. It is said that our Saviour made no distinctions among His disciples. It may be asked, on the other hand, are inspired Apostles in all things an example to uninspired missionaries?"

The establishment of an aggressive and vigorous native church became the soul burden of Charles Cowman. He felt, that if necessary he would gladly lay down his life for it. Often he was heard saying, "If I see this accomplished, I would feel, as far as my humble judgment is concerned, that my earth work to promote the glory and honor of my blessed Saviour was finished. I would be ready to exclaim with old Simeon, 'Now lettest Thou Thy servant depart in peace, for mine eyes have seen.'" God abundantly satisfied this desire and permitted him to see its accomplishment.

He placed his life beside that of his native brethren, fellow-servant of their common Lord, receiving from them and giving to them, counting it a very precious service that he could help them, by whatever experience God had given him in their sacred tasks of lifting up Jesus in their midst. "Silver and gold have I none, but such as

I have give I thee." He brought to them leadership, sympathy, and sound wisdom. His attitude was ever, "What can I do to best serve you?" not, "How can I direct, dominate, or dictate?" He found his place and would play his part. He was irrevocably committed to the enterprise. This was the burden of the Lord committed to Charles Cowman.

When God gives a man a conviction which he is willing to put into practice without haggling over the price, the effect is irresistible. Charles Cowman said, "I ask for nothing more than to spend my days in clearing the ground and laying foundations for the future years." He was content to build for the years which he would not see. Today the latest thought among missionary circles is swinging back to his strong emphasis of the value of a trained native ministry. Almost every missionary society is recognizing its value. Only let it have sufficient time and it will be productive of more important results than can be easily estimated.

Twenty-eight years ago he said to his native brethren, "If we will but stay true to the trust God has given us, hold fast to the doctrines which we believe and teach, God will let us see a fruitage right here in the Orient which will exceed our fondest imagination." God granted the exceeding abundantly, above all he asked or thought.

Hudson Taylor had a similar vision, and expressed himself on the subject as follows: "I look upon foreign missionaries as the scaffolding around a rising building; the sooner it can be dispensed with the better, or rather the sooner it can be transferred to other places, to serve the same temporary use."

Dr. Fulton, the Dean of the Presbyterian mission of China for forty years, said: "One thoroughly trained native missionary is of more value to China than *ten* missionaries from other countries." As early as 1901, Charles Cowman wrote to a friend in the homeland: "I cannot reach this vast multitude except through one thousand trained native workers, of stuff and caliber and spirit such as I am proud to work with; through them, one can expect to reach the multitudes." And after his Home-call a few lines in a leading periodical read thus: "In so far as Charles Cowman's successful achievements may be traced to correctness of policy, what is known as statesmanship, we are of the opinion that he should be credited with missionary genius of a high order."

A year before his Home-call it was stated by prominent missionaries that "The Oriental Missionary Society" was better equipped with native leaders than any other mission in the Orient, more than one thousand native preachers having been trained.

Successful demonstration is the best demonstration. A detailed account of the difficulties which were met and overcome, inaugurating this new experiment of training a native ministry, would be interesting, but space will not permit the story to be told. The difficulties encountered were many, some of them unpleasant; but success attended the enterprise, and year by year the Bible Training Institute gained in popularity and soon became widely known not only throughout Japan, but Korea, China, and even beyond. Its influence thus became very widely extended. It no longer stands alone, but similar schools have since opened in other parts of the country. It has thus accomplished a good work in serving as a model.

In addressing a native conference of pastors and evangelists, Charles Cowman made this statement, "The end toward which I am working is found in 1 Thess. 1. 8. 'For from *you* sounded out the word of the Lord . . In every place *your* faith to God-ward is spread abroad, so that *we* need not speak anything.'" Thus he encouraged them to step into positions of responsibility and to place their reliance upon Him. The outcome of the toil of these years has been that a native leadership has been raised up right frcm among the converts who are veritable flames of fire, possessed of such a true missionary spirit that they are pressing forth into the unoccupied places of their own land.

May a long line of native workers with a still greater burden be raised up to stand in the gap and to "build up the old waste places"!

"According to the New Testament, Jesus walked along the shores of a little sea known as the Sea of Galilee. And there He called Peter and Andrew and James and John and several others to be His followers, and they left all and followed Him. After they had followed Him they revered Him, and later on adored and worshipped Him. He left them on their faces, each man saying, 'My Lord and my God!' All that is in the New Testament.

"But put the New Testament away. Time passes; history widens; an unseen Presence walks up and down the shores of a larger sea—the sea called the Mediterranean—and this unseen Presence calls men to follow Him. Tertullian, Augustine, Anselm, Aquinas, Francis of Assisi, Thomas a Kempis, Savonarola, John Huss, Martin Luther, Philip Melancthon, Ulrich Zwingli, John Calvin—another twelve—and these all followed Him and cast themselves at His feet, saying, in the words of the earlier twelve, 'My Lord and My God!'

"Time passes; history advances; humanity lives its life around the circle of a larger sea—the Atlantic Ocean. An unseen Presence walks up and down the shores calling men to follow Him. He calls John Knox, John Wesley, George Whitefield, Charles Spurgeon, Henry Parry Liddon, Joseph Parker, Jonathan Edwards, Horace Bushnell, Henry Ward Beecher, Richard Salter Storrs, Phillips Brooks, Dwight L. Moody— another twelve—and these leave all and follow Him. We find them on their faces, each one saying 'My Lord and my God!'

"Time passes; history is widening; humanity is building its civilization round a still wider sea—we call it the Pacific Ocean. An unknown Presence moves up and down the shores calling men to follow Him, and they are doing it. Another company of twelve is forming. And what took place in Palestine nineteen centuries ago is taking place again in our own day and under our own eyes."

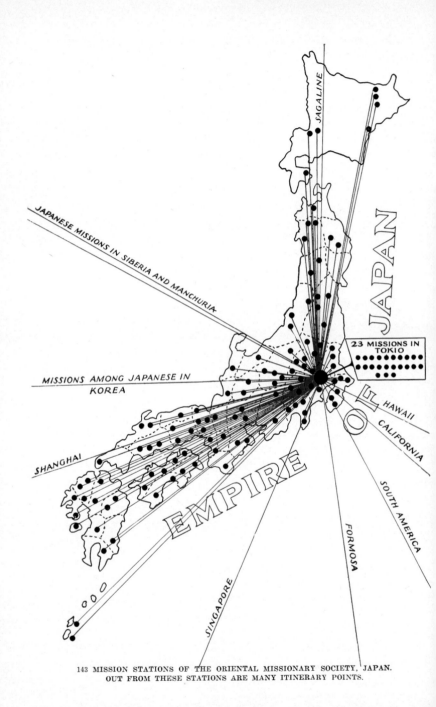

143 MISSION STATIONS OF THE ORIENTAL MISSIONARY SOCIETY, JAPAN.
OUT FROM THESE STATIONS ARE MANY ITINERARY POINTS.

EVANGELIZE

"Give us a watchword for the hour,
 A thrilling word, a word of power.
 A battle-cry, a flaming breath
 That calls to conquest or to death.

"A word to rouse the church from rest,
 To heed the Master's high behest.
 The call is given: Ye hosts arise,
 Our watchword is, EVANGELIZE!

"The glad Evangel now proclaim,
 Through all the earth, in Jesus' name.
 This word is ringing through the skies:
 EVANGELIZE! EVANGELIZE!

"To dying men, a fallen race,
 Make known the gift of Gospel grace.
 The world that now in darkness lies,
 EVANGELIZE! EVANGELIZE!"

CHAPTER XVI

EVANGELISTIC TOURS

Charles Cowman had been in Japan less than a year and a half when he began evangelistic touring which occupied much of the rest of his lifetime. Three native evangelists and seven students in training comprised the party on this first memorable trip, which, as it were, stimulated his faith in a native ministry. He became strongly convinced of its need so that no other work appealed to him as did the training of a native ministry. He dreamed of it by night and toiled for it by day. His letters and writings are filled with reference to it. Wherever he went in America, in England, or over the entire Orient, he was constantly presenting the claims for the native preachers.

Evangelistic services were held every day and evening during this trip, and about seven hundred souls sought Christ in less than six weeks. How he praised God for this new vision! Doors suddenly opened everywhere, whole towns and villages were given an opportunity of hearing the Gospel. His soul was set on fire afresh. He wrote to someone during this trip: "Oh, the luxury of roughing it! Tonight we are lodged in a room about six by twelve, four of us. The tatami (mats) look nice and clean and the inn-keeper is most cordial. He apologized greatly that he had no larger room, but I think that we four can lie down anyway and that will mean a whole lot after the ten-mile walk in the hot sun. We passed through fourteen wholly untouched villages today and preached in the streets, the people listening eagerly. Six splendid young men, students of a high school, asked us for New Testaments, saying they had given up idol worship, and had nothing to take its place. We pointed them to the Lamb of God, gave them Scriptures, told them where to begin reading the Word, and prayed with them. They accompanied us to the next village and as we walked along the roadway they opened their hearts to us. 'The order changeth' and may God help us to get ready for the new.

"We passed through a village where a lad had been brightly converted. He gathered his neighbors into his home, and so many came that the floor broke through, but he seemed little disturbed over it. They carried mats out into the yard, where for two hours the people sat quite still, listening as if their very lives depended on it. Two very aged grandmothers, toothless and slightly deaf, asked us to pray with them, as they wished to go to 'the Country of peace' when their earthly-life was ended. Oh, how the need of this land grips my heart! I cannot rest while they sit in darkness and the shadow of death!

"This kind of work brings us into close contact with the tremendous powers of darkness; however, the kingdom of the devil is under the power of our Heavenly Father, and only affords means by which His perfect will and counsel can be unfolded. This field is a real battle-ground. It seems all battle-ground, but it belongs to Jesus. Satan disputes the title, contends for every inch of ground and fights hard to cause a retreat, but, 'Fight on, my soul, till death!' We have had Japan's hundreds brought to Christ, we must have her thousands. The light is burning through the dense darkness and 'Jesus shall reign where'er the sun!' "

To another friend he wrote a few days later: "This has been a happy day to my soul. We began services this morning about seven o'clock. Many who heard for the first time last night, came early, thinking we were leaving today. Here, in this virgin soil, the Spirit of God has been doing a convicting work. It is wonderful to reach people who have never heard the Gospel before. I grasp afresh what Paul meant when he said, 'To preach the Gospel in the regions beyond you, and not to boast in another man's line of things made ready to our hand.' In this spot we have a parish of over one million souls. As we have walked through the country day after day, meeting hundreds and thousands who have never heard one word of the Gospel, my heart has been stirred to its very depth, and by the help and grace of God, *they shall hear* if it costs every drop of my life's blood. 'Here am I, Lord, send me, send me!'

"If our friends at home could but see the ripe opportunity,—so dead ripe, how they would stand back of us and help us to evangelize these millions. 'We want to find God. You won't leave us, will you, until we truly find Him?' said a dear aged man with bent form and whitened locks."

To a prayer-partner he wrote: "Two splendid young men came to me at the close of a service saying that they felt a real call to preach the Gospel. Both are graduates of the provincial high school. They have bright, keen minds. One is employed in a bank, the other in a silk store. I felt impressed to tell them to come straight to the Bible School, but they will need to be supported, as they will have to give up their positions. What an investment for someone, and what a small sum $90.00 (£18). (The cost of their support while in training).

"Calls are coming from other provinces and other districts. 'Give us a church or a small hall where we can worship the true God.' A deputation from a large cluster of villages plead with us, 'Send us a preacher. If you do not have one with long experience, send us some one who can read the Bible and pray and lead us to know God.' "

How was he to turn a deaf ear to such heart cries for help? What was he to do? As usual, he turned to God in prayer reminding Him that He had sent him to the Orient to do His work, without purse or scrip. Definite requests were made, plans were well laid, and God never failed him.

These trips inland, joyful as they were to him, invariably ended in some severe illness. One trip was taken which almost ended seriously. After an absence of some weeks "roughing it," on his return he was stricken with severe pleurisy, suffering untold agony for a number of days and nights. When barely able to be out of bed, he was at work again. This interesting note is found in his diary:

"Confined to the house for two weeks, but made a missionary map. Looking back to last year, a great advance has been made. New stations have been opened in Japan and Korea. Prayed much for the opening of China. Today have translators at work on the marked New Testament. Meditated on the Word, Matt. 28:17. *'But some doubted.'*

Several times during these inland trips his life had been miraculously preserved. Accompanied by several workers he visited a great untouched district in the North. He had gone with the purpose of opening a Mission Station and doing evangelistic work in the entire section, but on the night of his arrival, a great cyclone struck the town, completely demolishing parts of it. The door of the hotel was wrenched from its groove and hurled against him. The next morning when he was able to walk over the town he saw a great tree which had fallen across the entrance to one of the largest heathen temples. The aged priest was sitting upon it with a woe-begone expression, a picture of hopelessness and despair. The gods in the temples had been thrown from their shelves and the poor people were saying, "If they cannot protect themselves, how can they protect us?"

How splendid does pioneer work sound! In the very word there is glamour and glow; in the life itself there is nothing of the kind. One of the early missionary pioneers wrote: "The evangelization of the heathen world in the place where it is carried on, is certainly not a tissue of strange customs and adventures as thrilling as a romance; it is a desperate struggle with the prince of darkness, and with everything his rage can stir up in the shape of obstacles, vexations, oppositions, and hatred, whether by circumstances or by the hand of man. *It is a serious task.* Oh, it should mean a life of consecration and faith."

A visitor called at the home some weeks before the Home-call of our beloved missionary. He was shown into the study to look at a new map with its hundreds of mission stations dotted in red, the work of a quarter of a century. He remarked about the phenomenal success that had been made, when Charles Cowman said to him, "What *has* been done, we praise Him for, but what of the *unfinished task?*" For an hour he was leading him through the great untouched places of heathendom, away off into the interior, far off the beaten trail, hundreds of miles from coast cities and established mission stations, where millions of souls will forever be lost unless some-one with a passion for their salvation will leave all and "go quickly and tell."

Across the map was written in bold strong strokes, in the hand-writing known so well, " 'Without God and without hope.' 450,000,000 eternity-bound souls for whom I am responsible."

Turning to the visitor, he said, "What must the Master think as He looks down upon the map that represents the millions of heathendom? What does He think of me?"

This was his spirit, ever taking the blame to himself for this terrible condition; the spirit which burned out his very life.

Charles Cowman had a real passion for reaching out into untouched places, for God had not only given to him a vision of the millions without the Gospel, but also a vision of what could be accomplished through the scattered seed among them. He was not a dreamer nor a visionary person, but one whose heart was stirred to its depths over the unreached millions. He wrote to a friend in 1902, "I cannot rest while they die." His daily prayer was that God might give to him some plan by which they might be given at least one chance.

This first inland trip resulted in the opening of several mission stations. During the next twenty years which followed, 160 interior mission stations and an equal number of itinerary points were opened. There is now a chain of Mission Stations throughout the Empire. Thousands of heathen have been reached because Charles Cowman caught the vision and launched forth by faith to make the Name of Jesus known in places where naught but darkness prevailed. The hundreds of churches that he had been instrumental in opening and which are now flourishing all over the land were the first lights in the darkness of a dark land, pointing to Calvary's cross and to Jesus Himself. These are now being carried on by trained natives and many are entirely self-supporting.

A letter home tells his experience on this first inland trip. "It has been our great privilege to visit dear Brother and Sister Shimidzu who opened our first station. A party of seven left Tokyo on Monday last and traveled all

A PARTIAL VIEW OF AUDIENCE IN OUR CONVENTION HALL, TOKYO BIBLE INSTITUTE. IT SEATS 2,000, BUT AN ENLARGEMENT IS NECESSARY TO ACCOMMODATE THE CROWDS.

day, reaching a large city near the mountains ere nightfall. We stopped over night as it was a railway junction, and remained there until four in the morning, when we boarded another train which carried us on further into the chain of mountains. What an interesting journey! Our party traveled in a third-class compartment, and often the atmosphere was blue, as both men and women indulged in smoking. Our fellow-travelers were very friendly and the majority of them were country folk. A splendid opportunity was offered us for witnessing to them and we gave out tracts and preached in the train throughout the entire day. All seemed eager to listen and it would have done your heart good to have seen these raw heathen drinking in the precious old gospel truth. When alighting from the train one of our party suggested that as it was yet twilight, we hold a street meeting, so after partaking of our supper in a native inn we all went out and preached the Word on the various street corners in that heathen city. People flocked like doves to the windows and we had great liberty in telling them that there was no other name under Heaven given among men whereby they could be saved. When we returned to the inn a little past nine o'clock, all gathered into one small room and held a praise service. While we were singing the good songs of Zion, the inn-keeper came upstairs, entered the room and sat down quietly, bowing his head. He said, 'Please sing that song again.' We did so and then he asked us who we were, where were we going, and what had brought us to his city. It was a splendid opportunity to win a soul. We talked with him for two hours, as he had never heard of the Gospel. Then all retired as we had to start on our journey at three o'clock the following morning. This kind inn-keeper was up long ere we were, having maids prepare a hot breakfast for us and when we came down the stairs he met us with radiant countenance saying, 'I prayed to your God last night and peace came into my heart.' There was no need for his telling us as peace fairly beamed from his face. We praised God for this seal upon our first inland journey and we went on our way rejoicing. It was some time after noon when we reached Tateoka where our dear Brother and Sister Shimidzu met us at the train Quite a number of people were with them and when we went out of the gateway they all spoke to us saying, 'Welcome! Welcome!' Brother Shimidzu said, 'These are our Christians and they have come to the station to greet you.' We loved these-our first-fruit from the inland station and what a welcome we received!

"They had already gathered a number of converts and when our coming was known, this little handful began to tell others. This was better than printers' ink for advertising. The people walked to the services for miles up the valley and from far-off mountain fastnesses.

"Tateoka is a lovely little town and back of it is a mountain. We arrived in the afternoon, went out to this mountain, climbed to the top, and counted forty-two towns and villages within close range. Down the valley and beyond are more than one hundred thousand people, unreached, utterly untouched. Here they live and die without God and without hope.

"At our first service in the evening, the new converts testified and our hearts were filled with joy as we heard them tell of the way they heard, then sought and found. We had great liberty in preaching to this crowd and one old heathen woman listened as if her life depended on it. She came to me and said, *'I always knew that there ought to be a God like that.'*

"A man stood up at the close of the service and said in such a touching manner, 'I have been waiting for forty years to hear what I have heard tonight. I was sure there was nothing in Buddhism that could save me, and I felt that the great God must have some method by which the poor sinner might find salvation.'

"For three weeks we visited villages and towns, walking many miles every day, while the dear people just besieged us for literature. Although we had a large supply, it was soon exhausted and we had to wire for more to be sent to us from Tokyo. This order was also quickly given out. What readers these people are! We must throw in the Gospel seed!

"What beauty spots of nature! Mountains in all their stately grandeur and ever-changing charms; climbing woodland slopes and rushing torrents, fertile plains covered with paddy-fields or verdant with tea plantations; avenues of feathery bamboo and forests of pine; flowers of the deepest crimson and soft yellow, camellia, iris, chrysanthemum, such were the gifts flung—

> " ' . . . . . .—unrestrained and free
> O'er hill and dale and valley sod,
> That man at every step may see
> The footprint and the stamp of God.'

"But we saw something else as we stood on the crest of the mountain,—Satan's footprints. Idol temples dotted the hillsides and valley and the roadways were lined with stone images and wayside shrines. The people who lived in the quaint but picturesque little thatch-roofed homes knew nothing of the 'Man of Calvary.'

"Come with me to one of the towns we visited, a quiet town nestling in a fertile plain near the foothills of a chain of mountains. The mountains wear their winter robes of snow, and streams of snow water run along the steep gutters, to find the paddy-fields far below. There are not many lands where the people make more use of such tiny streams. The ducks swim in them; the little urchins wade and bathe in them; cabbages and carrots are washed in them; buckets of filth are emptied into them; clothes are washed in them; and lastly, coolies every hour dip their pails in them and carry refreshing contents to the tea shops and homes where fragrant tea is brewed. There are no wells in this place, as the people are very superstitious and fancy that if wells were dug, evil spirits would invade the place; hence the city is without wells.

"One morning just as we were starting out over the mountains we met two old men traveling to the temple at the top. We talked with them, asking if they had found peace in their hearts. Pathetic was their answer, 'I am feeling for the door, but cannot find it.'

"We had an experience one day that I am sure I shall never be able to erase from my mind. We were walking along from one village to another when we saw a large number of women working in a field. My wife beckoned to them to come to the roadside. They dropped their hoes and came as a foreign woman was to them a rare sight. They were asked if they had ever heard of God. Their reply was, 'Oh, yes, we have several gods right here in the field and in that small building yonder are numbers of gods whom we worship.' Wife and her Bible Woman then told them the sweet story in all of its simplicity and charm. They listened intently and soon were kneeling in prayer by the roadside. It was the first time for these dear women to have ever heard the name of Jesus.

"When we parted with them we said, 'Remember the name of the true God is Jesus.' They repeated it over

and over again and we left them repeating, 'Jesus, Jesus.'
We walked on, expecting to reach a large town ere night-
fall as there were no inns out in the open country where
we could stop for the night. We had gone but a few
yards when one of the women came running after us
almost breathless, crying out 'Wait, wait.' We waited
and when she came near to us she said, 'What did you say
that name was? Tell me His Name again.' Its strange
name had been forgotten, but we wrote it on a piece of
paper and she hobbled away saying, 'Jesus, Jesus, Jesus.'
I expect to meet that woman in the glory land.

"We passed through a large town and the Inn-keeper
where we stopped for our noon meal kindly permitted us
the use of the long veranda for a service. Our little party
of workers stood there singing, attracting quite a
crowd and for more than an hour we held a red-hot
Gospel service. It began to rain, but the people refused
to leave. They undoubtedly expected rain for the majority of them carried their oil-paper umbrellas. There they
stood for another hour under their dripping umbrellas. I
do not know when anything touched my heart more than
that sight. I doubt if one had ever before heard the name
of Jesus. It was a great privilege.

"When we reached the next town, some four miles
further down the valley, the rain had cleared away, and
here we gathered a crowd for an evening service. The
Inn-keepers are most cordial to us and everywhere we
have gone they have freely given us the use of their large
parlors for our services. It is the customary meeting
place in these lands, and they resemble great banqueting
halls. On this particular night we had about 500 people
indoors and more than that number out in the large front
yard. They were so orderly and quiet that it was a perfect luxury to preach to them. I asked one very aged man

if missionaries had visited this town and district. He replied, 'About twenty-five years ago a white man passed through here, but we have not seen one since that time.' These are the things that pull at the heart-strings. It is wearing on the physical to tramp miles every day and hold services almost continuously, but

> " 'It is great to be out where the fight is strong,
>   To be where the heaviest troops belong,
>   And to fight there for man and God.
>
> " 'It seams the face and it dries the brain,
>   It strains the arm till one's friend is Pain,
>   In the fight for man and God.
>
> " 'But it's great to be out where the fight is strong,
>   To be where the heaviest troops belong,
>   And to fight there for man and God.'

"There are so many open doors, so many pressing needs, and but one little human life, unable to accomplish one hundredth part of all we desire! I long to spend and be spent for their salvation."

These trips were made whenever funds would permit, and the result of the seed sowing was a harvest far surpassing any of his expectations. In a very short time after the opening of this first inland station, from among the converts out of darkest heathenism were seventeen young men who felt a call to the ministry. They were accepted as students in the Bible Training Institute where they spent several years in diligent study after which they were then sent out as evangels to their own people.

Charles Cowman often sang this song of faith:

> "Coming, coming, yes, they are,
>   Coming, coming, from afar;
>   From the wild and scorching desert,
>   Afric's sons of colour deep;
>   Jesus' love has drawn and won them,
>   At His cross, they bow and weep.

"Coming, coming, yes, they are,
Coming, coming, from afar;
From the fields and crowded cities,
    China gathers at His feet;
In His love Shem's gentle children
Now have found a safe retreat.

"Coming, coming, yes, they are,
Coming, coming, from afar;
From the Indies and the Ganges,
    Steady flows the living stream,
To love's ocean, to His bosom,
Calvary their wond'ring theme.

"Coming, coming, yes, they are,
Coming, coming, from afar;
From the steppes of Russia dreary,
    From Slavonia's scattered lands,
They are yielding soul and spirit,
Into Jesus' loving hands.

"Coming, coming, yes, they are,
Coming, coming, from afar;
All to meet in plains of glory,
All to sing His praises sweet;
What a chorus, what a meeting,
    With the family complete!"

"Extension or extinction is the Master's ultimatum."

HOLINESS TABERNACLE, SEOUL, KOREA.

O. M. S. BIBLE TRAINING INSTITUTE, SEOUL, KOREA.

STUDENTS OF THE O. M. S. BIBLE TRAINING INSTITUTE, SEOUL, KOREA.

CHAPTER XVII

THE ADVANCE INTO KOREA

A map of the Orient hanging on the wall of Charles Cowman's study had tracings of deep red letters denoting the population of the countries for which he prayed for years—these were: Korea, China, Siam, Annam, Tibet, Russia, and Formosa. To his missionary heart these figures spelled lost souls, dying millions. The map ever made its silent appeal. We little know, when praying, what we may be called upon to do for anyone for whom we plead, or for any country which is near to our hearts. Normal expansion of Christian work almost invariably leads to still wider expansion. Work begets work, and successes on one field seem to beckon onward to greater achievements on other fields.

When he returned from one of his deputational tours in America, he was greeted by three Koreans who had entered the Tokyo Bible Training Institute during his absence. They had heard of the school in Japan where students were equipped for aggressive soul-winning. Their names were Li, Kim, and Chung, well-known names in Korea. Although unfamiliar with the Japanese language, they had been accepted as students. How diligently they set to work to learn the language and in a brief time they were not only speaking brokenly, but understanding the lectures. Three years passed by; their Bible training was finished, and believing that God meant for them to have a similar school in their own country, they returned, praying that it might become a fact.

There was something remarkable in the chain of events which led to the opening of the Korea Bible Institute. These three brethren were sent back to the Capital city, Seoul, to open a mission, and on that day, God set His seal upon it by saving a number of souls. On Sabbath afternoons when Christians gathered at the meeting for the promotion of Scriptural Holiness, numbers sought and obtained the blessing, returning to their own churches veritable flames of fire. A rented building was occupied for one year, and the services were crowded with eager, earnest listeners. The workers begged us to erect for them a Bible Training institute where Korean native preachers might be trained, as numbers of these new converts desired to give their lives to preaching the Gospel to their own people.

When General Butler started on his great expedition, he sailed under sealed orders; the orders were not to be opened until after the expedition had been so many days at sea. But all on board had consecrated themselves so fully to the Federal Government that they had determined to go wherever the orders bade them. When God asked Charles Cowman to go to Korea for Him, he said, "It is part of the original contract to do the will of God as far as He shall make it known, and I accept this new requirement."

> "The light hath flashed from Heaven,
> And I must follow it."

It was not undertaken without very much prayer. Indeed, it never would have been undertaken apart from a feeling of divine constraint. A burden of this character is not lightly assumed by a man whose hands are already full. The call came at a time when there was not a dollar in the mission treasury for the opening up of such a new and extended work, but he was fully assured that God was able to care for the work in both countries, that His resources were equal to the new demand, and in this faith it was undertaken.

To how many places we come in life where there is nothing to be done but to *go forward!* There are times when we especially need God-given wisdom to see the guiding hand of God. How faithfully Charles Cowman followed the Lord when His way was made plain to him! The word so definitely given to him for Korea is found in Haggai, "Build the house; and I will take pleasure in it, and I will be glorified, saith the Lord." "Be strong and work, for I am with you." "Fear thou not." "The glory of this latter house shall be greater than the former, and in this place will I give peace."

God wonderfully worked in behalf of Korea! A missionary was needed for this new undertaking and He laid His Hand upon two choice souls over in England, John and Emily Thomas, and sent them out to Korea to take charge of the new work.

Through The Oriental Missionary Standard it was made known that the Society had extended its borders to Korea, and was expecting to erect a great Bible Training Institute there. How gladly the news was welcomed in the homelands, and gifts were received from hundreds of friends for this purpose. The gifts were not large, as the donors to the work are among God's humble children; but God put His multiplying touch to the loaves and fishes, and there was sufficient with which to purchase the location and erect several buildings.

We are not to look at natural possibilities or impossibilities; for with Him all things are possible, and they become possible to him that believeth, and who by faith becomes vitally one with the omnipotent God. We may attempt for Him, if we expect from Him, great things. Perhaps it yet remains for man to illustrate how great faith may be in its hold on God, and for God to demonstrate fully how He recognizes and rewards such faith. The possibilities of a believing heart and life lie among the unfathomed depths—unexplored secrets of God.

This step marked another crisis in Charles Cowman's life. He was conscious of God's call and there were countless indications that God was going before His servant, but he who would go forth as a pioneer missionary and assay to enter new territory, ventures over into the very possessions of Satan who for generations has held undisputed sway over the hearts of the people. What think you? Will he immediately give way when the missionary enters, offering no resistance? Whenever Satan acts as a hinderer, the obstacles which he piles up to block our pathway need not dismay us; they may call forth a fresh exercise of faith and patience, but in the end the Satanic hinderer will be met by the Divine Helper who will sweep out of our way all the obstacles, as with the breath of His mouth. Said Marshal Foch, "When one has faith, one does not retire. One stops the enemy where he finds him."

"The devil is not put to flight by a courteous request," wrote Charles Cowman to a close heart-friend during those days. "He meets us at every turn, contends for every inch, and our progress has to be registered in heart's blood and tears." Undaunted by difficulties, he refused to be turned aside from the plain path of duty, let come what may.

"A restful realization of the Lord's companionship," wrote Dr. Jowett, "has been the characteristic of men whose religious activity has been forceful, influential, and fertile in the purpose of the Kingdom. At the very heart of all their labors, in the very center of their stormiest days, there is a sphere of sure and restful intimacy with the Lord . . . Get a man who is restfully intimate with his Lord, and you have a man whose force is tremendous! Such men move in apparent ease, but it is the ease that is linked with the infinite; it is the very rest of God. They may be engaged in apparent trifles, but even in the doing of trifles there emerge the health-giving currents of the Kingdom of God."

"How I would tremble standing in this place of responsibility, if I had not known that God sent me here. I did not choose my position, nor did I seek it; it was placed in my hands by the Lord, and I shall not get up and leave it or flee as doth an hireling shepherd," were the words to a fellow-worker.

The splendid work in Korea is progressing, because Charles Cowman stood strong and firm in its cradle days when there was no small amount of persecution. He was at times acutely sensitive to the thrusts of sharp criticism dealt to him through misunderstanding of his motives. He was doubtless misjudged and stood under suspicion of false teaching, but he had no new-fangled religion to impart, only the Gospel as old as the ages. Accusations make wounds and leave scars; but even the scars were soon worn off by the remembrance of his Divine Master's tenderness and forgiveness. He could not bear uncharitableness.

There can be no Easter without a Good Friday, and there was a constant Calvary in his experience during the time the foundations were being laid for the Korea Bible Training Institute. The great adversary, knowing what was to happen in the lives of these people, did everything to hinder and to frustrate the plan, but great and mighty things happened in connection with the newly established

14

mission. There is always suffering connected with fruit bearing, and it may be written of the beginnings in Korea, that "the more they afflicted them, the more they grew," for the work advanced in a wonderful manner, and God continued to pour out His Spirit upon the new converts.

"Unless we maintain our standards, the whole work goes down," was a brief sentence to a prayer-partner.

"It is not enough to believe what you maintain. You must maintain what you believe, and maintain it because you believe it," wrote Archbishop Whateley.

The people in the homelands have but a small conception of the difficulties surrounding the securing of locations for Christian work in heathen countries. Intricacies that the Western mind can scarcely conceive of enter into the negotiations, and days, weeks, and months pass by very often, even after the location has been found, before the property is transferred.

Charles Cowman asked God for some particular promise upon which he could firmly pin his faith as he searched for locations. Two promises were especially given to him: "They got not the lands of the heathen by their own sword" (Psalms 44:3). This was underscored in his Bible. The other, "I will give you the good of the land of Egypt, and ye shall eat the fat of the land. Regard not your stuff; for the good of the land of Egypt is yours" (Genesis 45:18, 20).

He had searched two whole weeks for a suitable location for the Bible Training Institute, but every available hilltop in the city of Seoul was occupied, with the exception of one. The bargain was made for its purchase, when overnight a peculiar circumstance occurred. It seems sad to be obliged to paint a black cloud in the sky of this bright picture; but some mark of the enemy's presence might be expected to appear. Someone, upon learning that

The Oriental Missionary Society had contracted for that particular site, met the owner, offering him a very much larger sum, so the promise was broken. This was a strange test of faith indeed, but His servant was enabled to say, "God meant it unto good," then turning the seeming disappointment into His-appointment, he began another search. It was during the intense heat of summer. One morning quite early, while walking through the narrow streets, a Korean gentleman approached him with the question, "Are you the person looking for a plot of ground for a school?" He replied in the affirmative. The Korean then said, "I am employed in the former Emperor's household and my master has a plot of ground which he will sell to you."

Learning where it was located, Charles Cowman walked quickly outside the West Gate and climbed the beautiful hill overlooking the city of Seoul. There he had a magnificent view of the city, also miles and miles of valley which lay at the right. There was not a lovelier spot in the entire city and no place could have been better suited for the Bible Training Institute. It seemed to have stood there for ages just awaiting this time. What an ideal place it was for the training of students—away up on the hillside where the air was fresh and pure, far removed from the odors and filth of the valley below! And the price? It was almost less than half of the amount which would have been paid for the much smaller location. It was incidents like this that colored Charles Cowman's life with joy.

The next out-going steamer carried a letter to praying friends: "Praise God! Today the magistrates came as if by appointment and the land boundaries were determined, and all matters connected therewith amicably settled. We have the deed to the property in hand and I have already contracted for brick, stone and mortar and have engaged masons and carpenters. We begin the erection of the building this coming week. By the architect's drawings which I am sending you, you will notice we propose to erect substantial buildings. Such structures could not be erected in America for five times the cost of these. We have the most wonderful location, and to think that it has been truly God-given! Every time I step upon it, I feel like praising Him."

Well indeed might his cup of joy be filled to the very brim for was he not in a real sense "laying the foundation for future generations"? Some months later, when the buildings were up and occupied and when the students began to arrive from Inland Provinces, splendid young people who had heard the Lord's voice calling them to preach His word, overflowing was his cup indeed.

The beautiful buildings, with the lovely grounds, have all sprung from his willingness to "go up and possess the land." The temptation to say, "We are not able," must have been very great; however, the brave spirit flinched not, and he lived to see not scores, but hundreds of young men and women equipped for their life-work. In addition to this great joy, unlooked-for service opened for his beloved Master. New friends were given, new lessons taught, and many sweet surprises were planned for him by the Lord, causing him to see His dear Hand manifestly outstretched on his behalf. A large volume could be filled with details of interesting experiences. When God answers prayer, the answer is often given "exceeding abundantly above all we can ask or think," for with His multiplying touch one thing grows out of another.

Work opened up in the country districts of Korea, the people called for preachers, and it became necessary to pattern after the work in Japan, building churches and

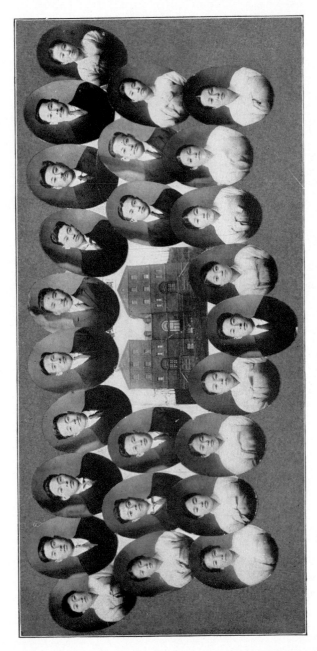

GRADUATING CLASS OF THE SEOUL, KOREA, BIBLE TRAINING INSTITUTE. DURING TWENTY-SEVEN YEARS THE O. M. S. HAVE TRAINED MORE THAN 1200 NATIVE PREACHERS. THE WATCHWORD OF THE SOCIETY IS, "THE ORIENT MUST BE EVANGELIZED BY HER OWN SONS AND DAUGHTERS."

opening interior stations. The story of the transformation of whole regions through the power of the Gospel, carried on by men of faith, constitutes a thrilling record. Up to the year 1927, fifty-seven churches had sprung up and scores of itinerary points, while about half of Korea has been visited by the Korea Village Campaign Bands, resulting in hundreds, yea, thousands of earnest seekers. The seekers in villages during 1927 numbered 5,564.

It was his joy not only to witness the growth of these Institutions beyond the most sanguine hopes he cherished when planting them, but to receive the grateful thanks of those who derived unspeakable benefit in partaking of their fruits.

A little success did not elate him, nor a measure of success prompt him to settle down in some quiet resting place. The ascendency he began to acquire, instead of making him vain, filled him with awe, and increased the rigor of self-discipline which he ever exercised over himself. A few lines found in his papers reveal the man.

"God must have looked all around to find a stick poor enough to use, and when he saw me he said, 'Here's one,' and that is why He picked me up. 'I have never been able to fathom *why* He passed by the many who, seemingly, were far better qualified, then gave me such an important place in the work of *training an army,* as it were, who, if our Lord tarry, 'shall build the old waste places and raise up the foundations of many generations'; but I humbly and obediently accept the trust and am 'plowing in hope' that this may literally come to pass through the native evangelists and Bible women who go forth from our Bible Training Institutes in the Orient. God grant it, until multitudes shall 'turn to God from idols to serve the living and true God, and to wait for His Son from

Heaven, whom He raised from the dead, even Jesus which delivered us from the wrath to come.' Amen!''

We find another convenant which he made at this date and into the Holy of Holies of his deeper heart life we venture to look with shrinking eyes.

" 'Now it is in mine heart to make a covenant with the God of Israel' (2 Chron. 29:10). 'I walked along the sea-shore at 11:30 P. M. The world was asleep and the stars shone quietly overhead. The murmur of the waves seemed to draw my heart closer to God and I knelt on the sands and gave myself to Him all over again, to live for Him, to die for Him. My little life, whether it be long or short in years, was laid down before His feet. Irrespective of what friends or foes or man may think, by Thy grace and power, I here and now determine henceforth to live for the purpose for which Thou didst send me to the Orient, with nothing between Thee and me. That 'I am with thee always,' is enough! (Signed)—Charles E. Cowman.''

With it these few lines were penned:

"Men may misjudge thy aim,
Think they have cause to blame, say thou art wrong—
Hold thou thy quiet way, heed not what men may say;
Christ is the Judge—not they; fear not, be strong!
Be brave, and dare to stand alone against the foe;
Thy Saviour stood alone for thee long, long ago.
Be not a coward in the fight, look up! be strong!
The morn of victory is near—the day of song."

"The best of all is, God is with us."—John Wesley.

We have to go—the Voice of Him,
　The dearest Lover of our soul, commands;
We have to go—His last great word
　Though so unheeded, unobeyed, yet stands.
When millions have no smaller chance to know,
　How shall we tie to things He counted loss,
The baubles of the earth-life here below?
　Yea, if we dally with their dross,
The joyance of the moment they bestow,
　How can we dream of glorying in the Cross?

We have to go—although we die,
　These temples bleaching on a desert sand,
Or in a distant lonely grave may lie;
　Although with struggle and a brave stand
We fall before an unknown banditry.
　But if such privilege now be granted men—
To view the martyr's crown with closing eye,
　We shall remember, and you also then,
That though the orders were to "Go, stand by,"
　We were not told that we must come again.
　　　　　　　　　　　—Opal Leonore Gibbs.

　"The nerve of missionary endeavour is the conviction that
in the Christian revelation there is something distinctive and vital,
which the world cannot do without."—*J. H. Oldham.*

CHAPTER XVIII

"IN JOURNEYINGS OFT"

The real value of the missionary tours made by Charles Cowman cannot be estimated by a mere glance at the surface. An observer might say that the principal object of such "journeyings" was that of raising funds for the needy enterprise. However, others soon recognized the real value of these tours, for Christians at home who gave of their substance received in return value, something which far outweighed their gifts. The leaders of the Holiness movement were centering their greatest attention upon work in the home lands. They were in danger of losing sight of the last and Great Commission. His heart was saddened over the fact that God's children needed a second conversion to cause them to take an interest in foreign missions.

A constant prayer on his lips was, "Oh that God would burn into Christian hearts the sense of their responsibility to the heathen!" He realized that there was a great lack of knowledge concerning conditions and needs of the darkened lands. Therefore God's children did not realize their responsibility and could not pray intelligently for the great work. Little did he dream that God would call him to girdle the globe time and time again to impart missionary information, spending months in heavy missionary campaigns in America and Great Britain; but in his life there was an ever-widening ministry that continued till his call Home.

His close friend Dr. A. T. Pierson once wrote him: "No greater need exists than that of the universal diffusion of information as to the facts of past and present missionary history. To know these facts and keep fully informed as to the march of God and His hosts in all the earth is, in effect, to quicken the pulse of the whole church of Christ. If we would have more prayer, we would know more to pray about; if we want more money, we must know what open doors God is placing before us for the investment of consecrated capital and what wondrous results He has wrought and is working with merchant's millions and the widows' mites. If we want more men and women as workers, the mind and heart and conscience of disciples must be awakened from sleep and sluggishness, by the electric touch of thrilling facts."

In many a church where the missionary fire was burning at low ebb, or in places where it had been extinguished altogether, God used his simple yet gripping messages to rekindle the slumbering embers. Many a Christian confessed with shame, after hearing his fervent appeals for the salvation of the heathen, that they had done so little for the cause of Christ. Many resolved that with the help of God, they would wake from their sleep and attempt to "redeem the time" and "buy up the opportunity." One could not enter his soul-stirring missionary meetings and thereafter not believe in foreign missions. Young people caught the vision and felt the divine urge. Whoever heard Charles Cowman saw the Orient; whoever talked with him felt the characteristic tone of Oriental life. He left an impression that will never be lost.

He had great faith in the use of missionary maps and seldom held a service without a large map of the Orient hanging in some conspicuous place. Once he was so impressed with their usefulness that he had hundreds of small maps printed. On these were the Mission Stations of the Society, marked in red. They were sent to the homeland helpers for their use while in prayer. After his Home-going an ardent missionary worker in the British Isles wrote as follows:

"I cannot forget Mr. Cowman and his missionary map. With a pointer in his hand and a large map of the Orient on the wall, he would take us from province to province and from city to city, naming the Stations which the Oriental Missionary Society had been privileged to plant. Then he would point out the vast districts where hundreds of villages remained unevangelized, and often he would turn around to say, 'Beloved friends, these villages must be reached, they can be reached, and by the grace of God we mean to reach them.'

"Leaving the map of Japan, he would take us over to Korea, telling of the work in the Hermit Kingdom, first to one station in a certain province, then to another, until fifty were visited, when again he would say, 'What about that great number who live out in villages and who will not be reached unless we go to them?'

"Then when he had finished with the map of Japan and Korea, we breathed a real sigh of relief, for we felt he was attempting too much for his limited strength; but when he continued, 'Now we shall leave these two smaller fields and take a jump over into China, where by the grace of God, we mean to put on a great evangelistic campaign and establish Bible Training Schools, as our call also includes that far stretch of land,' we were almost ready to say, 'Brother Cowman, we have gone just as far as our faith will permit us. Let us go home, think and pray, and we shall come back to the next service.'"

How calmly and confidently he spoke of the evangelization of China's millions! He spoke in terms of faith and expectation and it made one feel that God was very real to him, and his addresses were the greatest stimulus to one's faith. Wherever he went, people became profoundly interested in him and his work, in spite of his humility and unobtrusiveness. The quality of the man and the distinction that hung about him were too obvious to be hidden entirely, and those who came to know him discovered that missionary work commanded the highest type of manhood and devotion.

Such a volcano of conviction, enthusiasm, and activity as Charles Cowman possessed was certainly going to burn itself out early in life. No one could have heard him describe heathen lands, the part Christians are asked to take in their evangelization, the shortness of time in which to reach the unnumbered millions—without being convinced that he was terribly in earnest—that he was a true man. He was hall-marked with genuineness.

His second missionary tour was made to England— lasting four months. Altogether more than one hundred addresses were given in about twenty different towns and cities, all having been arranged by new friends whom he had never met before. One door opened another, until when he left England there were numbers of invitations which had to remain unaccepted. Hundreds of new friends were gained for the Mission and a lively interest was manifested everywhere.

From England he went to America, where doors opened on the right hand and on the left and every day was filled with engagements. A year was spent in traveling thousands of miles, one of the most strenuous campaigns of his life.

During these tours, his horizon was broadened and the whole wide world was included in his vision and field of service. Many mission fields and missionaries were on his prayer list. When questioned about it he would reply,

ABOVE—CHARLES COWMAN AND WIFE IN THE ORIENT.
BELOW—IN THE MOUNTAINS OF JAPAN WITH O. M. S. MISSIONARIES AND
DR. JOHN PAUL OF TAYLOR UNIVERSITY.

"I have given my life to God for the Orient, but I wish my sympathy to be as broad as that of my Master, who took in the whole wide world." He kept the cause of Christ and the great dying world far above the cause of his own particular organization. His joy was just as great when he heard of missionaries sailing for India, Africa, or the Islands of the Sea, as when they went out to his own beloved Orient.

He revelled in missionary biography and sought to acquaint himself with the needs and work of every field. Often when upon deputational tours he would be invited as a speaker at missionary conventions, thus he became acquainted with many of the Lord's ambassadors from the four corners of the earth and his missionary enthusiasm increased.

His messages at such conventions were the outpouring of his heart on the subject nearest to it, "the evangelization of the world in our generation,"—the watchword which the church has been so slow in adopting. Many earnest missionaries returned to their fields out on the far flung battle lines with a fresh vision that the Great Commission "to every creature" *could* be carried out.

When he left the mission field on these tours he would take with him work that would have overwhelmed an ordinary man. Piles of his letters were forwarded, and to carry out his policy of strictest economy no secretary traveled with him. No one understands more fully than the one who pens these lines, the cost in rest and sleep, that the hundreds of letters might have prompt replies. Often after a heavy missionary service, when the clock would strike the midnight hour he would still continue writing.

It would be difficult to state the number of letters which he wrote in the course of a year. It would seem almost incredible to those who did not follow him throughout his busy days. They were not brief letters either, for he kept in close touch with every detail of the work on the field, and with the workers. Were they not his life, his crown of rejoicing? It was a tie closer than blood that bound his heart to the native brethren. It was the Orient and the sleeping church at home that lay so heavily upon his heart.

During the summertime, when the thermometer registered from 95 to 100 degrees, he kept at his deputation work. During his homeland trips he took little or no rest, although no one needed it more than he. He possessed a nature that chafed at inactivity, for imbedded deeply in his heart was a great master passion for the salvation of the heathen. He loved to impart information and to solicit the prayers of God's people for the work. "No information, no inspiration," was his favorite saying.

Friends gained through these deputational tours have been the faithful helpers throughout the twenty-seven years, and often letters are received from them full of thanksgiving to God for sending His servant to them, thus putting them in touch with a work that stands for one thing—direct evangelization. People were encouraged to preach "by proxy" in foreign fields, while they enjoyed the privileges of the Gospel in their own fair homeland. As a result, gifts for the support of workers and students were received. The missionary society was put on a sound basis in the sympathies of the people, and his strenuous deputational tours have made a permanent place for it throughout the entire country. What he started out to do was done, but at what a price! For if anything is certain, it is that under the permissive will of God, his labors in the guidance and affairs of the rapidly growing society, in his "journeyings oft," the bearing of almost superhuman burdens, brought about his death.

He was greatly beloved in the homes where he was entertained, and made everyone feel at ease with his unaffected courtesy and pleasant conversation. He was preeminently one who commended himself to every man's conscience in the sight of God, being an incarnation of the things he proclaimed. What his Christlike life and influence meant to the work he represented cannot be measured. What the Bethany house must have been to our Lord, no one could better appreciate than the missionary coming to a strange place, homeless. The kind friends took Charles Cowman and his companion into their homes, rested them, nursed them back to health and strength and nerved them for their future service. May God reward them!

Two American homes which were very dear to him were those of Mr. and Mrs. Jacob Hoffman, in Philadelphia, and Mr. and Mrs. John Kimber, in Newport, Rhode Island. Every sojourn there was a spiritual renewal. To them and their kindness he owed much, and when he took leave of America, he was refreshed in brain, strengthened in health, enriched with beautiful memories, and in the possession of a friendship which was true to the last.

Like the great missionary Apostle of old, he was "in journeyings oft, in perils in water, in perils of robbers, in perils by the heathen, in perils in the city, in perils in the wilderness, in perils in the sea, in perils among false brethren, in weariness and painfulness, in watchings often, in hunger and thirst, in fastings often, in cold and nakedness." However, two things must be eliminated from the list, for he never suffered hunger, and as God clothed the lilies, so He clothed him; but this must be added, "Beside all these things that are without, that which came upon him daily, the care of the churches." Could he not say, "Follow me as I follow Christ?"

Each time that a missionary tour was undertaken there would occur some strange and sudden blockade. These became so numerous that he wondered in what form the enemy would come out against him the next time. Open doors he ever saw before him and just as true were the following three words, "but Satan hindered."

Enroute to Japan the first time, a great storm at sea, lasting three days made it look as if the good ship could not make port. But God—that is the sequel. During his first furlough in America he was in a great train wreck but was miraculously saved. On his second trip to England, the Suez canal was blockaded as the ship ahead had just been bombed by dynamite. Soon after the Titanic disaster, a huge iceberg came floating down almost striking the great ocean greyhound on which he was a traveler. While enroute to Japan the last time he stopped over in Honolulu for a day while the steamer lay in port. He was sitting under a large cocoanut tree in a park when suddenly he felt impressed to leave, and no sooner had he done so than a great limb crashed down immediately over the chair where he had been sitting. Thus was he saved from instant death. Again, on the Indian Ocean, enroute to Britain, a huge meteor fell within a few yards of the steamer on which he sailed. All the hounds of hell were seemingly after him, but God watched over His child. How oft is the saying quoted, "Man is immortal until his work is done." Nothing simply happens to the child of God, all is under His control. God still rides on the whirlwind and directs the storm.

Some beautiful incidents always followed these strange attacks of the enemy, and usually he would meet some one who would take a peculiar interest in the cause dearest to his heart,—the cause of missions.

God gives a return value for all that is truly sacrificed for His name's sake and when a man dares to leave friends, home and country, for the isolation of the mission field, he becomes a larger, better personality, with richer feelings, deeper thought and truer devotion. Losing his life, he finds it. Missionary biography becomes attractive, not because of adventure or romance, but the revealing of personality. Charles Cowman's life seemed to have come to him in the Orient. He was happy in the consciousness that he was in the very service and field where God would have him live and labor. Instead of "burying himself" in a heathen land, he came to a resurrection of himself. This remark was made after listening to an unusual missionary address. "What has not the Orient done for Charles Cowman! He has found himself there!" In building, he himself was built up as hundreds of others have been, and became great in his idealism and also great in service.

Charles Cowman ever looked upon himself as only a humble instrument carrying out the will of God. In his addresses he was wont to remark, "I am just a connecting link between the church at home and the heathen abroad. The work is His,—yours." In his heart was a deep love for the homeland helpers, and on the memorable night before the gates of glory swung open he exclaimed, "My fellow-helpers in the homelands! How I love them! The great work of the Oriental Missionary Society has not been the work of *only* one person. The homeland helpers have a large share in it, and it is just as truly theirs as mine. They have labored together with us in prayer and laid their offerings of love in the Master's hand. We have been at the battle-front seen of men, but they—they have been behind the scenes, living beautiful hidden lives, known only to God. In that great day when the rewards will be given we shall share alike."

15

The joy of the Lord is not all in the Orient and in heaven, but a great deal of it fills the hearts of men and women in the homeland who hold their wealth ready to use for God, who wait for Him, sensitive to His voice and eager to obey. God's providence works, like His Omnipotent power in creation, at all points alike. When He thrusts forth laborers into the field, He just as certainly raises up those in the homeland to provide for their needs. Charles Cowman never tried to extract from his audiences unwilling offerings; he never begged; but he ever held before his hearers the lofty privilege of giving, reminding them that they were debtors, and that bold giving to the kingdom was an investment which had the Master's sanction as He bids us lay up treasure beyond the reach of thief, moth, and rust. He enlarged their horizon in respect to the world and gave them a relish for its conquest. Here is an offering which represents the hard earned savings of a washerwoman; here, a small sum given by a child, his own money, gladly offered for the heathen; and here, a bereaved mother sends in a bank containing a few pennies, once the possession of her now departed boy or girl. The rank and file of the donors to the work of the Society are not rich in this world's goods, but they are rich in faith and love. The greater part of their missionary offerings is the result of rigid economy and the discipline of self-denial. Often indeed, they are the fruit of privation and suffering, but the gifts are given entirely voluntarily, in the noble spirit of sacrifice which would gladly lay down the life itself for Jesus' sake. Many a box of ointment, very precious, broken upon the feet of our Master for the sake of the perishing heathen, fills the house with the fragrant odor.

In the sixteenth year of the work, the entire amount of money received in response to simple faith in God, reached and passed the sum of one-half million dollars, and in the twenty-seventh year it went far beyond the two million mark. Eternity alone will reveal the many prayers of faith and the many gifts of faith represented by this sum which has been spent only in direct evangelism.

IF I HAD A MILLION

Someone once asked, "What would you do Mr. Cowman, if you were to fall heir to a million dollars?" He was staggered at first by such a question and did not reply at once, but that evening while sitting at his desk his thoughts upon the matter were put on paper. "What would I do if I fell heir to a million dollars?

"First of all I would lay it as a love offering in my Master's hands, saying, 'Lord, what woulds't Thou have me to do with it?' Such a gift would involve great responsibility, and an immediate handing it over to God would make it His and not mine. I would count myself but a steward, and 'it is required of a steward that he be found faithful.'

"I would reserve nothing for myself, lest the knowledge of possessing such a sum would hinder me in my God-called work of 'Faith Missionary.' 'Faith tried in the fire is *much more* precious than gold that perisheth.'

"I would not lay it up in the bank and allow it to remain there a long while, in order that it might accumulate interest for a possible future work. I would send it on its Master's business immediately and put it out to the exchangers, for too long have earth's millionaires been accumulating interest while the heathen perish.

"Following the light which I now have, if such a sum were in my possession today, I would immediately lay plans for the establishment of a number of Bible Training Institutes. I would add one more to Japan, down in

Formosa. This could be a small one. I would establish *five* in large centers in China, also one in Siam, where young men and women from the various tribes might receive a Bible training. Then I would go to Annam, French Indo China, Java and Russia and erect Bible Training Schools, secure the best trained missionaries possible, those who were full of the Holy Spirit and well versed in the Word of God. I would aim at the training of thousands of native workers, to work in their own lands.

"On the cover of my bank book I would write in bold letters 'THE ORIENT FOR JESUS WHOSE RIGHT IT IS TO REIGN.'"

Charles Cowman could talk thus, for he lived thus. Money never spread a glamour over his eyes. He looked to the Lord for the supply of his needs and thanked Him when it was received.

His favorite missionary hymn

O Zion, haste, thy mission high fulfilling,
To tell to all the world that God is Light!
That He who made all nations is not willing
One soul should perish, lost in shades of night.

Chorus.

Publish glad tidings, tidings of peace;
Tidings of Jesus, redemption and release.

Behold how many thousand still are lying
Bound in the darksome prison-house of sin!
With none to tell them of the Saviour's dying,
Or of the life He died for them to win.

'Tis Thine to save from peril of perdition
The souls for whom the Lord His life laid down,
Beware lest, slothful to fulfill thy mission,
Thou lose one jewel that should deck His crown.

Proclaim to every people, tongue and nation
That God, in whom they live and move, is love;
Tell how he stooped to save His lost creation,
And died on earth that men might live above.

Give of thy sons to bear the message glorious;
Give of thy wealth to speed them on their way;
Pour out thy soul for them in prayer victorious;
And all thou spendest, Jesus will repay.

He comes again; O Zion, ere thou meet Him,
Make known to every heart His saving grace;
Let none whom He ransomed fail to greet Him
Through thy neglect, unfit to see His face.

"Sir, lay the foundation thus, and ye shall not soon shrink, nor be shaken. Make tight work at the bottom, and your ship shall ride against all storms, if withal your anchor is fastened on good ground; I mean within the vail. And verily I think this is all, to gain Christ. All other things are shadows, dreams, fancies, and nothing."—Samuel Rutherford. 1637.

"Then began I greatly to commend them that stood stiffly for the name of God."

2 Esdras.

"You cannot drop great themes and create great saints."
—Dr. Jowett.

CHAPTER XIX

WHAT CHARLES COWMAN BELIEVED

A man's religious convictions are most important. Of all living men, the missionary, who stands in the midst of a people who do not bear the Christian name, needs to be able to say, "I know whom I have believed," needs to know whom he believes and what he believes. We shall see in the life of Charles Cowman, that it was what he believed that produced such a rich fruitage, not only in his life, but in his ministry.

The greatest thing about him was not what he did, but what he believed. When conviction seized him, he could not be turned from his course; neither could he be induced to relinquish his hold upon what he believed to be the truth and the right. It took hold of his own life until it perfectly saturated his thinking and all of his conduct. It was because he believed with such intensity that he could do the things that he did.

In the strictest and most literal sense the Bible was accepted as an inspired Book, a veritable sword from the Hand of God, put into the hand of man for the conquest of the world for Christ. It was the food which fed his soul. It put iron into his blood and enabled him for thirty-six years to face the foe without a question or doubt as to the final victory.

It is a real stimulus to one's faith to trace how wonderfully God honors men who dare to stand up for the highest truths in a skeptical and material age, and learn that to such souls rare treasure is given—"treasures in Heaven."

In these days when the authority and inspiration of the Scripture is being questioned and denied, and many find themselves in a perfect landslide of apostasy from "the faith once for all delivered to the saints," we appreciate characters such as Charles Cowman who had an uncompromising devotion to the Word of God. Charles Cowman's characteristics were his deep uncompromising and unswerving devotion to the Word of God. He believed that the Bible not only contained the Word of God but was the Word of God. He believed that in that blessed Word were the secrets of Heavenly vision, both for individual and organized work. He sought therefore every day to get fresh insight into the Holy Scriptures, and as it were a direction for each new day. He looked with strange wonderment upon the readiness of the so-called higher critics to make concessions to the enemies of the supernatural element in Scripture. He held firmly to the Word of God in its entirety to the last hour of his life. From the day of his conversion he never changed his theology, but stood steadfast for all the Bible taught. Untroubled by the battling of criticism, the words of the Book were to him an all-sufficient warrant for faith, a foundation on which he could stand as upon an impregnable rock. For the world's need, for his own individual need, there was no book to compare to that— it was the supreme authority.

Never in the contempt of the mass of men is the man who faithfully and in clear-cut terms preaches the message of Christ. He may be looked down upon and derided by a meager class that affects learning, up-to-dateness, and superior wisdom. But the sneer of this class is unqualified praise of the herald of the cross. Charles Cowman dared to be thought narrow and peculiar.

An oft-quoted and much-loved passage of Scripture was 2 Tim. 2:15. Way's translation gives it: "Be earnest to set yourself in God's presence tested by trial, a laborer who need not blush for his work, but who drives the ploughshare of truth in a straight furrow." Charles Cowman was valiant for the truth and was never known to relax his hold when thrown with those who differed widely from him. He was a true witness.

From an address which he gave at a ministers meeting we quote a few excerpts:

"We can have no real lasting peace until we are willing to unite upon the Bible as the infallible Word of God, for indeed, 'it is, and shall remain until the end of the world, the true center of Christian unity.' It is my firm belief, that if all of our ministers, missionaries, college professors, and Bible School teachers would proclaim to the world their unqualified belief in the Bible as the inspired Word of God and the supreme and only authority recognized in the church, and solemnly promise to proclaim its precious truths, until the stars melt from the firmament and the ocean beds are dry, that it would usher in the greatest revival the world has ever witnessed. Our prayer meetings would become veritable times of Pentecost. I believe it would bring our pastors into the finest fellowship known this side of Heaven, and the great body of laymen looking on from the side-lines would weep for joy. It may be permissible in our ministers' meetings to discuss such subjects as modernism and other isms, but when we stand in the sacred pulpit as the chosen representative of Jesus Christ, with three worlds listening in, and face to face with men and women of our common humanity, their lives blighted, their hopes blasted, their homes and hearts broken and their eyes stained with tears, looking to us for some message of hope that will send them back to their homes with new hopes and aspirations burning in their breasts, and a new light throbbing in their souls, let us remember that nothing but God's message of salvation, as revealed in Jesus Christ will meet their need.

"This is the holy warfare we are engaged in and we must fight it out on Bible lines until we are called Home or our Captain calls a halt. In these days there is an abundance of *destructive,* would that there were *constructive*—theology. Many a soul is left yearning for fundamental truths and rock-built systems, but is put off with negations and fantasies. Let us see to it that our feet tread only in His footprints. Let us make no new footprints of our own."

In the early days of his missionary career he was invited to join a movement for united revival services in the city of Tokyo. He heartily accepted such an invitation to promote a revival, but when he learned there would be those on the program who did not believe in the Deity of Jesus Christ, did not believe in the necessity for faith in His atonement, and who unduly exalted humanity to the place of practical Deity, he quietly withdrew. He was convinced that the message that such men carried to heathen lands was not the true Gospel.

> "There was no other good enough
> To pay the price of sin:
> He only could unlock the gate
> Of Heaven and let us in."

He was a real champion of the old faith. He was a positive man, a positive Christian.

It is said that the power of the preacher consists chiefly in the intensity of his beliefs. The words that move men are the words of burning conviction, the whole-hearted and unwavering faith in the central verities of the Gospel. That appeared in every utterance of his, whether by voice or pen. His correspondence was glowing with white heat and his intensity never cooled. A letter to a fellow-missionary gives us a glimpse of his attitude toward the new theology.

"Tokyo, Japan.

"My Beloved Brother:

"Your kind letter has been on my desk for several days unanswered as this has been convention week. There were early prayermeetings every morning and you know what the word 'early' means to the Japanese. Some of them met a little past midnight to pray and by daybreak there were several hundred in the chapel. What a prayermeeting! Real prayer is a rugged affair and I thought if some of the ministers in our homeland could have been here to have witnessed the fervor of our native brethren, they would have been greatly blessed. The evangelistic services were held down in the city in the Y. M. C. A. Hall, which was rented for the occasion. Last night there were about two thousand people packed in the hall and they sat there for two full hours.

"Two hundred seekers came right out to the altar. Nakada San preached with a powerful anointing upon him. Our army of students were on hand to do personal work and every one of them 'caught a fish' at the close. I saw one of our workers in a corner with twelve young men around him, another with seven, and there were prayer groups all over that large hall. I dealt with two dear old men. One was seventy-two, the other seventy. One was a Buddhist, the other a deep-rooted idolater. What hungry hearts they had and both came through bright and shining. The week has been very heavy beyond words, but such sights take out the tired.

"Now to your question. I, too, met Prof. . . . . and had a long talk with him. I found him very unsound in his doctrine and shaken in his faith. He would not fully admit to me that he did not believe in the Atonement, but I am quite fully convinced that he is all taken up with new theology. Have nothing to do with it, my brother! You do not even have to study it to meet them on their own ground. The best argument that I find for false doctrine is a red-hot testimony to the precious cleansing Blood.

"This is an age of skepticism, doubt, clouded philosophies, and mental entanglements. How few have retained the faith of their childhood, but I know of none who hold the new views, who are seeing altars lined with sinners, weeping their way to Zion. Their services are refined to an esthetic nicety. The charm of personality is still there, but the one vital thing is lacking, there is the 'lost chord.' No one is moved to attempt heroic service for Christ's sake, and yet we read great reports and they imagine they had great services, little realizing that 'the Lord has departed from them.' The great pity of it is that there are so many today who have sought after *new things* who are much like Samson with shorn locks, but all unconscious of the terrible fact. There are many in the pulpit today who have forgotten that the Lord placed them there, and instead of building up the most holy faith of our fathers, they are lending themselves to an unholy propaganda to largely tear down. Accepting the theory of organic evolution, they have become obsessed with an aversion to the supernatural in general; and consequently the miraculous birth of Christ, the miraculous resurrection, and all else miraculous, is no longer essential to the worship of God. I would advise you not to be seeking after new things. The 'old paths' have in them 'rest for your soul.' 'Remove not the landmarks which our fathers have made,' is the Scriptural injunction. The old paths were good enough for them, and should be sufficient for us. We must stand unshaken by all the winds that blow.

"Put down your feet where you mean to stand and be not carried about with every wind.

> "'I'm a little old fashioned you know,
>   When it comes to religion and God.'
> "So stand I here, God helping me.
> "Your fellow missionary in the best of bonds,
>   "Charles E. Cowman."

After thirty-six years of victorious warfare he could say with St. Paul, "I have fought a good fight, *I have kept the faith. Henceforth . . . . .* "

"In the valley of humiliation, Christian, meeting Apollyon, said to him concerning the Lord Jesus, 'I have given Him my faith, and sworn my allegiance to Him.' Apollyon replied. 'I am willing to pass by all, if now thou wilt yet turn again and go back.'"

Charles Cowman ever had a fear of looking backward and this made him hasten his steps and climb higher. He took others with him on his mountain climb and scores of men today are praising God for his aggressive spirit in the things that matter most, the spiritual, and for the compelling race in which he helped them also to "look from the top."

He never disguised his view on sanctification, and was often heard to remark, "I believe it right up to the hilt, that the Blood of Jesus Christ His Son cleanseth me from all sin." He did not believe that a child of God could *grow* into sanctification any more than that a sinner could *grow* into a saint. He believed and taught that a "born again" soul came to a place, if he walked in the light, when he would as truly cross over into the promised land as did Joshua when he set up a heap of stones as a witness of the crisis step taken. He never deviated one jot from that standard.

A missionary once asked one of the natives what he understood by the word "Holiness." The native replied, "When copious showers have descended during the night and all the earth and leaves and cattle are washed clean, and the sun rising shows a drop of dew on every blade of grass, and the air breathes fresh—that is Holiness."

"Many people have been frightened away from Holiness because some one had called them specialists" said Dr. C. J. Fowler, President of the National Holiness Association. "They have been so afraid of being specialists on the subject of Holiness that they have avoided it altogether. It is true that no man can really have the experience of heart-holiness without being a specialist, for Holiness is the specialty of the religion of Jesus Christ, the specialty of the Bible, the specialty of Heaven."

Charles Cowman never glossed over anything. When controversy came up he stated his belief in a clear-cut manner, proving often that "a faithful witness delivers souls." He was honest in his convictions at every cost. No one ever had a doubt as to where he stood, and this with no shadow of bravado or self-assertion, but in "meekness and wisdom," the very gentleness, the "sweet reasonableness of Christ." His convictions on the subject of heart holiness were grounded upon a close study of the Word, and he never failed to let his belief in the blessed experience be well understood, often in circles where it cost something to be firm and true.

He was never known to compromise the truth for the sake of prestige. He did not forget the purpose of his journey, nor his life that had been committed to the sacred trust. He never sold the truth to save the hour. There is too much compromising and trimming in this our day; the age needs men of stern fidelity to God and His cause. A Chinese proverb reads thus, "Do not try to stand with one foot in two boats."

"But I'll tell you this," quaintly wrote Owen Marston, A middlin' doctor is a pore thing, and a middlin' lawyer is a pore thing, but keep me from a middlin' man of God."

"Conservatism" is often only another name for "compromise," when it comes to matters of heart purity or salvation. Had Peter and Paul and Stephen been conservative they would never have won a martyr's crown, and if John the Baptist had been conservative, no doubt he could have had the friendship of Herod. There was no conservatism in those who were "sawn asunder, stoned, imprisoned for Christ's sake." They were radical and will not be sorry on that blessed resurrection morning that they gave up their lives rather than compromise.

This limitation, call it narrow, call it rigid, call it what you please, how strong it made him! Men of one purpose are mighty! What marks they leave in the world long after they are gone! Take note of this fact, if not in the short run, yet always in the long run, the men who dare to be true to their convictions whatever the cost, who so value a close fellowship with God that they will not yield one inch of honor, not one iota of truth in order to please men or to find favor with those who oppose them, are the men whom God honors with His own Hand, and gives to them the power to lead the hosts.

His own faith and experience never seemed to separate him from others who did not feel and think as he did. No one felt at a distance from him because he believed in holiness of heart and life. His was a purity that attracted, not one that repelled. He believed it possible to be both sane and holy. Men might, if they pleased, oppose his arguments with doubts and objections; but no one could question the purity of his life, the practical embodiment of holiness.

"The great beauty of Charles Cowman's life," wrote a well known Bible expositor, "was its symmetry. He was all over alike. The first constituent of his character was his remarkable common sense and the completeness of it was his intelligent piety. He was a man who never varied, and his steadfastness helped to steady others. I have met with few men so even and constant in their religious walk."

One of the finest tributes that was received after his Home-call came from a native brother who attempted to express his appreciation in English. He wrote after this quaint fashion. "Brother Cowman always alike, all over alike, never change, no fall down, no wobble, all the same every year. For this I like very much. Five year, no matter, ten year no matter, twenty-five year no matter. Christianity never change for him. I see him every day, always smile, always work, always try to get souls. Praise the Lord!"

And that expressed it exactly. Was it because he sought to follow closely the One "with whom is no variableness neither shadow of turning" that he was held so steady that his life steadied others,—that drew forth from the natives the simple but wonderful testimony "all over alike, never change"? How often was he heard to admonish his fellow-workers with such words as "Let the world take us as they may, we must not change our road." As he led the way by example and kept one straight path, he made it easier for others to keep to the truth without deviation.

One Sabbath morning he attended the Moody church in Chicago where Dr. Torrey was giving an address on the subject of "The Second Coming of Christ." Before this time Christ's Second Coming had been a misty belief. He had been taught, that by the means of the Gospel, the entire world was to be converted. How he thanked God for unveiling to him this blessed truth, as it brought to him the knowledge of God's purpose for the age, not in converting the world, but in gathering a people from every tribe and nation. The Bible from that day became a new Book to him; old and familiar passages suddenly became fraught with new force, henceforth exercising a power over his whole being. Some years later he said, "I do not know of any truth that has been a greater blessing to me through life than this. If our teaching and living were more in harmony with the blessed truth that the coming of our Lord draweth nigh, Christians would not be so worldly as so many of them are."

To him this was not a truth for mere disputation, but a purifying and enlivening hope, in the light of which he journeyed and wrought and which shone brightly as his days upon earth drew to a close. He longed to be alive when the Lord Jesus came, to be caught up to meet him, but to him it was not given. Rather will it be his to return with the Lord and with those tarrying within the veil, when the trump of the arch-angel shall arouse the whole earth.

"There is no mockery more sad and inconsistent," said Dr. A. B. Simpson, "than that of believing and speaking of the Blessed Hope with folded hands and selfish heart. No man can rightly believe in the coming of Jesus without expending all the strength of his being in preparing for it by sending the Gospel to all nations. God is summoning those who hold this hope today to a great missionary

16

crusade and there are enough to make it effectual before the close of the generation, perhaps before the end of the century."

The subject of Divine Healing was very closely studied, especially during his later years. He saw it in the atonement as a blessed privilege of the child of God.

He loved the words of the hymn written by the saintly Horatius Bonar:

> "Look to thine armour well!
>   Thine the one panoply no blow that fears;
> Ours is the day of rusted swords and shields,
>   Of loosened helmets and of broken spears,
> Heed not the throng of foes!
>   To fight 'gainst hosts is still the Church's lot.
> Side thou with God, and thou must win the day;
>   Woe to the man 'gainst whom hell fighteth not!
> Say not the fight is long:
>   'Tis but one battle and the fight is o'er;
> No second warfare mars thy victory,
>   And the one triumph is for evermore."

The life of Charles Cowman would be utterly incomplete if we did not take into account his childlike, unswerving confidence in and dependence upon the Holy Scriptures as the infallible rule and practice, as the all-sufficient manual of the Christian workman, fully inspired and adapted to all the world throughout all time. "Back to the Bible," was a much loved watchword. When he was converted, he became as a little child in his attitude towards God's revelation and this continued with him through life.

His faith was simple, almost childlike. He obtained it by constant converse with God in the reading of His Word, a habit which begun when he first met the Lord. Whenever a subject for controversy came up, he would invariably say, "Let us go to the Word of God for the answer." It gave him direction in all the affairs of the mission as well as those of his own life. The Bible was to him, complete, authoritative, final. "Hath God spoken?" To the very last, every word of Scripture was to him a treasure of wealth and knowledge.

The Bible he frequently used and carried with him to the mission field, contains hundreds of cross-references, with numerous comments, chapter analyses and inter-lineations. A book could be compiled from the many rich thoughts. His own circumstances formed the key to the many marked passages. Many of these texts refer to missions and they seem to have been his choicest nuggets for he saw in the Bible more about missions than any other subject.

He did not attempt to measure up to men of letters, but he did "seek to excel to the edifying of the church," and he was one of the keenest Bible students of our day.

No book in the Bible was read more than the Acts of the Apostles, and it was his belief that the Gospel is just as effective now as in the Apostolic days, and just as surely as we live a life as consecrated as that of the Apostle Paul, will there be spiritual fruit enjoyed as in Apostolic days. The Epistles of Paul are a mass of notes and interlineations and he studied them for the enriching of his spiritual life.

He followed a rather unique method of Bible study which he ever recommended to others, especially to students and ministers. He would read through one book of the Bible at a sitting. The next day he would re-read it and this was often continued for a week at a time, sometimes longer, till the contents were thoroughly mastered. He likened this method of study to a landscape painter who first draws an outline or perspective, then adds a tree, a flower, and a brook. Many have testified to the great worth of this simple method of study.

The systematic study of the Bible had a great effect upon his own spiritual life, and more and more he came to regard the Word of God, not only as a book of doctrine, but as a living counsellor and a Book of Life. When he needed close guidance over the many perplexing problems that came into his life, he found it in these pages. It was pre-eminently a missionary Bible and every promise or word that referred to missions was doubly underscored. In his tense, memorable manner, he wrote some notes beside the texts that lay at the root of his life.

"Redeeming the time." Eph. 5:16. (Buying up the opportunity). "Be spiritually alert. God keep us from duties evaded, capacities wasted, opportunities neglected, the God-given life slipping away from our grasp! May we 'redeem the time' while redemption is yet possible. There are great crisis-hours in our history,—golden opportunities, chances, only once given, never to return. Let us not forget them. It may be to our eternal detriment. It was the wail of the old woman, 'I have lost a day.' See to it that we have not in bitterness of soul to say, 'I have lost a life.' Let us arise and shake off from us the dust of inactivity. Let us go to Calvary's hill. Behold He dies!"

"Ask of me and I will give thee the heathen for thine inheritance." Psalms 2:8.

"Who would not be an inheritor among the heathen and rejoice in "that great day" in their precious God-given heritage? Who will dare to stand before God empty-handed when He said, 'Ask, and I will give'?"

"Wherewithal shall a young man cleanse his way? by taking heed thereto according to Thy Word. Psalms 119:9.

"I know of no better guide for a young man, who wants to steer clear of failure, than the Bible. The good old Book has lost none of its helpfulness in the on-rolling centuries, and is today the best chart extant for the youthful voyager on life's stormy sea. Let a young man study the wisdom of the Bible, and acquaint himself with its naked, strenuous truth, and he cannot go far wrong in his every-day life."

"We believe and are SURE. John 6:69.

"How grateful we should be that instead of expressing opinions, we can testify to facts which are matters of personal consciousness. Instead of saying, 'we believe,' we can humbly declare, 'We know.' 'We believe and are SURE.'"

"But Prayer." Acts 12:5.

"Our prayers are God's opportunities."

"He went out not knowing whither he went."

"The opportunity is often lost through deliberation."

"And they went forth, preaching the Word, the Lord working with them confirming the Word with signs following." Mark 16:20.

"It is a glorious privilege to be 'workers together *with Him.'* To be worker *with* Him and not *for* Him. What a partnership! The victory is always His and always sure."

"Except a corn of wheat fall into the ground and die, it abideth alone, but if it die, it bringeth forth much fruit." (John 12:24).

"Of all *qualifications* for missionary work, love is the most excellent. Of all *methods* of attaining to a position of usefulness and honor, the only safe and sure one is to fit ourselves for it by purging our hearts from worldliness, selfishness, and being sanctified wholly. Of all *plans* for ensuring success, the most certain is Christ's own—becoming a corn of wheat and falling into the ground and dying."

"There hath not failed one word of all His good promise which He spoke . . all come to pass." 1 Kings 8:56.

This was a favorite word and at the close of life's little day, he could testify to its truth.

The Bibles which he used for study, were marked with scrupulous neatness, showing how diligently they were studied. One had a broad margin for notes. What a thrill of joy he experienced when he found some fresh-lit promise. Many a time I would be called from a room on an upper floor to listen to a promise he had newly discovered. No excavator for buried treasure could have had greater delight than he, in the "treasures" which he discovered by digging down deep.

His small study-room was a model of neatness, which characterized the man. Over the built-in bookcase was a shelf which contained twenty volumes of the translations of the Bible. Although he had never had the opportunity of studying Greek and Hebrew, he secured the various translations, Weymouth, Murdock, Godbey, Sawyer, Way, and others, but he loved the King James version best of all.

His library contained Matthew Henry's Commentaries, such as Adam Clark's, Gray's, and a number of others less popular. Those silent friends, good books, that speak to us when we turn to them in our need, were a large factor in his growth, but he found the Book of all books the quintessence of them all. He greatly loved his friend Dr. Arthur T. Pierson and his books were eagerly read, especially as they referred so often to foreign missions. Several books which made a deep impression upon his life were "The Life of Chas. G. Finney" and the devoted "David Brainerd." These two latter books seem to have given him a greater impulse toward missionary work. He read widely and diligently, morning, noon, and night, not only when traveling, but while walking, or out for a stroll in the fresh air. Dr. A. M. Hill's book, "Holiness and Power," also Wood's "Perfect Love" and "Purity and Maturity" were among his favorites. There were few books written on the subject of Heart Purity that were not found in his library.

While living in the Orient, when arranging his traveling bags for long or short journeys, both the Old and New Testaments were included in the necessaries, also the Japanese New Testament, of which he was exceedingly fond. On the train, on board steamers, he was found with a copy of the Scriptures and fragments of time were never allowed to go to waste.

How often were those journeys made! *"In journeyings oft . . . in weariness and painfulness."* 2 Cor. 11. How well he knew that part of it!

He loved the Word to his dying day. "I am fully persuaded that I could never have lived through the terrible sufferings and sorrows appointed for me without the Word of the living God, revealing, by the Holy Spirit's power, His great love, His glorious attributes, and His marvelous purposes, not only in creation and redemption, but in the most minute circumstances, affecting the daily lives of His children" were the words he wrote sometime before His Home-call.

A few texts adorned the walls of his study-room. *"There they dwelt with the King for His work,"* and, *"No man having put his hand to the plough and looking back is fit for the kingdom of God."*

A map of the Orient with the mission-stations of the Oriental Missionary Society marked in red, hung in a conspicuous place in the study, and here, daily, during his last years away from his deeply-loved work, he spent hours alone with God. It is a sacred little spot and much of the biography has been written here.

"I would fain die sword in hand."—*George Whitefield*.

CHAPTER XX

AS A WORKER

It is needless to write of Charles Cowman as a worker. The founding of the Bible Training Institutes, the Great Village Campaign, and Evangelistic tours throughout the world are instances in a life whose course was steady and determined, of a personality which was firm in its resolve, invincible in its purpose, unremittent in its endeavors. Not only did he work but he worked with a faith that brought results.

He was a perfect dynamo of energy. His hours were always filled with all kinds of useful activity; his enthusiasm and undaunted courage were infectious; they begat like qualities in his fellow-workers. He became very worn, but his pace never slackened. There was something within him that fairly leaped at the call of battle. Nothing discouraged him, nothing baffled him, and difficulties always attracted him. He gloried in hard nerve-racking toil and said very often, "I never feel better than when I am on the full stretch for God." Suffering seemed to have a certain ingredient of joy, and he would not shrink from the most strenuous task. He endured changes of climate, diet, and habits of life, and went through labors that would have tried the metal of an iron constitution; and very much of his toil was accomplished in the face of weakness and suffering.

Nothing could have been greater punishment to him than a prolonged rest. He was often heard to remark, "Leisure I do not anticipate nor desire until reaching the fair land where it is said of the redeemed, that 'they rest from their labors.'" He had tested the joy of labor for Christ—full, vigorous, and prayerful labor, and he could not be happy in any other mode of life.

How much it meant to have such a leader for an example! His life was completely stripped of every appearance of self-indulgence and self-consideration. He did not ask others to endure hardships while he himself lived at ease. No, he led the way. The secret of his unparalleled success was the blood-earnestness of his heart. A heathen convert once said to him, "We want more men with red-hot hearts like yours, to come here and tell us of the love of Christ."

A young missionary, watching his life, wrote to him, seeking his advice about afternoon social times, and he replied to his letter: "I would advise you to shun the afternoon social times. While they may be right in themselves, they murder time, unless you accept invitations to go where you have every reason to believe that your presence will be a witness and where you can let your light shine. Things may be legitimate in themselves, but God has a far higher plan for His ambassadors whom He has scattered far off among the heathen."

Well may the missionary be a miser, so far as time is concerned as he considers the immensity of the work and the meagerness of human agency. In the oppressive weather, when the leaves on the trees were sere and dying, when everything was lifeless, Charles Cowman kept at his work. When remonstrated with for keeping the city missions open every night during the hot season, his usual reply was, "Satan never rests and dare we?" Many a basket of summer fruit was plucked during those months, and summer time became the greatest harvest time.

Naturally he was often judged harshly. Did he not by example encourage the weary and worn missionary to undertake what was too strenuous for him? "Should not powers like his be treated with respect and guarded?" Such were the criticisms, but his life was a torrent of divine intensity sweeping through the narrow channels of a single hearted consecration and concentrating all his powers upon the evangelization of the Orient.

The minor tones of the temple bells as they rang to awaken the gods, always brought a pained look into his face. He never became accustomed to heathenism. That the people for whose sake he had given his life were seeking peace, by worshipping gods made of stone and wood, gods who could not hear or help them, ever sent a pang of pain to his heart, and it is little wonder that he felt that he could not rest amid such surroundings. When he met the Lord Jesus, do you think that because he loved the heathen so well, caring that they perish, the Master would reprove him for over-working and sacrificing even life?

The Christian experiences no greater joy than that which comes from laying down his best and dearest at the nail-pierced feet of the world's Redeemer—his blessed Lord and Master! There is something of magnificence in the thought of working only for the pleasure of the Divine eye and the satisfaction of the Divine heart. Duty done for love grows lovely and clothes it with worshippers in noble lines.

How often was Charles Cowman heard to remark, "I am serving God out of pure joy!" He had an absorbing love for his work and put his very heart and soul into it. Service done for the Master alone has a much finer finish, and the best work was never done for money. "We are not working as slaves at a task, but as partners in a blessed fellowship, in which we share all the plans and thoughts of our Lord respecting His work," were the words to a fellow worker.

He was a man of method. He believed that no missionary society deserved the support of business men, unless it was on a business basis. Many attributed the marvelous growth of the Society to its thorough business management. His ways of business were careful and methodical, a pattern to others in safeguarding funds. He was a careful administrator of the Lord's money. A common saying of his was, "I wish to transact the business of the Missionary Society in such a careful manner that the angels may look over my ledger at the close of the day."

He hated wrong and was resolutely sincere. Those who came in contact with him recognized his transparent integrity. It is a high privilege to be a man that God can trust, knowing that he will always be loyal and will do his duty without wavering. It is also a great honor to be a man that men can trust, yet this honor brings a serious responsibility. No other motive for fidelity and truth makes a stronger appeal to our hearts, than the consciousness that others are trusting us, taking us for a guiding example, leaning upon us, following us. A man who occupies such a place among men needs to keep a most careful watch upon himself. "What would happen," asked the visitor of a lighthouse keeper, "if your lamp should go out some night?" "Impossible!" replied the old man in a startled tone. Men who are trusted by others, occupy a position of still greater responsibility than the keeper of lighthouses.

Public funds were to him a sacred trust, demanding greatest care and fidelity in their administration. The very fact that he was handling trust funds and that he

was acting as a trustee made him rigidly scrupulous. He was not the kind of man who indulged in extravagance because someone else was paying for it. A plain method of living was natural to him; self-denial was his habitual rule; and sometimes things perfectly allowable, he was induced to forego for the good of others and the sake of the work. The work was administered with a conscientious frugality, almost incredible, and it was largely on account of his close attention to detail that the Society was carried through times of great financial testings, without a station having to be closed or a native worker dismissed. This mastery of details, coupled with imagination and broad grasp, a blend that makes the administrative mind, wherever applied, made his twenty-five years of leadership a marvel of management. Said a noted visitor to the work, "I count it a privilege of a life-time to have seen Charles Cowman in his capacity as an administrator of the Lord's money."

Many hundreds of letters were received and answered in the course of a year and he dispatched business with great facility. He dreaded an accumulation of letters and made it a practice to answer them as soon as received, although this often kept him at his desk long into the hours of the night. Life for him meant tireless activity, but anything that meant the furtherance of the kingdom, was not thought by him to be work, no matter how strenuous. Every moment was capitalized. This ceaseless round left him little time for rest or recuperation. For thirty-six years he scarcely knew the meaning of a holiday and his summers were his busiest months. He went just a pace further than many others, presenting a striking picture of a worker ever pressing onward with an entire Missionary Society following along. Wherever he went there was life and activity, for he created a type that reproduced itself.

"Not the cry, but the flight of the wild duck," says the Chinese author, "leads the flock to fly and follow." What we do tells infinitely more than what we say.

The influence of such a life does not end when the grave covers him from our sight. Such men, it has been well said, "create an epidemic of nobleness," and by looking at such examples we are more ready and willing to lift our eyes out of the mire of selfishness, and the dust of anxiety and toil, more brave to try whether we also cannot scale the toppling crags of duty and hold converse with those loftier brethren upon

> "the shining tablelands
> To which our God Himself is moon and sun."

These lines were found among his papers after his Home-call:

> "When I am dying how glad I will be
> That the lamp of my life has been blazed out for Thee.
> I shall not mind in whatever I gave,
> Labor or money, one heathen to save.
> I shall not mind that the way has been rough!
> That Thy dear Feet led the way was enough.
> When I am dying how glad I shall be
> That the lamp of my life has been blazed out for Thee."

Of an old hero the minstrel sang—

> "With his Yemen sword for aid;
> Ornament it carried none,
> But the notches on the blade."

What nobler decoration of honor can any godly man seek after than his scars of service, his losses for the crown, his reproaches for Christ's sake, his being worn out in the Master's service?

Charles often sang the hymn for workers:

"Shall I empty handed be,
　When beside the crystal sea
I shall stand before the everlasting throne?
　Must I have a heart of shame
As I answer to my name,
　With no works that my Redeemer
　　There can own?

"What regret must then be mine
　When I meet my Lord Divine,
If I've wasted all the talents He doth lend?
　If no soul to me can say,
'I am glad you passed my way;
　For 'twas you who told me
　　Of the sinner's Friend.'

"If my gratitude I'd show
　Unto Him who loves me so,
Let me labor till the evening shadows fall;
　That some little gift of love
I may bear to realms above,
　And not empty-handed be
　　When comes the call.

"When the harvest days are past,
　Shall I hear Him say at last,
'Welcome, toiler, I've prepared for thee a place?'
　Shall I bring Him golden sheaves,
Ripened fruit, not faded leaves,
　When I see the blessed Saviour
　　Face to face?

"When the books are opened wide,
　And the deeds of all are tried,
May I have a record whiter than the snow;
　When my race on earth is run,
May I hear Him say 'Well done!'
　Take the crown that love
　　Immortal doth bestow."

"Let us build for the years we shall not see."—Newbolt.

CHAPTER XXI

AS A MISSIONARY LEADER

"Missionary leadership, to my mind" wrote Rev. S. M. Sweimer, "is the one solution of the whole missionary problem. Not money, but men; not statistics, but dynamics; not how many we can enlist, but how much we can enlist in this enterprise, will give us the victory."

What is the price of missionary leadership? The first price is *vision*. What is a leader? John R. Mott says, "A leader is a man who knows the road, who can keep ahead and who can pull others after him."

In that wonderful chapter, the eleventh of Hebrews, I notice that seeing the invisible is God's baptism into leadership. As soon as you see something that everybody else cannot see and won't see, then God is baptizing you into leadership in that thing. Carey saw the whole world, when Sidney Smith only saw the pavements of London. Henry Martyn saw India and Persia and Arabia and North Africa, a vision of the Moslem world, when the rest of the church was blind.

Vision alone makes a man visionary, and may God deliver us from men visionary on missions.

After vision comes *decision*. Every one of those great heroes in the eleventh of Hebrews was a man of decision. They saw and then they considered. When Moses saw the burning bush he did not write poetry. He went out and led God's people through the weary wilderness. When Abraham saw the city that hath foundations, he laid the foundations for God's Church right there in his own household. And if you and I catch the vision of the

17

missionary possibilities, then, like Carey, we must put that vision in our cobbler's shop and start to realize it.

Passion for souls is a necessary qualification for a missionary leader. Think of John Knox, that great missionary leader of Scotland. It is said that he used to pray in his little room, and he would call out to God and say, "Oh, God, give me Scotland, or I die!" God did give him Scotland, though he died, and John Knox has Scotland today. And so if we pray in that fashion and live in that fashion, with the passion in our hearts for missions, we shall be leaders.

The next price to pay is *sacrifice*. This is where leaders particularly fail, in self-sacrifice; nothing pulls so much as the print of the nails and the mark of the spear. It takes life and blood to be to the people the thing that they need. In a lumber camp in Michigan some time ago a man was hurt; his limbs and body were badly skinned, torn off in large patches, and some of his blood had been lost, and the proprietor said, "We must send him to the hospital." They raised a little sum of money to send him off to the hospital, but just before he went, his chum, who was a leader in the camp among the men came to him and said, "Jim, I ain't got no money to send you away; the boss and his friends have given the money, but you know that I like you well, and I want to do something for you; I can't do much but when you get down there to the hospital you are going to need some skin and blood. Say, Jim, if you do, will you send for me?" No one is a leader who is not ready to lay down his life for those he represents. Our Master Leader laid down His life for us.

Leadership costs. Leadership means misunderstanding and loneliness and suffering. Often the crowd does not recognize a leader until he has gone, and then they build a monument for him with the stones which they threw at him in life. A leader must be ready for ridicule. He must accept anguish. Our best plans will often be rejected by those for whom they were made.

Charles Cowman was a man of vision. Throughout his life he seemed to see what the crowd did not see and to see wider and further than many of his own day. He was a man of far-horizons.

It is said of President McKinley that he was a great statesman, because he had the faculty of putting his ear to the ground, and listening for the things that were coming. It was a remarkable capacity. Is it any wonder that men of prayer catch foregleams of the day while the east is still dark? The man on the watch-tower with clarified vision cries, "the morning cometh," even though it seems foolish to the man in the deep shadows below. The day will come when "every man's work shall be made manifest; for the day will declare it." Granted that Charles Cowman gambled with his life, who shall dare say that it was not worth while? If it had not been for a long chain of labors of the early pioneers we would not have the Gospel; and we cannot expect in any other way than by adding one link to that chain to have the glory of handing it down to others.

God waits and the world waits also, for men who will greatly believe and greatly dare. "All things are possible to him who believes." It is a fact as certain as when the apostles and leaders of the reformation proved it. We look at the records, and see that enterprises are undertaken and schemes matured in the physical world undreamt of a generation ago while the cause of foreign missions marches along at a snail's pace, when it ought to be taking the lead.

The evangelization of the world in our generation was was not the idle dream of man. Such men as Dr. Arthur

T. Pierson, John R. Mott, D. L. Moody, A. J. Gordon, Hudson Taylor, A. B. Simpson, and Dr. Blackstone firmly believed that the seemingly impossible could be done, because it was God's command and would be attained by His enablings.

"I loved Charles Cowman" said a noted missionary leader, "and it was one of the pleasures of my life to spend an hour or two with him, but whenever the evangelization of the Orient was mentioned his soul took fire and you felt that he would die a martyr through his own fervidness before he reached the sunset of life, and it was even so. He belonged to the class of early martyrs, whose passionate souls made an early holocaust of the physical man."

Some months before his Home-call a request came to him from a teacher of a missionary study class for a brief article from his pen on the subject of "A Missionary's Qualification." The following lines were found on his desk and as they so fully express his thought, the high standard he ever held for an ambassador of Christ, a place has been found in the biography. They may answer the query in the mind of many a young life who stands looking longingly into the future.

"We have rated the scale of missionary qualifications too low; instead of advancing the missionary character *up* to the fulness of the stature of the New Testament standards, we have been disposed to make it *subordinate* to the pastoral calling at home. We send forth to the heathen world young and inexperienced persons who have not been sufficiently tried at home to be trusted with any weighty responsibility. God forbid that we should discourage the ardor of youthful enthusiasm, but truth compels us to express our honest apprehension, that amid the blaze of popular excitement, and the splendor with which

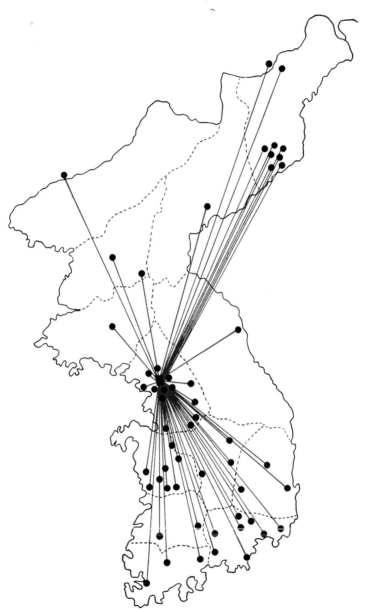

MAP OF KOREA, SHOWING MISSION STATIONS OF THE
ORIENTAL MISSIONARY SOCIETY. (57 STATIONS.)

the distant and magnificent scenes of missionary enterprise are ever invested, many young and ardent minds, suffering their imagination to overrule judgment, and their zeal to outrun their knowledge, have rushed upon a work for which they found, when it was too late, they were morally and spiritually unfit; thus disappointed in themselves, they have been a burden on the missionary cause, and a stumbling-block to the attempts of others.

"For this I know of no remedy but a general diffusion of correct views of the missionary office and the missionary work. We must *raise* the standard of the missionary character. A New Testament missionary! I hesitate not to say, that a heaven-called, heaven-inspired, and heaven-sent missionary of modern times, bears a close relation to the apostles of ancient days; or, to say the least, is fully equivalent to the evangelist of the primitive church; he stands preeminent in the first order of the Christian ministry; he towers above all bishops, elders and deacons, he is the chosen vessel to the *Gentiles,* the great spiritual pioneer in the wilderness of the heathen world. Can he be an ordinary, every-day minister, who is sent by the Lord of the church to the dark-skinned African, or to bear the message of mercy to the Oriental? He goes to lands "unknown to song," over which the foot of the prophet or apostle never trod; he goes to beard the lion in his den; to grapple with the fierceness and obstinacy of paganism in all the primary elements of its native and gigantic strength. Can he be an ordinary character, who, as the chosen champion of the Lord, advances to the attack in the teeth of the heaviest fire of the enemy's strongest batteries, and when the victory is won, is appointed to lay the broad foundations of the Christian empire abroad?

"Shall the Christian church intrust this momentous enterprize to the raw conscripts of the camp, or demands it not the most experienced and determined veterans we can send forth? Else why did the Lord and Prince of all missionaries call the fishermen of Galilee, men in *middle life,* to this arduous work? Who can forget that Luther and Knox and Calvin and the Wesleys were not employed in the *morning,* but in the meridian of their age.

"The *spiritual* qualifications of such a missionary should be scarcely less than apostolic. If deep and genuine piety be indispensable to the pastoral office at home, how much more to the missionary abroad! Who can estimate the spiritual burden of the missionary alone amid the dreary solitudes of the pagan world? Who but himself knoweth the heart-rending trials, the soul-harassing temptations of such a life? Separated from friends, and home, and country, cut off from the consolations of Christian fellowship, a stranger in a strange land, begirt by an unknown tongue, surrounded by scenes of lust and blood, think you that the dwarfish piety of a modern religionist will sustain, or the ephemeral fervors of youthful enthusiasm will endure the wear and tear of such a herculean undertaking as this?

"He who adventures forth to this dangerous and desperate post must aspire after the apostolic zeal and devotion which adorned the primitive champions of the church. Is he the messenger of God? Then he must be a man of God. Is he the trumpet of the Lord to the nations? Then he must be sanctified to the Master's use. Preaches he Christ crucified? Then he must himself be crucified with Christ, baptized not only *into* the faith, but *unto* the death; He must possess resources within himself sufficient to sustain him single-handed against the com-

bined powers of earth and hell. Though heart and flesh
may fail, he must feel that God is the strength of his
heart and his portion forever. His must be a victorious
faith that laughs at impossibilities; a love omnipotent; a
zeal unquenchable, an industry untiring; a disinterested-
ness unimpeachable. He must have a lion's heart and an
eagle's wing and a serpent's wisdom and a dove-like
charity which 'beareth all things, believeth all things,
hopeth all things, endureth all things.' He must approve
himself as a minister of God, 'in much patience, in
afflictions, in necessities, in distresses, in stripes, in im-
prisonments, in tumults, in labours, in watchings, in fastings; by pureness, by knowledge, by long-suffering, by
kindness, by the Holy Ghost, by love unfeigned. By the
Word of truth by the power of God, by the armour of
righteousness on the right hand and on the left. As
sorrowful, yet always rejoicing; as poor, yet making many
rich, having nothing, yet possessing all things.'

"And to the *natural* qualifications of a missionary:
Let him be a *practical* man rather than a theorist. Let
him have a body inured to labour, and a mind prompt to
decide; for rest assured his life will be a life of action
rather than a life of contemplation. Not that we would
exclude the aids of learning from the scale of missionary
qualifications: it has its place, and it ought to have a
place, but the *practical qualities* of the missionary are the
primary qualities.

"The missionary must be a man of decision, a man
of one purpose. He must keep his eyes singly fixed on the
one great object, and all inferior things count but loss, so
he may win the missionary crown. He is separated,
devoted, consecrated to the sublime and godlike work. In
him the missionary spirit burns like fire, and the love of
Christ is the master-passion. He is determined to know

nothing save Jesus Christ, and Him crucified. Forgetting
the things behind, he presses toward the mark. He thirsts
for souls, he pants for spiritual empire. He shuts his
ears and steels his heart against the entreaties of friendship at home, or the anathemas of opposition abroad.
His cry is "Onward!" Though mountains rear their
rugged heads, and oceans roll their tempestuous surges,
and pestilence breathes its deadly poison, yet, in the name
of that Divine Master whose he is, and whom he serves,
he embarks his health, his reputation, his hopes, his
interests, his life, his all, and having landed on the enemy's
opposite shore, he disdains a retreat. Like the great Athen-
ian commander, he burns the ships behind him, he draws
the sword and throws away the scabbard, inscribing on
his banners, "Victory or death." He rushes to the
imminent deadly breach, and victoriously scales the loftiest
battlement of the enemy's strongest hold.

"This is not an imaginary character. We have the
bold and graphic original embodied in the person of St.
Paul and his apostolic coadjutors. 'These be the men
that turn the world upside down;'—I pray God that they
may 'come hither also.'

"Cannot God raise up such men? I believe it, I
expect it. What the great Head of the church has done
before He can surely do again. I firmly believe ere the
bursting glories of the coming of Jesus to take up His
reign upon earth, the breath of the eternal Spirit shall
come from the four winds and breathe upon His own,
and we shall behold 'an exceeding great army' of such
heaven-inspired, and heaven-qualified men, marching
forth to the conquest of the heathen world."

Charles Cowman continually combated the idea that
missionaries were a low, ill-educated, and fanatical set

of people. He invariably took the high line, that the missionary enterprise lay at the very heart of the Gospel, and ought to enlist the ablest and most experienced men. He also urged that the very difficulty and complexity of the problems faced by the missionaries demanded the application of the finest intelligence of the church. Everything in Christianity should be in the superlative degree. The best of men are the men Christ wants—the best morally, the best mentally, the best spiritually.

> "Give me men to match my mountains,
> Give me men to match my plains,
> Men with empires in their purpose
> Men with eras in their brains."

Men of this stamp are not to be manufactured; they are God made. They are not to be *found;* they must be God-sought and God-given, but the Master who has need of them is able to provide them.

He had but little sympathy with young people, who, hearing God's call to preach, neglected the study of the Word of God and a thorough preparation for their work. Especially did he advise prospective missionaries to "study to show themselves approved unto God, workmen that needeth not be ashamed, rightly dividing the Word of truth." Among his papers the following bit of advice was found, evidently written to some ardent young soul who wished to take a short cut in training.

"We have no right to think that while all the other vocations of life, of doctor, of lawyer, of business man, demand preparatory hard work and training, that we can successfully put untrained men into the work of the ministry. If God takes hold of a man He has called to a certain work, and he becomes a veritable flame of fire, there is no reason why other men should shirk training and slip carelessly into the work of the ministry. The

very magnificence of the Gospel, the very majesty of
your work demands that you should take time, take your
whole being, and make it a fit instrument for the procla-
mation of the great and glorious tidings. My dear brother,
gird up the loins of your mind and do not try to hurry
through your training in order to get into the work more
quickly, but along with your training go down into the
city missions and preach and teach, exercising the gift
that is within you or it will burn down into ashes. And
when you become a full-fledged missionary, if you ever
consider yourself as anything bigger and better than a
messenger boy, you are above your business."

Someone was asked to name three essential qualifications of a successful missionary. They did so, in the
following order:

1. Holy deadness.
2. Holy daring.
3. Holy drudgery.

The first of these stand out pre-eminently, *Holy deadness*. Paul expressed it over and over with a special
emphasis. "Always bearing about in the body the dying
of the Lord Jesus." The outstanding need of the present
hour is not so much those who talk of the "old man dead,"
but someone who can *show* us the crucified life. It is
not enough that we are able to refer in eloquent terms to
the clean and empty vessel; our ceaseless prayer should
be that God will bless us with men whose one great concern shall be that they shall stand before the Lord as
clean and empty vessels—not popular, not self-seeking
and self-pleasing, not even great and successful, but clean,
empty, filled, poured-forth.

"*Holy daring* is the inseparable companion of all
sober, God-rooted faith when energized by the Holy

Ghost. Isaiah complained that "there is none that stirreth up himself to call upon thee," and David warned of old, "Yea, they spake against God and said, Can God?"

Holy daring was a quality in the life of Charles Cowman. His joyous, venturesome, enthusiastic spirit was a perpetual inspiration. He was always ready to spring into the van when it required sacrifice. With him a vision of possibilities became action. The moment he found that it was possible to do a thing he was uneasy until it was in the course of execution. The evangelization of the world did not seem to him to be an impossible task. He spoke of it in the greatest faith. Often was he seen during the last six years of his life, walking the floor and saying, "It can be done," and his prayers were fire-lit over the thought. Our visions after all are the strength of our lives. If a man has a vision then difficulties and death are mere details in themselves. He is not thinking of what opposes him or how few are his resources because he is absorbed in his vision. Christ was the supreme visionary. His eye pierced the centuries. God grant that we may be literally absorbed with the visions of the unevangelized world with its suffering, sin, and sorrow. May we never become calloused to the vision.

Holy drudgery occupies the third place and without it, holy daring, however consecrated, must inevitably fail. These qualifications were most marked in the life of Charles Cowman. The mightiest force in all our work is to know, and to have men know, that our life is back of our work. How often was he heard to remark, "I am so tired of seeing people live by halves." Of all things under the sun, the most amazing and most shameful to him was a luke-warm professor of Him who trod the wine-press alone. The master-passion of his life was to live wholly for Him, and he was in blood-earnestness in his dedication to Him.

All service ranks the same with God and it is quite true that "the finest life lies oft in doing finely a multitude of unromantic things." Charles Cowman was an indefatigable worker. Even when traveling he would carry on a voluminous correspondence and type letters in trains and while waiting in stations. Not only did he work, but he injected the spirit of work into those with whom he was associated. Missionaries and native workers would drop into his office in Tokyo for a few minutes' conference and go away with suggestions and outlines for work that would keep them busy for weeks and months. His own example of hard work was calculated to dismay any who might feel called to follow him, unless God was with him also.

A few stray lines in his diary read thus:

"Today is the anniversary of our happy marriage. The entire day from earliest dawn was filled with just a little of every kind of service. For weeks we had looked forward to our wedding anniversary, planning to spend it together, but breakfast was scarcely over when three of the workers came in from their country stations with loads of difficulties. In the afternoon, we were summoned in haste to the printing house in Yokohama. We did not return until dark. However, at ten o'clock, wife and I went out for a moonlight stroll and lived over again June 8, 1889."

"I feel very weary," runs his diary. "It was long after midnight before I could retire. The new converts wished to sit up and talk and it would have appeared very rude to them had I left them. At two o'clock I finally crept into bed, but when the morning dawned, a delegation of Christians were outside my paper door waiting for further conversation."

ON THE LAWN OF THE O. M. S. COMPOUND, SEOUL, KOREA. A FAREWELL TO OUR CHINESE STUDENTS ERE THEY LEFT FOR THE OPENING OF THE COWMAN MEMORIAL BIBLE TRAINING INSTITUTE, SHANGHAI, CHINA.

Brief, but full of meaning are the extracts from his diary which give a picture of unceasing labor. The service was so joyfully rendered that he was rarely conscious of the mental and physical overstrain incurred. Many of his friends felt that he was undertaking too much work and frankly told him so. One might have almost believed that he was trying to illustrate the proverb "the more light a torch gives, the less times it burns." The men and women who make history romantic and picturesque are but few. The men who are prepared to die, if need be, will win a record in valor and be crowned with a fadeless wreath, when the jeweled crown of earth melts in the fire that shall consume the universe.

It was the beautiful thought of the early Church that there were three forms of martyrdom and that every Christian could be a martyr in one of these three ways:

First, a martyr in will but not in deed, like St. John, living longest of all the little band of Apostles, and yet always willing and ready to lay his life down when the Lord should desire. But in his case the will was taken for the deed, and the long life was ended peacefully by a natural death.

Second, a martyr in deed, but not in will, like the innocent babes of Bethlehem, dying as children for the Lord Jesus without knowing it.

Third, a martyr in deed and in will like St. Stephen, facing death in the fulness of his manhood, and freely giving his life to and for Jesus, his Life-Giver.

Charles Cowman was a victor, and he bore the scars of conflict to the close of life. No doubt the heavy labors of those early days laid the foundation for ill health in later years.

He never boasted of his achievements. Humility is the brightest gem in his crown, as in the diadem of every disciple. Many an otherwise useful man tarnishes his service for God by self-consciousness and self-conceit. When the temptation to glory was greatest, and its justification most abundant, his humility was only the more noticeable. He always depreciated his abilities. He might have written the most thrilling stories of actual life in the Orient and was often urged to do so, but shrank from self-advertisement.

"The beginning of greatness is to be LITTLE, the increase of greatness is to be LESS, and the perfection of greatness is to be NOTHING," were words of the oft-quoted Moody.

You may expect to be greatly applauded if you make a sure success, but beware of flattery and human praise which is a dangerous thing. Better is persecution than too much praise. This is the kind of trial which one has seen wither some of the finest characters, and distract others from the simplicity and resolution of their youth. The glory of the Master is often obscured by the glory of the servant. Charles Cowman passed through unscathed. It neither warped his spirit nor turned him from the old paths in which he ever sought to walk.

A man is not made by honors men bestow upon him; he is made before men bestow any honor. Was not his humble-mindedness the secret of his fruitful service? "There is no limit to what God will do with a man, providing he does not touch the glory." One evening he was called upon to give an address in a well-known city church. He was fresh from the battlefront, after the completion of the Great Village Campaign. The crowds were eagerly waiting for a glimpse of the man who had been advertised in the daily paper as having "put over" one of the greatest campaigns since apostolic days. As he stepped to the platform, the audience rose, took out their handkerchiefs and began waving. He was their missionary; they had prayed for him; they had followed him through the five years of the campaign and now their joy knew no bounds. How did he receive this ovation? A pained look came into his face and he quietly fell upon his knees behind the pulpit and buried his face in his hands. There was one person in the vast audience who understood what was passing through his mind and heart. The hardest of tests he successfully met in his humble, modest manner.

> "Great duties are before me and great sorrows;
> And whether crowned or crownless when I fall
> It matters not, so as God's work is done."

A small book which he read perhaps more than another was one written by Andrew Murray. Its title is "Humility." It had been his great privilege to know the author personally, and during his student days this great missionary from South Africa would lecture to the Bible students for a month or more. They too caught his spirit.

Charles Cowman in an hour of triumph remained simply himself. The glory of the hour did not upset him. Unprecedented honors were showered upon him, but he did not lose his head. "I have done nothing," was the reply to the praises, and the people loved him for that self-effacing statement.

To a great audience he once said, "When I think of myself in the Gloryland and hear Jesus saying, 'that is the man whom I washed from his sins in my own Blood,' I shall not want any glory for myself, but all for Him. It was God who looked upon me the chief of sinners to make me an example of the cleansing power of the precious Blood." ("Forbid it Lord, that I should boast, save in the death of Christ my Lord!"

Charles Cowman hated sin with a perfect hatred— hated falsehood or pretense, anything with veneer, anything that looked like pushing himself forward. How greatly he disliked anything like petty jealousies between missionaries. Once, during a summer deputational tour, he was invited to give a missionary address at a large campmeeting on a Sabbath morning. He had traveled a long distance to keep his appointment at that particular place, but on Friday a dear missionary and his wife from South Africa had dropped in. They greeted him with "and you are here, Brother Cowman?" There was pathos in their very tone. The African missionary had toiled long and hard in that far-off land, but had not witnessed the revivals and the visible results in his harvest field.

Sabbath morning came, a great crowd assembled to listen to an address on "The Orient," and Charles Cowman went to the platform. Taking his place among the speakers, he said, "this is a missionary meeting and I am going to ask my wife to sing 'Dark Africa'." She wondered why she was not asked to sing "Beautiful Japan," but she obeyed her kind husband and when the message in song was finished, he said, "We have with us this morning our dear Brother and Sister Fuge, from the Dark Continent. I wish them to come to the platform and take the service." They came with tears to plead for dark Africa while Charles Cowman prayed for them, helping forward that meeting without as much as saying one word about his own fields—Japan, Korea and China. When a few years later a friend asked him to what mission field he should send a gift, he replied "To the Fuges in Africa."

He had a passion for the whole wide-world and this one instance will give the reader a glimpse of his large heartedness and his absolute unselfishness, a lovely trait of character—the character formed in him by the indwelling Holy Spirit.

"Let it once be fixed that a man's one ambition is to fit into God's plan for Him, and He has a North Star ever in sight to guide him steadily over any sea, however shoreless it seems. He has a compass that points true in the thickest fog, and fiercest storm, and regardless of magnetic rocks."—S. D. Gordon.

CHAPTER XXII

LETTERS

Few missionaries of our day worked harder than Charles Cowman, yet he found time to carry on a voluminous correspondence, the letters of one year numbering into the thousands. Many wrote to him sending gifts for the work, others asking for advice and sympathy. He always found time to reply to them.

Quite often after a heavy day's work, a little trip into the country might have been taken, as invitations were received from friends asking him to accompany them, but these were usually declined, with the excuse, "I still have unfinished work on my desk." Often the midnight hour would find him there before the last letter had been finished. Long after his body and mind craved rest, he toiled on, far beyond his strength. How many letters might have been dated "midnight," "two o'clock A. M.," how many missionaries at their lone outposts were cheered because he made time to write them, and how many native workers were lifted over some rough bit of road by his cheery words of encouragement.

It was not known until long after his Home-call that he had written to many at the crisis of their lives. There was a breadth in his sympathies, which influenced many a defeated soul to seek a shelter in his wide heart. His advice was widely sought upon all kinds of subjects. He would throw himself into a round of circumstances, disentangling complicated threads, with a prayer to God for wisdom which was granted.

A number of the friends to whom he had written, kindly sent copies of his letters, hoping they might find a corner somewhere in the biography. As they so unconsciously revealed the man, several have been copied. A man reveals himself in his intimate letters as in no other way and declares himself in the messages which come from the heart. Would the world know the real Charles Cowman, let it see him in his unconscious declarations.

It has seemed best to open to the readers enough of the correspondence to enable them to gather from his own language what took place during his missionary days. Several letters, written to the one dearest to him, are shared with the readers, as they contain items of much moment to his work. In them, as in a mirror, his whole soul is reflected, and the noblest and purest aspirations of his heart were breathed into the ears of the one whom he loved most.

It was during a summer when he was in America on a deputational tour that a very peculiar temptation was thrown in his way. One of Satan's employees is the switchman, who likes nothing better than to sidetrack one of God's express trains, sent on some blessed mission and filled with the fire of a holy purpose.

He had diligently labored in Japan, laying the foundation for the great work of training native evangelists and preachers. There were years of aggressive service, without seasons of relaxation or rest. The temptation came at a time when faith was being tested to the uttermost.

The needs of the fast growing work were great, the Society was not well known. The month of August arrived, bringing a peculiarly trying experience. The heat was extreme, he was weary and worn, but willingly permitted himself to be broken for the One whom he so supremely loved. It was a time of darkness and Satan must have known that Charles Cowman was about to enter on one of the most fruitful periods of his life, rich in blessing for his own soul through an increase in faith, rich in blessing for thousands of others, as well as for the multitudes in heathen lands. Is it any wonder that the enemy came in like a flood?

No untried life has triumphed, and it often takes crisis hours to discover God, but, "thanks be unto God who always causes us to triumph."

Two letters written to me during those days, state the nature of the testing, and through them we catch a glimpse of God's child under hot fire.

"New York City, August 11.

"My dearest Lettie:

"The train was almost forty minutes late, but I arrived in New York yesterday just at noon hour, dusty and very weary. The weather is unbearably hot, over one hundred degrees in the shade. How the New Yorkers exist through it is a mystery. Surely God never meant that such masses should be huddled up in great cities like this when He has made such vast prairies and plains. Such weary looking men, tired faced women, and poor kiddies! How I wish that they might have a whiff of real country air!

"After luncheon I went to the Bible Society's Headquarters and met Dr. Haven, manager, a very courteous gentleman, who was much pleased to see the copy of the marked New Testament in Japanese. He thought the idea quite unique and when I left the building, I had a very distinct impression, which I believe was from the Lord, that it should be printed in Korean also. It will take several thousands of dollars to do it, and of course the enemy was on hand to whisper, 'Where is the money to come from?' Well, we need have no fear whatever about the funds for printing, if God has really spoken, so let us keep this before Him in believing prayer. If you have received any letters from Japan, please forward them tomorrow, care of the Missionary Alliance Hotel.

"I have something real amusing to tell you as a very peculiar temptation was thrown in my way, and yet it was not a temptation, as I was not tempted with it. I just called it a device of the enemy.

"After I had visited the Bible Society, I went up to the Telegraph Office to see the old friends. I found them in a new and magnificent building, and you should see their elegant offices—no. 1 right down to the last minute— liveried messengers, spick and span, everything up to date for first class business! Mr.————was in an inner office somewhere, as he is now one of the officials and holds an important position. When I asked to see him, the clerk looked at me as much as to say, 'Who are you anyway, that you wish to see Mr.————?' He doubtless mistook me for an agent and promptly said, 'You cannot see him, nobody can.' I handed him my card and said, 'Will you kindly hand him this?' He went away, returning in about five minutes, his face all smiles as he said, 'This way, sir.' He escorted me through long corridors and offices, and finally into an elegantly appointed suite of office rooms and soon I was in Mr.————'s presence. What a greeting he gave me! I thought surely he would shake my hand off, he was so cordial. His first words were, 'Well, Cowman, coming back to us are you, I have been thinking of you today and wishing that I could see you, but imagined you were over in Japan somewhere.'

"He then told me of their great difficulty in finding capable men for official positions. He was in a great quandary as some of his principal men had left him that very morning, and for an hour he sat there trying his utmost to convince me that I was more needed in the telegraph office than in the mission field. He begged me to stop and help them out and offered me a position that fairly took my breath away for the moment. An alluring prospect it was indeed. Lovely office, luxury, little to do but look wise and draw a large salary every month. Just imagine it!

"Poor ————— is still unsaved and I do covet him for the Lord. You will remember that I used to talk to him a great deal. His mother was an old-time Methodist, but he is far from the fold, and now since all of his associates are among the "four hundred" there is not much hope for him, but we must never stop praying for him for God's arm is not shortened.

"Are you wondering what I told him? 'When I get the Gospel message to our five hundred million of the Orient, then you may talk to me about coming back to the telegraph service.'

The enemy suggested that if I accepted this position, I might supply the need of the work in that way. How could I leave those dear people without violating the most solemn convictions of conscience? I would not exchange my humble toil among them for all the positions of earth and He knows how to supply the need. Glory to His name! Don't overdo this hot weather. Please write me every day.

With all my love,
Forever yours,
Charlie."

Are we to suppose that the race of spiritual athletes is extinct, and, that amidst the comfort and luxury of the

age, stern, uncompromising deadness to the world cannot
be maintained?

Charles Cowman might have remained in the homeland and lived at the heart of the commercial world; he
might have had prestige and honor; he might have climbed
to the height of fame and fortune, but he chose the way
of the Cross, "choosing rather" to go to the weary hearted
and burdened heathen, to whisper to them words of love
and hope. He believed that he was in the will and plan of
God and kept steadily on in this plan without a single
break to the end of his life. The hand of faith trembled at
times, but kept hold of the promises and would not let
them go. Well might he feel himself strong and
courageous when he felt himself within the sweep of God's
purpose. A man sure of himself, because sure of God, a
man who felt himself a co-partner with God for the high
ends of His kingdom.

> "I had rather stand,
> A prophet of my God, with all the thrills
> Of trembling, which must shake the heart of one
> Who, in earth's garments, in the vesture frail
> Of flesh and blood, is called to minister
> As seraphs do with fire, than bear the palm
> Of any other triumph. This my joy
> The Lord fulfilled."

New York City, August 15th.

"My Dearest:—

"Was all packed up to leave when your letter came.
I went out to a little park near the hotel and read and
re-read it, and there lived a long hour in that letter and
thoughts of you. Perhaps there was some moisture in
my eyes. I knew that you would say, 'Get thee behind me,
Satan,' when you heard of Mr.———'s proposition. All
the morning, I have been pondering over these words,
'He that putteth his hand to the plow and looking back
is unfit for the kingdom of God.' I know a lot of young

men who are out of the ministry because they met some kind of testing and 'looked back,' allowing Satan to take their crown.

"You and I may not have some things that the world offers, but 'Bread shall be given and water sure.' *Sure and shall* are firmer than the rock of Gibraltar, and if God sees fit to bring us into severe testings, He is able to sustain us on such fare and we shall rejoice and be glad. We are God-called missionaries and there is no discharge in this war. I would not exchange places with the wealthiest men of earth, for I have learned that I can be rich without money.

"How I wish that you were here with me, although I am sure you could not endure this extreme heat, but I am like a ship with torn sails without you and have longed that we might pray unitedly over some of these new problems. 'Oh God our help in ages past' has been singing itself in my heart and He will not fail us in this crisis hour. Somehow I feel that He is allowing the situation to become desperate before He steps in, but we shall wait and pray and 'He will show Himself strong on behalf of those whose hearts are perfect toward Him.'

"Let us keep under the cleansing fountain continually, our eyes fixed upon Him alone.

"I thought of running down to Philadelphia yesterday and spending the day with dear Brother and Sister Hoffman, but felt that if I did, I might be tempted to tell them about some of our testings, so I remained in and told Jesus. Went to the Water Street Mission this evening and was scarcely inside the door when the leader invited me to come to the platform and give the message.

"What a motley crowd, far worse than our old crowds in 'Little Hell,' but the same type of men, drunkards and down and outs. I spoke to them of the love of God, for the poor fellows looked as if they needed a little bit of love. I told them how He had found me, and as I was leaving the Hall, had to hurry away as I was engaged to speak to another crowd at the Midnight Mission, a man grasped my hand and said with tears, 'I accepted Jesus Christ as my Saviour while you were talking.' It did my heart good. Praise God for one more soul!

"The fine crowd of young folks from a Bible Institute, who had charge of the music, said just before I left that they wished to sing a special song for 'the missionary visitor.' I had never heard it before, but copied two of the verses and will try and secure the music for you.

> " 'I have enlisted for life in the service of the Lord,
> Though the fight may be long and the struggle fierce
> and hard,
> With the armour of God and the Spirit's trusted sword
> At the front of the battle you will find me.

> " 'With the banner of love and Holiness unfurled,
> Full salvation proclaim in a sinful dying world;
> Though the darts thick and fast from the enemy be
> hurled,
> At the front of the battle you will find me."

"As I walked along to the hotel I thought of the words in 2 Chron. 20:15, 'The battle is not your's but God's!' And over this promise my soul rolled its notes of triumph. I slept very little last night. Somehow the cry of the heathen rang in my ears all through the night. Before I retired I read, 'He came and found them sleeping.' And the picture of the sleeping church and eternity bound souls drove the last bit of sleep away.

"No matter, my dearest, whether storm or sunshine be our lot, whether our cup be bitter or sweet, we have a work to do in the Orient, and by the grace and help of God, we *must* do it. Let us covenant together anew to do our utmost to bring the heathen to Christ, even though it may bring us to early graves. Our lives may be short, but they must be fruitful. I trust this burden may soon be lifted and we shall be able to go back home, for America has no charms for me. Expecting to see you on Saturday evening, D. V.

"With all my love, forever yours,

"Charlie."

How seldom we see souls of the mould we read about in ancient story. We hear much of the saints and heroes of old, we famish for the saintly heroes of today, the life silently surrendering everything to the spirit of truth; rejecting the gain which comes at the cost of conscience, crucifying every lust of evil, and even turning from friendship and dear society, when they seduce the soul from its simplicity. When a man comes to live such a life as this, the Heavens are open, his ear hears the voice of the Spirit, his heart is full of love, his hands of kindly deeds.

Charles Cowman came through this test and trial a positive gainer, for soon there came a complete reverse, when every need was met, when every student's support had been assumed by friends in the homeland as well as all of the workers who were in charge of Interior Stations. Prayer had also been abundantly answered for the printing of the Marked New Testament in the Korean language. Above all, Charles Cowman went forward with a consciousness that he had obeyed his Lord and His command for life. The pathway was often very narrow, but he followed and found that the Lord was ever beside him, even through the darkest days, the testing days, but thanks be to His name, the triumphant days.

To a Missionary passing through financial testings.

"My dear Friends:

"I sympathize with you greatly in the test of faith through which you are now passing, but, when the fire is hottest, hold still. The Lord will not come too late. He may come in an entirely different manner than what you expect. I have found in the walk of faith, that I cannot make a program for God, He will not run on man's tracks.

"How often we ask Him for deliverance when in the midst of a tremendous testing, expecting that He will come on the scene in some strangely grand manner, showing forth His power and majesty, but His ways are not ours, and more often He delivers in some truly simple way that does not seem as if it was Himself at all.

"When God called wife and me to the work, what seemed to shine with celestial glory as a life of faith, we found to be a very commonplace thing and God's deliverances often came in a very ordinary way. He sent some poor widow sometimes to give a little gift that would meet the hour of crisis, or even the contents of a child's penny bank. One special gift was received from a servant girl who had saved her nickels and dimes for nearly twenty years and the amount was exactly what was needed that day to meet a great emergency.

"We need to watch for God and to find Him in the very ordinary things. Do not make the mistake in thinking that because you are in line with God's will, you will never be tested. Paul was right in line with God's will, but God permitted the storm to continue for two long weeks. Now He could have invented an aeroplane, just as He prepared a great fish, or He could have sent a life-boat

STILL CALLING
CHARLES E. COWMAN

with an angel-crew, for here was a great passenger, but we see nothing of the kind. Paul had to jump overboard and swim along just the same as the others.

"Several times God has used heathen people to answer our prayers and supply our daily needs. We shall join you in believing prayers. Rest your whole weight upon the everlasting Arms.

"Faithfully His and yours,
"Charles Cowman."

"Within a day's journey of every mission station" wrote one, "may be found a wilderness with a juniper tree, where men of 'like passions' with Elijah, are apt to repair." In times of weariness and despondency the "accuser of the brethren" brings his cruel charges against the soul. How often they lie wounded and weaponless on the battle-field, courage, not *almost* gone, but altogether gone, hope gone, strength gone, then the suggestion comes, "pity thyself and return home." Many a dear missionary is writing "lost" beside his name, when all that is needed is a change of air and rest. How like an angel visit is a cheery friendly letter from a fellow-worker at such a time!

To a sufferer with "missionary blues" he wrote.

"Dear Fellow-worker:

"Pardon a hastily written note in a railway station, but am on my way to Kyushu, where we have a hundred workers just entering that great district. I forgot to fill my fountain pen before starting, so please pardon this penciled note.

"Stop all your nonsense this minute about being 'lost.' What you need is a change of atmosphere and a few days away from your work. Jesus, while on the Cross, appeared to have been deserted by His Father, and you are tempted to think the same thing. His supreme triumph consisted in His trust in God through the shadows; your victory will be won on the same road.

"I fear that work is allowed to come between us and the Lord quite often. Could you not get right off in the mountains to some native hotel? 'Come ye yourselves apart and rest a while,' said the Master to His own. How often our souls get so dry that we need to get off alone in some desert to be rejuvenated. We cannot minister to our fellowmen if we are not constantly ministered to by Jesus Himself. We must keep our lives in tune with the Infinite at any cost.

"How about your private prayer life, and are you attending the testimony meetings? I find that such meetings with the native brethren are a great help to my own soul. I find it also a great and lasting help just to forget that I am a missionary, and to go with a simple heart to receive instruction from my native pastor. God always gives me something fresh.

"Write me at Kagoshima. Wife is with me and our Headquarters will be at that native inn near Torai Mon. Come down for a day or two. 'I believe in the communion of saints.' Praying and believing for great victory for you.

"Faithfully Yours,

"Charles Cowman."

To a Missionary tempted to leave his flock.

"My dear————

"And you are really returning to the home land? I can scarcely grasp it and I confess to you that I feel disappointed. Full well do I know something of the hot trials through which you are now passing, for we too went through many testings in our earlier years and I sympathize greatly with you.

"Forgive me if I write plainly right out of my heart. You have met a life crisis to be sure, but should such a man as you, redeemed, sanctified, called of God to be an ambassador to the heathen, flee from your corner of the field, just because the battle waxed hot?

"The other day I read a really good thing which I shall pass on. It said that an American traveler was in Italy when one day he stood watching a lumberman, who, as the logs floated down the swift mountain stream, occasionally jabbed his hook into one and drew it carefully aside. He said to the man, 'Why do you pick out these few, for they all look alike?' The lumberman replied, 'They all look alike, but they are not all alike, signior. The logs I let pass are grown in the valley where they have been protected all their lives. Their grain is coarse; they are good only for lumber. But, these logs, signior, grew on the mountains. From the time they were sprouts and saplings they were lashed and buffeted by the winds, and so they grew strong with fine grain. We save them for choice work; they are not lumber, signior.'

"I somehow believe that the Lord has chosen you for some 'fine work,' which the devil wants to thwart. Hold steady a bit longer. You tell me there is darkness in your soul. Here is a rule that I copied in my Bible when I first found the Lord. It is a safe rule.

"In times of darkness, be concerned about two things. First, is my consecration entire? Second, do I this moment trust in Jesus as my perfect Saviour and Sanctifier? Yes. Then all is well. I am on the Rock. The homeland does not need you, but God does need you right where you are. 'Oh for wings,' we cry, 'to fly away and be at rest.' But if Christ had said that, where would our redemption have been? Wings await us only as they awaited Him—only when like Him, we have finished the work He has given us to do and fought the battle to the end. Let us never become battle-weary! Who had ever so sore a fight as Jesus? Whoever kept up that fight until the very last, as Jesus? If He had given up the conflict, had folded His weary hands, what then? And what was the review of His life when almost done? 'I have glorified Thee on the earth, I have finished the work that Thou gavest me to do.' That was all, but that was enough.

"I would not dare go back. Would not God say to me, Charles Cowman, where hast thou left the souls of the heathen? Oh Brother, let us not appear in His presence without them! Your letter burdened me very much and I spread it out before the Lord this morning asking Him for a word and was somehow impressed with 1 Kings 20: 39-40. *"If he be missing, then shall thy life be for his life."* What a word of warning to us all! With God's help no heathen shall miss Heaven if I can help it by throwing my life into the breach for them. You are not going home. I know you are not. Write me fully and freely and come down at any time."

> "I am ever and always your brother,
>
> > "Charles Cowman."

Charles Cowman was loyal to his friends and his loyalty manifested itself in faithfulness and downright frankness. How direct and free from hypocrisy his dealing with them. The foreign field is no hot-bed for saints. Rather it is a place of dreadful spiritual tragedy. He had a supreme pity for a man who is in the church today, in the world, tomorrow—one who is having a constant spiritual struggle. While he possessed a very gentle spirit, he would not gloss over anything wrong when dealing with souls. Some of his letters may seem harsh to those who did not know the man, but to those who knew him and had written out of their hearts to him, his messages were received in the kindliest spirit, recognizing that "faithful are the wounds of a friend."

"My dear Brother:

"It is just the 'wee sma' hour of the morning, but as I awakened my thoughts were of you, so before the day dawns will send you a few lines. Would have replied earlier, but wife and I were out with an itinerating party to some villages and did not arrive home until after midnight. The rain came down in torrents and we had five miles to walk to the nearest railway station, so you can imagine what a sight we were on our arrival home.

"We spent a blessed day and saw four souls pray clear through. Some of our students had gone up to these villages, but the people had never seen a missionary. I would rather be here than in Heaven, and hope the Lord will yet grant me a few years in this greatest business on earth—that of winning precious souls.

"Now to your letter. 'Out of much anguish of heart and with many tears,' I am replying, confident you will not take offense. You tell me that your experience has 'cooled off,' that you are 'lean in your soul.' Forgive me Brother . . . . but I have known it for months. The natives have even mentioned it to me and we all have carried a burden regarding your need. I fear that you have been mixing up in too many things, lawful in themselves but not expedient. Children of the King, of the true blood-royal, hold too lofty a place in the kingdom to

19

mix up in secondary things. Keep in mind that we are the spiritual aristrocracy of these mission fields and never let us come down from our position to dabble with anything on the side. God has in His great love sent us here for one purpose and we have no strength, no time for anything else but soul-saving. We have left friends, home, money, and all else, and have traveled five thousand miles to do this work. We are after but one thing—perishing souls.

"Forgive me for telling you, but I am sure that there are many things in your life that are only waste; these ought to be cut right off. 'Narrow' shall you be called? Yes, doubtless, but I would make a clean sweep of everything and be content to be termed 'narrow-minded.'

"God does not want you to be passing through days of drought here in this, the greatest harvest field of the world. He wants your life to be a power, but if you want His power, you must be separated unto God. If you want the electric current you must be insulated. Won't you begin right now while you read this to separate yourself from the things that hinder, the social hours that are sapping your very life and let Him separate you unto himself? He can make you gloriously free, from all the power of the enemy—utterly, absolutely, and forever free! Not one thread of the old bonds should remain on the child of God, but we should be free, from the sole of our feet to the crown of our head; spirit, soul, body, mind, heart, will, completely and entirely free, now and forever.

"Bring your wife and run down to our Holiness Convention. Rev. John Paul from Asbury College is to be with us and all of the native brethren are expected in from our Stations for a 'Ten Days with God.' It will be a real old-fashioned Holiness meeting. Come with us.

We will do thee good. Send a wire and someone will be at the station to meet you.

"All for Jesus and the Orient,

"Charles Cowman."

Charles Cowman could write thus because he lived thus. His greatest service lay in his own character. The warmth and glow of his first love never subsided.

To a discouraged missionary.

"My beloved Brother:

"Your letter has just been handed to me by Saji San. So glad you have written to me for I perceive you have been associating with one named 'Giant Despair,' and his brood of gloomy faced children. I realize full well that you are in a stiff battle, that you often feel as David did that 'all thy waves and billows have dashed over me.' God bless you, my dear brother, look up. He is with you. Often these 'extra-sized waves' roll over us, but let us be like the Iceland ducks whose spirits rise in a storm and who sing in the face of a blizzard.

"I would put right out of my mind the thought of returning to the homeland to find spiritual food. Did you ever hear the story of the ship's crew that were half famished for water? Again and again, they signaled to a ship near, 'Oh, give us water!' Each time the ship signaled back, 'Dip down where you are.' This seemed like cruel mockery, but finally, in sheer despair they dipped down, and to their astonishment, found they were in the mouth of the Amazon river and they knew it not. God knows how to direct you to 'water springs in the wilderness.' The long, boundless river is free; it is free at the mouth, at the little stream, and free all the way along. Anybody can come and drink and anybody can come and bathe in its boundless waters. Are you going to believe it? Am posting a parcel of books. Please get alone and read them. Come down for a week-end with us and bring your wife and children. There is plenty of room here.

"Faithfully Yours,

"Charles Cowman."

One of the choicest traits of Charles Cowman's character was that of his unfailing optimism. He always saw the sun when it did not shine and was

"One who never turned his back but marched breast forward
Never doubted clouds would break."

A search through his manuscripts and papers for texts that would hint at discouragement has been in vain, for a note of victory rings through every letter, every sentence. His simple trust in God made him always confident of His care. Only once can I recall his giving way to anything like discouragement and that was during the days when he first broke down in health and was laid aside. His sister called to see him and found him helplessly ill. He lay quite still, a tear trickled over his cheek as he said to her, "It is so very difficult to lie here absolutely helpless, when so much work remains to be done." After she had left the room he said to me, "Oh forgive me for saying what I did. It sounded as if I were murmuring and God knows I did not mean it that way."

As we trace his life, let us notice the wonderful persistence of the faith that God had given him. Where others might have turned aside, he seemed to be more directed of God than ever; where others would have been cast down, he seemed to be carried along by a power from above.

Said the Rev. Oswald Chambers of Scotland; "The thing that strikes you about Charles Cowman, is not his holiness, but his absolutely reckless, careless, defiant abandonment to Jesus Christ."

To an Episcopalian Missionary.

"Beloved Brother:

"I wish you might run down to Tokyo for a day or two, as letters are poor things indeed, when you wish to help a person living four hundred miles distant. I deeply sympathize with you in your soul-trouble, but were I in your place, I would not be eternally dying, but would yield myself right up to God and have done with the consecration forever. It is so easy to keep marching round and round in a beaten path and get nowhere. The reason many Christians have so much fighting to do, is because they do not have one sharp decisive battle to begin with. It is far easier to have one great battle than to keep on skirmishing all your life. I know Christians who have actually spent forty years fighting what they term their besetting sin, and on which they have wasted strength enough to have evangelized the world. Have one big battle, one glorious victory, then shout His praises the rest of your life. The height is steep, the way of the Cross is not an easy one, but 'let us labour to enter in.'

"The fire cannot consume the gift that is not placed on the altar, but after it is placed there, we can walk through the midst of each smoking sacrifice, and along each path of holy duty, cheerily singing, 'I'm free, free, gloriously free.'

"God offers us Himself with all of His resources, but to possess them, there must be a complete separation from the earthly. The manifestation of His glorious presence is ours only to the extent that we are found willing to withdraw from the world, living, working, and walking alone with God.

"Come down soon if possible. We are having some glorious times in our afternoon services.

"In the best of bonds,

"Charles E. Cowman."

Excerpts from a Letter to a Missionary Leader, who was dealing with an erring brother:

"What is needed is a baptism of passionate love for our Lord and for lost souls. It is possible for us to speak with the tongues of men and of angels, but without love, it is but sounding brass and tinkling cymbal. It is possible for us to have the gift of prophecy, to know all mysteries, and to have the faith that removes mountains, and not have love. Because of this lack we are nothing—not something, but nothing. Yes, it is possible for us to give all our goods to feed the poor and to be martyrs, giving our bodies to be burned; but without this love, it all profiteth nothing. It is not just a patronizing pity for the heathen, a kind of condescending compassion that we need, but a real passion for the souls of men.

" 'I beseech you by the gentleness of Christ,' said Paul. Have you ever marked Christ's steps—Christ's gentleness when bringing a painful message? Often the way to conquer is to submit.

"Hard missionaries are not of much use; they are not like the Master. He is never hard. It is better to be trusting, gentle, and sympathizing, even if often taken in, than to be sharp and hard. The converts of Paul saw that the Apostle deemed it a small thing to die for them. Let it not be said of us, my brother, that 'we are holy, but hard.' "

To a fellow-missionary whose furlough was due.

Tokyo, Japan, April 17th.

"My dear Brother:

"Your letter containing the news of your sailing reached me last evening. I cannot offer you congratulations, for I am sure you will not be in America twenty-four hours until you will wish yourself back again among the native brethren. It was thus with us and it would rejoice our hearts could we be permitted to remain right here until 'finis' is written to our life-work.

"You will have many and varied experiences in your missionary services. When wife and I were on our first furlough, people looked upon us with pity, as if they thought we had made some great sacrifice. Some came to our meetings as if they were coming to a funeral. Now why should a missionary meeting be a gloomy one? Tell the people of the victories we are seeing out here, give them the glory side and exalt Jesus. Tell them of the glorious answers to prayer and don't allow your meetings to be sombre and melancholy. Tell the people that we who are 'scattered far off among the heathen' are in a winning battle. Tell them we never expect to lower the banner which has been placed in our hands, and as the years pass along, we constantly expect to see the stronghold of sin and Satan beaten down and temples of righteousness rise up on our right hand and on our left, for we 'plow in hope.' May the Lord use you and your beloved companion in lifting up the drooping missionary banners.

"You will find much to sadden your hearts for many of God's children are settled down, 'rich and increased in goods and needing nothing.' May the Holy Spirit aid you in shaking them up. Keep a warm heart, with God's blessings upon you. We shall look for you home again. Remember that home is out here.

"His and yours for the speedy evangelization of the Orient.

"Charles Cowman."

P. S. "Met Mr.———— today. He told me that he no longer believed that sinners were lost, but that all were

God's children. He further added that he could not believe that there was a devil. This is Satan's latest trick, to play that he is dead, but if he is really dead, I would like to know who carries on his business out here."

Charles Cowman could be bold and brotherly, but he never ceased to be indignant over the denial of the Divinity of His Lord and often spoke in very strong terms to those who termed themselves "Modernists."

A favorite and oft-told story in the hand-writing so familiar to thousands.

That Hand has never lost a Man!

A traveler, following his guide amid the Alpine heights, reached a place where the path was narrowed, by a jutting rock on one side and a deep precipice on the other. The guide passed around and then holding on to the rock with one hand, extended the other out over the precipice for the traveler to step upon, and so pass around the jutting rock. He hesitated, but the guide called back, saying, "That hand has never lost a man!" The traveler stepped on to the hand and was soon safely past the danger."

I Peter 1: 5

Charles Cowman slipped leaflets in his letters. The following are samples:

"Jesus was full of the Holy Spirit, and yet He was tempted. Temptation often comes upon a man with its strongest power when he is nearest to God. As someone has said, 'The devil aims high.' He got one apostle to say he did not know Christ.

"Very few men have such conflicts with the devil as Martin Luther had. Why? Because Martin Luther was going to shake the very kingdom of hell. Oh, what conflicts John Bunyan had! If a man has much of the Spirit of God, he will have a great conflict with the Tempter. God permits temptation because it does for us what the storms do for the oaks—it roots us; and what the fire does for the paintings on the porcelain—it makes it permanent.

"You never know that you have a grip on Christ, or that He has a grip on you, as well as when the devil is using all his force to attract you from Him; then you feel the pull of Christ's right hand."

"Extraordinary afflictions are not always the punishment of extraordinary sins, but sometimes the trial of extraordinary graces. God hath many sharp-cutting instruments, and rough files for the polishing of His jewels; and those He especially loves, and means to make the most resplendent, He hath oftenest His tools upon."

"An' when He hears yo' sing, He bends down wid a smile on His kin' face an' listens mighty keerful, an' He says, 'Sing on, chile, I hears, an' I's coming down to deliber yo'; I'll tote dat load fer ye; jest lean hawd on me and de road will get smoother bime by.'"

The man who recognizes new duties above those he has been taught to observe, who sees beyond the circle of conventional obligation the dim form of new claimants on his heart and service, is a moral innovator, an enlarger of human life. How many such have still to rise!—*Cotter Morrison.*

"We ask for toys when we should ask for continents, and be claiming the world for Christ."—Rev. Thomas Payne.

"I did not think of doing a great thing. I did not wish to be famous. It came upon me, and I did what I *must,* and wrote it out, but I was only *the pen in the hand of God."*
                              —Author of Uncle Tom's Cabin.

CHAPTER XXIII

THE GREAT VILLAGE CAMPAIGN

One day, two of the Lord's children climbed up a high mountain near a large city in Japan. It was just as the last lingering rays of the sun were sinking, and ere the evening shades began to fall. Wearied with the hard climb, they sat quietly without talking to each other. A silence fell upon them as they looked out over the long broad valley, one great stretching plain for miles and miles. In every direction were villages and hamlets, by scores, yea hundreds, *untouched, unreached*. They sat thus till darkness enwrapped them. There seemed to be standing in their midst some One Who said to them, "Seest thou those villages yonder? I have been there today and have seen the broken-hearted people, have stood beside the weary pilgrims as they have bowed down before the cold blocks of stone, seeking for peace. I have longed to comfort the sorrowing, the sinsick, but I passed by unnoticed—no one was there to tell them of Me. I gave my life for them also, but I chose men, I thought that I could depend upon them, but they have failed Me." A sweet still Voice whispered, "Will *you* not go to the villagers and tell them of Me, tell them that I care when their hearts ache and break, tell them that I will be their Comforter, their Saviour?"

Charles Cowman said a glad, "Yes, Lord." His attitude was ever, "Speak, for thy servant heareth."

It was during this time that he read again "The Evangelization of the World in our Generation," by Dr. John

R. Mott. It was like a winged seed that flew down the years and reached his receptive heart and influenced his life as no other human words could possibly have done. The words *"To every creature,"* literally took possession of him and burned like a fire in his bones. He prayed over them, asked others what the words meant to them. God had said it and He never meant less than He said. He would not give His servants an impossible task, then why had the last commission not been undertaken?

God's plan unfolded in this way. A little company of our new missionaries met one evening for language study. Charles Cowman was instructing them and none were permitted to speak a word of English during this study hour. A young missionary asked him in broken Japanese this question, "Brother Cowman, have the villagers of Japan been given an opportunity to hear the Gospel? If not, why not?" The words were like an arrow and pierced his heart. The language study class was changed into a prayer service. At ten o'clock he went to his room and the midnight hour found him at his desk. I remonstrated with him, urging him to retire, but he said, "I cannot, the burden upon my heart is too great and I wish to be alone." When the first streaks of dawn stole over the hills ushering in the new day he was still at his desk. He greeted me with a cheery good morning and told me he had met the Lord in the night silence; that He had unfolded to him a plan whereby every person in Japan might be reached with the Gospel during the next five years.

"We have only skirted the borders of Japan," said Charles Cowman to his fellow-missionaries, "eighty percent of the people have never heard one word of the Gospel and this condition exists after sixty years of missionary effort. At whose door lieth this sin? God said to Joshua, 'Get thee up; Israel hath sinned' (Joshua

THIRTY-EIGHT OF THE ONE HUNDRED WORKERS WHO WERE ENGAGED IN PLACING THE SCRIPTURES IN THE 10,320,000 HOMES OF JAPAN.

7:10-11). There is no need for us to wait for councils, conferences and committees. To get at the work and do it, that's the thing. We act as if we had a lifetime in which to evangelize the world. We just leisurely take our time to it, when

> "The work that centuries might have done,
> Must crowd the hours of setting sun."

From an overflowing heart he made this announcement to the little company of missionaries assembled in the dining room, "We are going to place the Word of God in every home in Japan and this is the plan which He gave me. In his businesslike manner he had jotted down statistics and figures, the number of provinces in Japan and their population, also the number of homes. It read like this:

> Population of Japan.......................58,000,000
> Number of homes...........................10,320,000
> Cost of Scripture Portions and
>   expense of workers......$100,000.00 (£20,000)

Two special texts of Scripture had been impressed upon his heart during the night, while alone in prayer. "I will give thee the treasures of darkness" (Isa. 45:3). "Have faith in God" (Mark 11:23).

A systematic campaign was planned. The provinces were to be taken one by one, as there could be sent to each a force of workers who would visit every town, village and hamlet, also every home. He believed that two missionaries and ten Japanese workers could visit the homes in one entire province in six months' time. If the force could be doubled and trebled several provinces could be undertaken at one time. He was quite assured that fifty missionaries and two hundred and fifty Japanese workers could complete the work in one year, however, among our number only one or two missionaries could be spared for this particular work. The plan he proposed seemed audacious for those days, but his faith and vision had grasped it. It was a plan that had been God-given, God-inspired, and he committed himself to it in humble and definite faith that was ever his way. He waited until he had light from the Lord, then went forward and made no plans for retreating or turning aside. They were so well laid that nothing seemed left to do but to carry them out.

"I have a very strong conviction," he said, "that this is God's set time for the speedy evangelization of Japan and we ought to accomplish in a few weeks what ordinarily would take months. I feel that we must act as if we were the only ones to act and wait no longer. Why not, in these days of business schemes that are colossal in capital, magnificent in plan, and world-wide in their extent, why not undertake the King's business as something that requires haste, and should summon to its prompt prosecution every loyal disciple?"

In spiritual warfare, as in the strife of armies, very much depends on the plan of the campaign which is adopted. If no plan is formed, if no systematic method is pursued, if the efforts put forth are desultory and disconnected, and if the field of operations is contracted almost to the verge of absolute insignificance, no great result can be expected, and success on a wide scale cannot be hoped for.

In the life of Charles Cowman were no great bursts of soon-spent enthusiasm, flying before every passing breeze and dying down into a calm, but the steady motion of a steamer, that goes on day and night without stopping, until it at last drops anchor in port, receiving an abundant entrance into the desired haven. He dreamed dreams, and had ability to change those dreams into reality, but he did not dream of great harvests and neglect the toil that produces them.

He was not self-confident. Indeed there was nothing in his character that was less manifest than self-confidence. He was ever leaning upon the arm of God, fearing to take a step which was not at His command or clear direction. He prayed that every home in Japan might be reached, and no common faith was needed for such a claim. The step he had taken was wholly taken in the belief that God was leading him, and he dared to trust Him for all. To an inner circle of friends he wrote:

"The Great Village Campaign has been launched, and the Mission committed to a program which is the subject of much comment throughout missionary circles. It was quickly noised abroad that the Oriental Missionary Society, a 'Faith Mission' that had no guaranteed funds or influential home committees to back it up in case of an emergency, a Mission that would not go in debt even if the worst came to worst and there would be nothing in the treasury, had undertaken to place the Gospel into the ten million, three hundred thousand homes in Japan." Someone said, "What can Charles Cowman be thinking of?" He was thinking of heathen souls waiting for one crumb of the Bread of Life, and the Master's "Go ye."

Men crowd upon one another's steps, and the nobleness of individuality is lacking, few daring to brave the sneer of being peculiar in doing each his own duty in obedience to the Word of God. The men who succeed are sure to be criticized. Is he therefore to abstain from going forward in his efforts to be obedient to the heavenly vision? We are responsible to God alone, and cannot regulate our lives to other people's ideas. "The essence of faith lies in this," said Rev. James Wood, "a deep sense of conviction, that in what we do, though it were single-handed, with all men standing aloof, and even saying 'Nay!' to it, we have God and all the universe at our back."

After a thing has been done, everybody is ready to declare it easy, but before it has been done, it is called impossible. One reason why people fear to embark great enterprises is that they see all the difficulties at once. They know they could succeed in the initial tasks, but they shrink from what is to follow.

When the news reached the homeland of the vast undertaking, it created a thrill of surprise and wonder. There were letters of encouragement, letters also of discouragement. To the latter he boldly replied:

"The dangers and difficulties in our way will be neither few nor small, but with Jesus as our Captain and Leader, we may follow safely on, without a single fear. Can we accomplish anything great or good without encountering difficulties? No, let us look difficulties in the face and then, 'Let us go up at once and possess the land for we are well able.' Faith will be staggered even by loose stones in the way if we look manward; if we look Godward, faith will not be staggered, even by inaccessible mountains, stretching across and obstructing apparently our onward progress. 'Go forward' is the voice from heaven; and 'God with us' is our watchword."

The zeal which burned in his heart gradually communicated its glow to others. They, too, took up the slogan, "The Gospel in every home in Japan during the next five years."

A lover of missions wrote him, "I have been longing to see something just like this for years; a forward movement in a heathen land on a gigantic scale, one that we believe pleaseth God and will greatly glorify Him."

Warm hearted friends, knowing his physical limitations urged him not to attempt it, fearing it would result in a complete breakdown, but he felt that God had called him; it was His voice to him, and he went forward at once and for five years the last commission of our Saviour controlled his very life. He responded to it with an unquestioning obedience, and if ever any person on earth attempted to pay his debt to the heathen world it was Charles Cowman. Full well he knew that the work to be done could not be done without prayers, tears, and a real crucifixion, yea, even death itself if that come in the carrying out of God's purpose.

"What if we lose our lives in the undertaking?" he said to his companion, "be it so, thank God! None of these things move me, neither count I my life dear unto myself."

There can be no great achievement "without shedding of blood" and he did not consider the price too great.

The day of advance had dawned and he responded to the call, which commanded dauntless resolution and fixedness of purpose. Forward he went with a swing of a mighty urge. The Great Village Campaign was no longer a venture but a fact.

It was undertaken with $5.00 (£1) in the treasury, and faith in God. The first distribution of the Scriptures began in Jerusalem (Tokyo) his home city, and the homes of three million people were visited. Workers were then sent out into the provinces, who daily visited the homes. At the end of four months the first province, comprising more than one million souls had been reached with the printed message and nine hundred souls had definitely sought the Christ, flinging away their idols. The practical evidence that he was in line with God's purpose was so manifest that letters began to pour in from hundreds of people. They, too, had heard the songs of joy afar off and were filled with praise. The letters that came from the little band of workers were so full of victory that one's

20

heart was fairly thrilled when the news was read. Daily they were tramping to hundreds of homes, where the Word of God was being received with gladness. There were seekers and converts everywhere, scores and hundreds of them right amid raw heathenism. Through these visible results, God showed that His smile of approval was upon the movement and that alone spurred His servant onward in the blessed soul-saving plan.

Funds began to come in from the homeland, small amounts, but gifts watered with prayers and tears, and the distribution of the Scripture in another province was undertaken with an added corps of workers. At the close of three months when another million people had been given one chance to hear the Gospel, the report which the village workers sent in more than repaid for all the toil and hardship. It read: "The work closed in a blaze of glory. We have seen twelve hundred seeking Christ. Scores have prayed through in their homes. What a hallelujah march we have had around that province until the walls fell flat!"

"It is your Father's good pleasure to give you the kingdom," wrote Charles Cowman to a sympathizer. "Thank God for this promise. The grants of God are not cramped up quarters but kingdoms and we claim a land which He has called His people to possess for Him."

The enemy contended for every inch of ground and pressure of every conceivable kind was brought to bear upon the leader of this movement. Several years went by when the distribution work in six large provinces had been finished and glorious had been the results. There was no scarcity of workers, for earnest young Japanese Christians felt the call and heartily responded, but funds began to fail and it looked as if the Village Campaign was at an end. What was to be done? But one thing—to pray. New lessons were being learned in trust, leaning upon the strong arm of God, upon Him alone. And while he was trusting, God was working. Upon the hearts of hundreds in the homeland came a fresh burden for the evangelization of Japan, and the small gifts of the many were laid at the Master's feet. There came an hour when larger sums were needed if the work was to advance speedily. A fine old southern judge was tossing upon his bed one night, sleep having left him. He had just received a letter from his friend Charles Cowman and the villagers of Japan seemed to be standing about him. Would he dare to leave them to perish for the lack of the help he might give? And what about his missionary friend out there who had given up all to go to the lost and dying with the words of Life? He was laying down his life for them. The judgment would have no terror for him, for without hesitancy could he lift his face to God and say, "I have done my utmost." The Word in Ezekiel came forcibly to the mind of the judge, "If I say to the wicked, thou shalt surely die, and thou givest him no warning, he shall die, but his blood will I require at thy hand."

Judge Strouse knew his Lord's voice and he arose in the dim light of dawn, went to his desk and wrote:

"My dear Brother Cowman:

"My heart is stirred over the work you are doing in giving the Gospel to those who have never heard. Will you evangelize one entire province for me? I enclose a check for $3,000.00 for the purpose."

Over in Japan the weary missionary received the letter which brought fresh hope and courage to press on. The great Province of Saitama was entered and the following lines were written and sent to his good friend and helper.

"Our Village Campaign Bands began their work in Saitama Province last week by distributing a large number of Scripture portions and tracts. The first day we preached twice in heathen temples, the priests giving us a royal welcome. One of the old priests said, 'I believe that what you have told me today is the truth, and that my efforts to lead my people for the last twenty-five years have been altogether in vain. I have led thousands on the wrong roadway, and now I wish to learn the real truth that I may begin even now to turn them into the right road.' The second day of our work, twelve young men grasped the plan of salvation clearly as we told them the story in a simple manner. Five fine old men said to us, 'Stay here with us in our village and teach us more.' Ten of our workers were out in a great village center all day returning at night with glowing reports of the day's labor, and we feel abundantly encouraged."

The following report will give you a glimpse of a day's work.

May 2nd. "A cloudless morning. Before starting down the valley to the village homes, we had a precious season of prayer with the workers. One of them broke down and wept like a child, while we were singing, 'The Ninety and Nine.' Between his sobs he said to me, 'Brother Cowman, not only the *one* sheep in my country are far off from the gates of gold, they are here by the million.' Thank God, we are out searching for them and He is helping us to find them.

"One band of our workers entered a town, held a street meeting, and the leader of the young men's club became so interested that he invited them to hold a service in the club-room the following day. He sent out personal invitations to all of the members and fifty came, bright young fellows, everyone of them Buddhists. Five of

A PERPLEXING MOMENT. A LETTER HAD BEEN RECEIVED FROM THE VILLAGE
CAMPAIGN BANDS WHICH READ: "WE ARE JUST ENTERING ANOTHER LARGE
PROVINCE. PLEASE FORWARD AT ONCE 200,000 SCRIPTURE PORTIONS AND SUP-
PLIES." THE ACCOUNT BOOK SHOWED NO FUNDS IN THE TREASURY.

them publicly sought the Lord and knelt simply before their fellows, confessing their sins and calling upon God to save them. They told us that if we would send them a preacher, they would open the club-room for religious services, absolutely free of charge. What calls from everywhere! Would that we had a thousand native preachers ready to thrust into this white harvest. They are the only hope for the evangelization of their land!

"In one place, the town council was in session and a large crowd of people gathered. Business was suspended for an hour and a half in order to hear the wonderful story of Jesus and His love. Five sought the Lord right there.

"In another town, when the Village Bands entered, they found that the policemen of the entire district had met for a convention. The Chief courteously invited the band to hold a meeting with his men. They sat quietly listening to the Gospel story, when the chief arose and with much dignity said, 'Will you please stay with us awhile and teach us more. There is a welcome in our homes for you and we need just such a message as you have been telling us, one that will help our people to stop sinning.'

"The worker asked them to fall upon their knees and he would pray to the Living God for them. Everyone of them obeyed, simple as little children, while the Chief prayed, 'O God, who lives in the heavens, please come and save us from our sins.' When he arose his face was wet with tears.

"Those days and weeks stood out above all others in Charles Cowman's life. It was a time of mighty visitation of the Spirit and entire villages were swayed as a field of wheat is swayed before the passing of a mighty wind. How often during his last days did he say, 'What a wonderful time we had during the Great Village Campaign. What wonderful meetings! I feel the thrill of them still!' "

When the distribution work in Saitama Province was completed, he wrote again to Judge Strouse: "Through your gift, we have been enabled to carry the blessed Word of Life to one entire province, representing approximately 1,436,895 souls. There have been hundreds of seekers after God, and many genuine conversions. It has occupied four months' time. Numbers of splendid outstations and centers have been opened. The cost of the work has not exceeded $3,300.00."

There came a reply from the judge to this letter: "I have found no better place to invest my Lord's money, and have decided to evangelize another province." A check for $2,000.00 was enclosed. He further stated, "I will stand behind you until the entire land of Japan is reached," but this was his last gift. God had another plan and ere the distribution in the second province was completed he was suddenly called to his heavenly Home.

Today I fancy that Judge Strouse and Charles Cowman are walking the streets of glory talking over those days. Do you think he was sorry that his treasures were laid up above?

"God buries His workmen but carries on His work" is a true saying, and to those who walk closely by His side, there will be no disappointments when the human arm fails through any cause. "Help us, O our Lord, our God, for our eyes are upon Thee," was often pleaded during those days.

The Children of America and England wished to have a part in the Village Campaign and sent $3,000.00 (£600) for the evangelization of a province. The women also took it upon themselves to have a share and one thousand women sent $5.00 (£1) each, as a love-offering.

God seemed to let His little ones who are poor as to earthly possessions have the privilege of doing the major part of this work and many gave out of their poverty. $5.00 (£1) was a sufficient amount to purchase Scripture portions and pay the worker's traveling expenses and thus one large or two small villages were reached with the Gospel story.

A number of friends who had heard of this widespread campaign wrote a letter to Charles Cowman inquiring about the results of the Scripture distribution. His reply read as follows:

"My dear Brother:

"In replying to the question as to the results, a consideration of the following statistics will give you a very comprehensive idea:

Population of Japan latest census, about	57,976,322
Of these we have reached about	35,047,791
Number remaining to be reached	22,928,531
Number of houses in Japan about	10,376,700
Number already visited about	6,234,792
Number remaining to be visited	4,141,908
Number of provinces in Japan	47
Number of provinces finished	28
Number remaining	19
Number of counties in Japan	640
Number of Counties finished	338
Number remaining to be visited	302

"The area to be covered is 161,000 square miles including in it about 4,000 islands, all mountainous. More than one-half of the territory has been covered.

"Between 5,000 and 6,000 names of seekers have been sent in to headquarters at Tokyo. Thousands of others have been dealt with.

"Hundreds of New Testaments have been sold or given to those who received a 'portion' and wanted more.

"Hundreds of letters have been received from inquirers, and hundreds of replies sent out, together with thousands of other tracts and periodicals to seekers to instruct and lead them on. Thousands of sermons have been preached in the open air, hotels, and halls. In fact, Japan is being literally sown with Gospel seed.

"And all this has been accomplished for $55,000.00. (£11,000). All has been done in answer to your prayers and ours—praise God! Balance needed, about $45,000 (£9,000)."

MARCHING ON THROUGH THE PROVINCES

Charles Cowman was wholly absorbed in the undertaking and his spirit was straitened until it should be accomplished. This pioneer work proved to be much more difficult than he had ever dreamed, but his heart was with the Christless multitudes and self-ease was not permitted to come between them and his responsibility.

The year 1914 was rapidly nearing its close when funds went down to the last penny. Scores of splendid native workers were offering themselves for the Village Campaign. They, too, were longing to plunge into the battle, but an empty treasury was looked into morning after morning. Hard work, heavy responsibility, and the impossibility of any escape from either in the Orient, were telling on his health. The new year began in a semi-breakdown and fearing it would be complete, he left Japan for America expecting to remain a brief time. The short ocean voyage so invigorated him that he was able after a few days to be out in deputation work.

"I feel that God is holding me responsible for the thirty million souls in the provinces who are yet unreached," were the words in a letter sent to a prayer-helper.

After a few brief months in the homeland during which he was busy in conventions and campmeetings, traveling thousands of miles, speaking in hundreds of places, he bade farewell to his friends with apparently a buoyant heart, and set out for his field of labor with the air of one leaving a foreign land for a loved and longed-for father-land. In a peculiar sense he felt he was going home. His heart and his treasures were far away "near the golden gate of day," and while his affection for his native land had never waned, the new affection which had taken root in his heart for the land of his adoption had been stronger than his attachment to the land of his birth. A friend who accompanied him to the steamer said to him, "Brother Cowman, I fear that you will never come back." His quick reply was, "I do not need to come back."

Leaving the attack on Naples, Gonsolvo, the captain of the besieging band, declared that he would rather die one foot foremost than preserve life with one step of retreat. There are occasions when no other alternative is offered. It may not be necessary that we should live. It is imperative that we should stand firm. The motto of David Livingstone was in these words: "I determined never to stop until I have come to the end and achieved my purpose."

A much loved Chinese proverb was often quoted by our beloved missionary. "If you set out on a journey of ten miles, remember that nine miles is only half way." Also a Tibetan proverb, "As you go forth to the fight be in the front; as you return be the last to come." He returned to his task with unabated diligence. A man of his nature could not go slow. The doctor was anxious about him. "Charles Cowman is burning away," he said, "and he has no fuel, but it does no good to blame him, he could not help it with a fire in his bones for perishing souls."

If we could forget what we know of the lands and the people where the evil one reigns, we might for a time live in a dream-world, but having once known even a part of the woe of the sin-cursed world, we never can forget again, until its redemption is complete in its finished workings, as well as in its Divine plan. But they are there and they are our brothers and sisters, left to our care and love by One who loved them and us even unto death.

Instead of making the fact of his being leader an excuse for considering his own comfort and health, it was the very opposite, and he felt that he must remain at his post of duty even if it meant the loss of all. Often he quoted, "He that saveth his life shall lose it." He had very strong views about a missionary's duty to his work.

He started out in the new year with the thought deeply implanted in his heart that if the Village Bands could be increased to one hundred workers, (ten new missionaries and ninety native workers), the entire work could be completed in one year.

The dying words of a missionary veteran were, "It is my deep conviction and I say it again and again, that if the church of Christ were what she ought to be, twenty years would not pass by till the story of the cross was uttered in the ears of every living man." If this veteran had a vision of twenty years for the evangelization of the entire world, then why not touch every home in Japan in one year, was his argument.

He prayed, "Lord, send laborers, send us one hundred men," and in a remarkable manner that prayer was answered, for almost immediately ten splendid young men in America came forward offering themselves for this particular work, also ninety native workers. These were accepted, and during the year that followed they were engaged in the most intense activity out in the villages of Japan.

What an object lesson to the native Christians these young missionaries were, in their willingness to endure hardships, in their zeal, in their deep interest in souls! How persistently they pressed their way through rice plains, over mountains, wading rivers and swollen streams, in the dead heat of the summer and the piercing cold of the winter, for Christ counting everything but loss. The millions were hearing and responding to the Gospel message.

Think of the progress made in Paul's day! If the pace established in his day had been continued, the world would have been evangelized long ago. Paul never pitied himself from the moment he got the vision; there was no more love of ease, for the passion seized him and whether in shipwreck, under the lash, or in prison, the love of Christ constrained him, and passion for souls pulled him on. It is a continual drinking in of this compassion in the fulness of the Holy Spirit that keeps one's life a living sacrifice, a constantly burning flame.

Requests came from several parts of the world for a story of the Village Campaign as to its inception, progress, faith aspect, and results, as it had become quite well known. It was talked of in pulpits, in campmeetings, and by firesides, and people wished to hear more, but Charles Cowman was too busy to make notes of what he was doing. The record of the Great Village Campaign would make a thrilling volume of answered prayer, and we trust that some day time will be given for writing such a volume.

A note in his diary at sea enroute to Japan, his last voyage there, reads, "I have resolved by God's grace, never to untie my loins, but keep them girded until I hear my Master's call, 'My heart is fixed, O God.'"

> "Think not of rest; though dreams be sweet,
> Start up and ply your Heavenward feet.
> Is not God's oath upon your head?
> Ne'er to slink back on slothful bed.
> Never again your loins untie,
> Nor let your torches waste and die.
> Till, when the shadows thickest fall.
> Ye hear your Master's midnight call."

He worked rapidly and finished a magnificent course in holy haste, as if under a presentiment that he must crowd much into a brief space.

A small booklet was sent out to praying friends bearing the title, "Thirty Million People to be Evangelized during 1916."

"An unprecedented opportunity lies just before us. Our Great Village Campaign Bands during the past two and a half years, have reached almost ONE HALF of the fifty-eight millions of people of Japan, going from house-to-house with the Gospel message.

"THOUSANDS of souls have been won to Jesus by these workers as they have spoken with them 'by the way.' After tramping all day to the homes, with great packs of Gospel Portions on their backs, and coming in to their lodgings at night-fall, weary and foot-sore, they have preached on the streets of their village and labored with earnest seekers, often until midnight. Then, retiring to get a few hours sleep and rest (on the hard floor—no beds), they were roused at early dawn by seeking souls, ere they started to repeat the work of another day.

"EIGHT THOUSAND letters have already been received at our Tokyo office, from other seeking souls, desiring to know more of 'this way.'

"NEVER before in the history of Foreign-Missions, has such a stupendous effort been put forth—to evangelize a whole nation of people, individually, but the very fact that our bands of evangelists have already reached almost half of Japan in such a brief period of time, only proves it CAN BE DONE, and by the grace of God and help of His people, we mean to do it."

The dream of Charles Cowman was being realized. One hundred workers were scattered about in the villages and neglected districts of the Island Empire.

Can the reader grasp the full meaning of that sentence? One hundred at work every day from early morning till long into the night, scattering precious seed by the wayside, winning souls by the hundreds, yea, thousands. Eternity alone will reveal the vast number who were brought out of darkness into light.

It was then that his resourcefulness, generalship, and persistence were made manifest. He wished to be at the front with the workers, and in the springtime of 1917, a temporary headquarters was established in the large Island of Kyushu. Nine million souls were there to be reached and with full assurance that God was in the front, the distribution of the Scriptures in this island began.

How often do people fancy that the way of the heroic man is all peace and pleasure, but what a mistaken idea. From first to last there is the battle with obstacles, blockades, and other adverse conditions. "The hero is not fed on sweets." Envy no man his place. His well-earned success has been paid for with tears and with blood. The *missionary's life!* Ah! an archangel would come down from his throne if he might, and feel himself honored to give up the felicities of Heaven for the toil of a missionary's life!

Charles Cowman was often heard to remark, "Oh, how I wish that I never had to leave the field again. How I would love to live and spend the rest of my days among this needy people."

To another prayer-partner he wrote:

"We have entered the fourth year of the Village Campaign and this morning, remembering all the way the Lord has led us, I was moved to tears which could not be suppressed. They were tears of joy and thankfulness to our wonder-working God. 'What hath God wrought!' How I thank Him that He has given grace for these heavy years. The evangelization of the world is our Lord's dearest purpose and He will not fail to supply us with resources as we co-operate with Him. God Himself is with us and He will not fail. I never took hold of the work with more faith, with unshaken confidence of success, than at this time, and I never saw the Arm of the Lord made so bare. Jesus *shall* reign."

"Refreshing news was received this morning from the village evangelists. The distribution work in twelve more large counties has been completed. While summing up the number of seekers the figures startled me. I read, 'We have seen more than four hundred souls seeking Christ during the past thirty days.' This alone compensates for all the scoffs and jeers of those who said, 'It cannot be done' and 'It will not pay.'

"Compare this sort of evangelizing with hammering away weekly at Gospel-hardened people who have as much made up their minds to reject Christ as did Chorazin and Bethsaida!"

Four months later he wrote to homeland friends:

"It is with very grateful hearts and deepest thanksgiving and praise to God that we are able to tell you that the nine million precious souls who reside in the Island of Kyushu have been reached. 'Unto Him be glory world without end.' The work has been done by twelve missionaries and fifty native brethren who have marched through the land, their faces set like a flint in fulfilling the last commission. All classes have been reached, the high and low; coolies, college professors, heathen priests, merchants, and most of all, the splendid student class.

"One of the most pathetic stories we have heard in a long time was told us by one of the missionaries. He was out in the mountains searching out the little huts and homes scattered over them, when he came to a group of houses off by itself. Each home was visited, the Gospel booklet presented, when he discovered a cage or prison in one corner of a garden. It was built of poles and peering through the bars was a fine looking young man. He held out his hand and a Scripture portion was given to him. Our missionary brother started down the mountain, the young man calling after him as far as he could hear, 'Arigato, Arigato' (Thank you, thank you). This so touched our brother's heart that he began to pray earnestly for this young man who was evidently suffering mentally. As there are no asylums in these far-off country places the distressed parents had erected this cage in a garden near their house in which to keep him from doing violence to others.

"It was learned that he had been confined to this place for six years. Other mountain homes were visited and the missionary returned again after a time to the roadway near which this unfortunate man was in prison. He heard a voice as if in prayer. The young man had read the portions, its truth had taken hold upon him and he was calling upon God at the very top of his voice. It was now growing dark and our missionary fearing he would lose his way started down the mountain; on and on he went but still he heard the man praying louder and louder. The night grew still, the foot of the mountain was reached but echoing down through the cliffs was the sound of the man still at prayer. Oh the marvelous power of the Name of Jesus which can break every fetter and set the captives free." Two weeks later he wrote again:

"Seventy-eight men are now engaged in the Great Village Campaign. These faithful bands of young men are walking to about 20,000 homes daily so that every day means another 100,000 souls have the 'Word of this Life,' which Peter also was commissioned to proclaim. Acts 5:20.

"Every member of our Bands is keenly alive to the urgency of the work. Although many of the provinces are very mountainous and difficult, they are marching on victoriously with the great object in view—to complete the work by Christmas. Hundreds of seekers have been the result.

"Although the work has extended over the best part of five years, yet the amount accomplished during the past year since we have had the means for the large force of men at work, has been remarkable. The ten, sometimes twelve missionaries and their bands of Japanese helpers have gone over almost half of the Empire during the year, walking over 50,000 miles equal to twice around the world, over mountain paths and muddy rice fields in all kinds of weather. It has not been easy on the physical, but we have proved how simple is the task set the church in the last great commission of Jesus Christ, to go into all the world and preach the Gospel to every creature.

"On July 3, the village Bands began their exodus from the Island of Kyushu, forty-seven of the number going to the extreme northern part of Japan, the great Island of Hokkaido, away up near Russia. We arranged with the railroad officials for a whole coach for the party. They were two nights and a day journeying to Tokyo and although very worn on arrival, we are sure that all along the line they fulfilled the Word, 'As ye go, preach.' There were song services and testimony meetings on the train and one of the missionaries said: 'We had a gloriously good time even though the seats were hard boards and we had to sit up all the way.' The Hokkaido Band stopped a day and a night in Tokyo and then resumed their journey to the far north, another day and night's journey by train and boat.

"They were re-enforced there by some splendid Christian young men. Two of the number are sons of a blind preacher, others are from our thrifty mission stations in the far northland. The work has had a good beginning, and we fully expect that the two million souls of Hokkaido will have had 'the Gospel as a witness' ere this issue of the Standard reaches you.

"The other bands are hard at work on the mainland, the dear faithful men not counting their lives dear unto themselves that they might fulfil the ministry given to them by the Lord Himself.

"As the work progresses, we are more and more convinced of the power of the Word of God. We need have no anxious thought as to its outcome. Ours is to sow the seed, the Lord of the harvest brings it forth to full fruition. We are seeing results, marvelous indeed. From seven to eight orders a day for Bibles come from out-lying dis-

21

tricts where the village bands have been distributing the Scriptures. Today a letter came from a young man in a far-off lone village saying, 'I received a Scripture Portion and it was the first time I ever heard that there was a true and living God. I want Him, lead me to Him.' Another writes, 'I received a Scripture Portion and read the wonderful words which led me straight to him, the Way, the Truth, and the Life.'

"Yes, right in this time with the thunders of war rolling all around, God's tender voice is speaking peace, sweet peace, His gift to the lost and sinning world and men are finding Him. We feel more determined than ever to spend the last hour of our earthly day in scattering the Word of God to the heathen world—scattering it broadcast into village, town, and city with every ounce of strength we possess. Little wonder that the devil hates and fights us inch by inch for he, too, knows and trembles at the power of the Word.

"They tell us that the last words spoken by the dying soldier boys on the battle fields are words from the Book of Life.

"We read of Cromwell and his Puritan warriors in the midst of one of their fiercest battles, stopping long enough to read the 117th Psalm; and John Huss, dying at the stake, choked by flames, repeating with his last breath the words used by Christ when He hung upon the Cross, 'Into Thy hands I commend my spirit; and Savonarola on the night before his death, with his left arm broken and his shoulder pulled from its socket by his tormentors, falling asleep repeating, 'The Lord is my Light and my salvation, whom shall I fear? the Lord is the strength of my life, of whom shall I be afraid?'; and brave Martin Luther in one of the dark hours of struggles for right and truth said to Melancthon, 'Come Philip, let us sing the 46th Psalm, 'A mighty fortress is our God.'

"Ah, those old saints and martyrs knew the power of the Word of God and we missionaries are getting visions too of old heathen temples transformed into chapels and churches, of heathen homes and heathen communities transformed by 'the Word that liveth and abideth forever.' "

A few weeks later he wrote again to dear homeland friends:

"From snow-capped Fuji to coral-reefed Loo Choo, the neglected peoples are coming, coming in by the hundreds to the Saviour who died for them. Thirty workers are in Hokkaido among the three million there, seventy of the campaign band are scattered about on the mainland. We have proved beyond a doubt that the pure, unmixed Gospel-message, accompanied with faith and prayer, makes converts anywhere and everywhere, and that in the most unlikely places and districts, where idolatry has held undisputed sway for centuries, resisting all attempts at uprooting, the sweet story of the Cross of Christ has proved equal to its displacement. Another very noticeable thing: the greatest success has not been attained by the greatest of our native preachers. It has not been the fruit of skilled labor. The simple story told in a simple manner has brought the hundreds to the feet of Jesus."

How could the work help but develop and increase born in the soul travail of a man who had seen a vision and had paid the price of his dream! The months that followed after his return to Japan were very busy ones and were perhaps the most critical, yet the most fruitful of his life on the field.

One of the greatest tests during the Village Campaign was met during this time. The treasury again became completely depleted. One hundred men were out campaigning. "No funds" were the words in a wire from Tokyo. "Lord, to whom shall we go?" was often upon his lips. Where? To his never-failing Friend. To the One Who had said to him twenty-five years before, "Go ye also into the vineyard and whatsoever is right I will give you." Yes, to the One who said, "Go ye. . . . to every creature" and he had gone. Could God fail Him? Perish the very thought!

Telegrams were sent to each leader of the bands informing them of the test and on Sabbath morning they gathered their native workers about them and made the need known. Some went to the mountains where they could be quite alone, others remained in their rooms in the native inns to wrestle and prevail. On Monday morning a note of victory was received from each leader. "We prayed through" wrote one. "God gave us assurance" wrote another. Charles Cowman had spent the night alone with his Lord, but there had been no wrestling. A deep settled peace stole into his heart and an assurance came that prayer was heard and the answer was on the way.

How often was he heard to remark, "Let us take the promises to mean just what they say; let us look into His marred face and commit ourselves unreservedly to Him and let us do it now, right now. Why do we delay? Then let us expect a response, and go forth quickly to put it into use in our every day life."

A favorite promise was, "My people shall never be put to shame." It held good at this particular time. Monday morning arrived when a wire from Tokyo conveyed the joyful news, "Dr. Blackstone has cabled $8,000.00 for the Village Campaign."

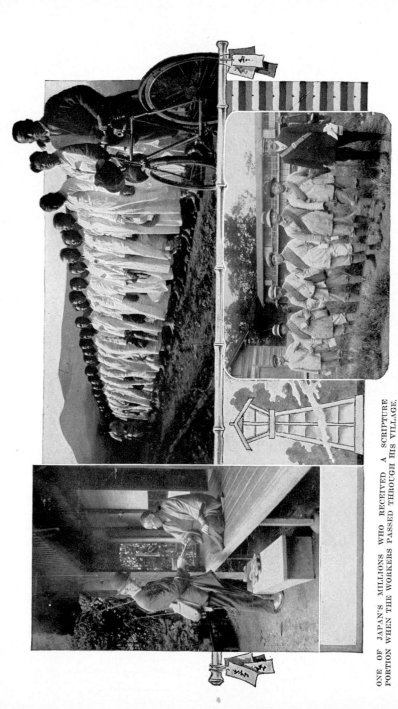

ONE OF JAPAN'S MILLIONS WHO RECEIVED A SCRIPTURE PORTION WHEN THE WORKERS PASSED THROUGH HIS VILLAGE.

ABOVE—A GROUP OF VILLAGERS WHO CAME OUT TO MEET OUR MISSIONARY.
BELOW—ONE OF THE FOURTEEN VILLAGE CAMPAIGN BANDS.

What a doxology of praise rose from grateful hearts for His unfailing love! He had not moved too late behind the scenes. God's little ones, here and there over the world were moved to send their humble gifts and the treasury was replenished like the barrel of meal that wasted not, and the work went on.

His most trying fight was not over funds, but with ill health. Through what pain and weariness were gathered the gems for his crown! He was making a desperate fight with physical weakness and loving friends in the homeland knowing about it were writing, "Come home and take a good, long, well-earned rest," but he was gazing into the homes where precious souls were living and dying in the dark. He thought he saw a Hand guiding him to those lowly homes and he followed the gleam.

How often during those days he sang the Christian's bracing battle hymns. "Onward Christian Soldiers, marching as to war," and "Soldiers of Christ, arise and gird your armour on." Like David "he encouraged himself in the Lord" and marched forward. How often he said, "Christ can scatter the darkness, if His children with kindled torches shall speed forth."

"The idle man does not count in the plan of the Campaign. Let us not be too careful of the physical man," were the words he wrote to a relative. A few sentences in the same letter were "Put yourself in my place for one brief day, come close to the heart of heathendom, see and feel their deep need, and then see what your answer will be. How can I do otherwise than what I am doing? If strength fails, if life itself goes out, I shall fall where I am, and feel that I have paid my debt, and how great is that debt. I must pay it to the full with the last ounce of my blood."

"The dead have been awakened—shall I sleep?
The harvest's ripe—and shall I pause to reap?
I slumber not—the thorn is in my couch.
Each day a trumpet soundeth in mine ear,
Its echo in my heart."

Rest? Settle down in the homeland? Impossible for such a man as Charles Cowman, but he was so cheerful always, so happy, that it was difficult for anyone to believe that he was overworking; yet in my heart there were misgivings as to how the end would come. He loved his work so dearly, loved the people, and there was such a joy in serving the Master that it fairly radiated from him. Often we were away together on trips and at these times we were quite alone, a rare experience for us; and then, without interruptions, in the sequestered domain of some native inn, he would admit me into the wonderland of his inner hopes, his plans for the extension of the work, his ideas about the evangelization of the Oriental peoples. Ever I looked forward to such times as one might look forward to an excursion into some new unexpected transport of existence, for he always had new plans and wonderful things upon his heart to reveal in these byways we explored together. These were the hours that one puts away in the secret chamber of unwritten and untold feeling.

The burden of souls was ever with him and he never slipped from beneath it for one moment and it remained with him to the very end of his day.

It happened on a Sabbath morning when we were far up in the mountains with our village workers. Suddenly he said to me, "I feel very ill." A doctor was hastily summoned and after a thorough examination said, "You had better stop right now and return to the homeland." The heart was ceasing to function properly. There was no one to take his place and he believed that with care he might be able to continue a few weeks longer. A passage of Scripture made a strange impression upon him at this time (Zech. 4:9). "The hands of Zerubbabel have laid the foundation of this house; his hands shall finish it." His own name seemed to be written in this text. It came to him that day radiant with light. The words were like a diamond flash.

The fresh mountain air seemed for a time to invigorate him. There was new vitality and he continued to work, but little bits in his private diary written for no eyes but his own, told of some inner battles.

August 15. "Experienced a strange pain in my heart in the night, but prayed and it left me. I can see no place to stop in the work."

August 20. "Fight on my soul till death. God grant that 'I may see my pilot face to face, when I have crossed the bar!' "

> "How oft at the touch of that nail-scarred palm,
>   My storm-troubled soul has at once grown calm.
> The tempest that surges I will not fear,
>   For how can I sink if that Hand is near."

And the next day he said to me, "It will be so wonderful to look into the face of Christ. To see the same Face that we have seen throughout all our earthly pilgrimage,— the Christ with whom we have grown so sacredly familiar out here during these twenty years. He will be the very One who will meet us when we cross the boundary line."

Beautiful life, lived to the glory of God!

And the task of us who are left is to shape the issues of these days that the sacrifice of such a man may yet seem to have been right.

THE COMPLETION OF THE TASK

The Autumn of 1918 had come, the distribution of the Word of God to the 10,320,000 homes of Japan was nearing completion, but the leader of the Village Campaign Bands was having a battle with illness. A change of climate seemed to be an absolute necessity and after very much prayer it was decided that he should leave Japan for a few months. His only human hope was across the sea in the homeland.

"Worn out" was the term which the physician used when he called to see him ere he took the steamer for his last journey.

Those who were present in Tokyo during his last week can never forget his closing ministries. Though extremely weak in body, with his usual self-forgetfulness, he was planning for first one, then another, writing letters to his fellow-workers who were out somewhere tramping over the mountains to lone village homes. His words of counsel, his prayer, his benediction—all seemed prophetic of a veiled but most fitting farewell. Some hearts were then taken with a sharp apprehension of some momentous change to occur before they met again.

The final parting was in the early morning. A group of workers and students had already arrived at the Missionary Home, coming early from their prayer-meeting, the shine still on their faces. They felt a strange presentiment that their next meeting would be in the presence of the King, but he bade them farewell with the same old cheery smile, assuring them that he would soon be well and back at his post again, but to those who were left behind there was a premonition that they would see his face no more. There was a pathos too deep for words as he left his Tokyo home for the last time.

We boarded the steamer, but she lay in anchor the entire day. Numbers of friends and missionaries came to bid him farewell. It was night when the boat lifted anchor and put to sea and his last look at Japan was under the stars in the moonlight. Long he watched the receding shore-line, as fainter and fainter it grew. A farewell tear dropped upon the hand of her who held his and he hurried to his cabin,—to sleep? No, to pray as did his Master in the Garden when He was about to be separated from His disciples.

"I love them so dearly" were the words spoken between sobs, and his great heart was outpoured for his brethren. "Oh, how utterly vain to express the emotions of my soul! No, never, can any finite being know! Never!" were the words he said to the one at his side. He was leaving Japan for the last time. His work on the mission field was finished; the work his Father had given him to do.

The month of November was spent in Honolulu and he seemed to grow stronger, when a letter came from his dear mother conveying the news that she needed him at her side, as father was very ill. The remainder of the journey was taken. Several times the climate of sunny California had restored his nerves and renewed his strength and sent him back to the Orient a different man physically. Would it not do it again? He never ceased to pray and believe that it might. Never for a moment had the hope of returning been given up—but his closest friends knew that his missionary career was ended, that his powers of recuperation which had served him so well in the past were now spent, that his health was shattered beyond all possibility of repair.

Those who were intimately associated with him during those days could not help noticing a character mellowed and rounded out by all the work and all the suffering of his life. None could meet him without feeling the deep, strong, steady purpose of his life which was wholly consecrated to God and his fellowmen.

There is a deep truth in the words of Illingsworth: "The pleasures of each generation evaporate in air, it is their pains that increase the spiritual momentum of the world."

> "If on the brow of each were writ his heart,
> Now should the revelation make us start,
> And pity those who play the envied part."

When the steamer brought him to his native country again, it was just at the time when America was at the feet of a great explorer. The one had explored for science, the other for Christ; the one had risked life for curiosity, fame, adventure, the other to win souls to the crucified, risen, ascended, and glorified Saviour of the lost. Thousands upon thousands were doing honor to a man who lived for the world, while, excepting to the few saints even the name of Charles Cowman was unknown! Meanwhile, the noble missionary has verified the promise: "The people who do know their God shall be strong, and do exploits." Yes, exploits worth doing, and exploits infinitely greater than the discovery of continents, for the exploits of God's chosen ambassador will bring glory to Him, and joy to the redeemed through the countless ages of eternity, long after the judgment fires have passed upon this earth.

"Not unto us, O Lord, not unto us, but unto Thy Name, be the glory!"

On the first page of The Oriental Missionary Standard dated January 1918 was the word HALLELUJAH in deep outlined letters. Following it was this interesting item.

THE JAPAN VILLAGE CAMPAIGN IS FINISHED

"By the time this reaches our Homeland readers the great work of taking the Gospel to every home in Japan will have been completed. We may not have time to stop and 'celebrate,' for the very momentum of its joy, its privileges, and its newly revealed responsibilities and re- sults has pushed us right over into the beginning of a similar campaign in needy, ripe Korea where already about 10,000 homes have been reached. Beloved fellow-helpers, you who have made this work possible shout the victory with us and give Jesus all the praise that the 60,000,000 of Japanese have had the Gospel put into their individual homes, and so there is added to the marvelous ripeness of this Empire an infusion of the Word of God that awaits but the touch of fervent prayer to set this land aflame with a mighty revival. As we shout the victory and earnestly pray for the sown seed, let it be while we ad- vance and let us altogether mingle with our shouts and prayers the faith inspired cry, 'On to Korea!' "

The area of Japan is about 161,000 square miles and it has all been covered by our workers and every road and almost every foot-path traversed in seeking to reach every one of the 60,000,000 souls of Japan domiciled in over 9,000,000 homes. The total cost has been about $100,000 (£20,000). This amount has been received in answer to believing prayer.

As to the results, the day shall declare them. We leave them where Charles Cowman would have wished them to be left, at the feet of the Lord.

> "Oh, matchless honor, all unsought,
> High privilege surpassing thought,
> That Thou shouldst call me, O Lord, to be
> Linked in such work, O God, with Thee!
> To carry out Thy wondrous plan
> To bear Thy message unto man;
> In trust with Christ's own word of Grace,
> To each soul of the human race."

Space forbids writing in detail of the Korea Village Campaign which has been in progress since 1918. God's

seal has been upon it in a remarkable manner. Thousands
of villages have been reached and tens of thousands have
heard the name of Jesus for the first time through our
Korean Village Bands. Almost half of the Hermit Nation
has been completed and the glorious work goes forward
at this time (November 1928). An effort is being put
forth to reach every remaining village in Korea during
the next twelve months—then we hope to begin the greater
task—the China Village Campaign. The same plan which
God gave to Charles Cowman in 1912 is being followed.
Bands of workers are scattered about in the provinces of
Korea. They are tramping daily to the homes, carrying the
wonderful words of Life to the thirsty souls. The saints in
the homelands whose heart God touches send gifts of
$5.00 (£1) for the evangelization of a village and upon
these gifts depend the furtherance of the work. To "every
creature" said our Master. Shall we not do our best to
fulfil the commission?

HIS LAST PUBLIC SERVICE

He apparently regained his health and for a time he
seemed to recuperate greatly, but when numerous calls
for missionary meetings came they proved too much for
his fiery spirit. He made an attempt to answer them all.
Everywhere doors opened for the recital of the story of
"How the Gospel was placed in the 10,300,000 homes of
the Orient." It was indeed a great privilege to be able to
stand before great audiences and show them the map of
Japan painted a vivid red, from Hokkaido to Loo Choo,
from east to west and to say, "Our Great Village Campaign workers walked over the entire Empire, placing a
portion of the Word of God in each home. Often he
would break down in the middle of his story and weep
like a child, as the days of battle and glorious triumphs

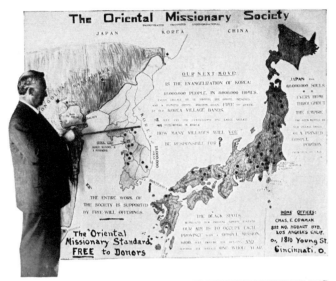

CHARLES COWMAN WAS KNOWN AS THE MAN WITH THE MISSIONARY MAP

O. M. S. BIBLE TRAINING INSTITUTE, TOKYO.

were recalled. Many a minister and audience caught a glimpse of what one man who dared believe God could accomplish, and many dear missionaries went back to their fields of labor with a fresh vision after listening to this thrilling address.

For six months he traveled incessantly in service, meeting crowds of people. Someone remarked that he must have a body of steel, as he looked the picture of health, but the candle was slowly burning down to the socket.

It was summer-time and he was traveling from a campmeeting near Toledo, Ohio, to Owosso, Michigan when a severe heart pain seized him and he was unable to proceed further. We discontinued the train journey, and hastily summoned a doctor who said to him, "You must stop your public work at once. Return to California and rest awhile." He frankly told him that his work was ended.

He obeyed the doctor, returned to California, but the heart attacks continued growing in violence and he faced the fact that he was an invalid. I marveled at the way he received the blow but found the secret long afterwards in a penciled note in his diary. "We had the sentence of death in ourselves, that we should not trust in ourselves, but in God which raiseth the dead. In whom we trust that He will yet deliver us." It was this faith that carried him through in such a calm and marvelous manner. Activity is not the only kind of service which fulfills God's will. "They also serve who only stand and wait," wrote blind Milton. Not always, however, do we accept the Master's guidance with submission and joy when He calls us away from the white fields to the lonely desert.

What a change for this keen active man! From the din of the battle to the seclusion of the sick chamber. From the glow and the glory of the work he loved so dearly, to the utter abandonment of it all. Would his faith fail now at this crucial point? Would he love Him only when the blue was in the sky and the fragrance of summer roses filled the air? Would he trust His leadings only when they led through flower-decked valleys and over sun-kissed hills? Now when the rain was falling, and the mists hung in the air, the road dark and lonely. Would he still trust on? Ah, a triumphant faith was needed just here. God gave it and he found that it was possible to bless God in the darkest hour that ever swept a human life. To rejoice with joy unspeakable and full of glory, to be ever "sorrowful, yet always rejoicing." If God was to give him songs in the night He must first make it night.

Hearts all over the world were aching and many letters were received which contained such sentences as these, "Why should such a valuable worker be cut down so suddenly? Why this stroke? Why, when the work needed such a missionary? Why? Why? That cruel word is as old as the hills.

"Dumb, because Thou didst it." *Thou.* "Even so, Father, as seemeth good in Thy sight."

The doctors would say after special diagnosis, "If we had seen you five years ago, this might have been averted. It has been caused through overwork." After they would leave the room there was usually a long silence which would be broken only by prayer, "Oh my Father, Thou knowest and it is all right." Not knowing, but trusting, Praise God!

Without those sharps and flats, the full compass of his life's music could not have been brought out. It was that stroke which gave the weapon that edge and point, that temper and polish, without which it could not have done its proper work. If the great adversary sought by that bruise to mar or destroy a chosen instrument, he was certainly disappointed; and if he thought, by making the Lord's servant often go heavily, to arrest his work, he was foiled. Charles Cowman stood still beneath the shadow of the Cross.

> "What was the answer of God's love
> Of old, when in the olive-grove
> In anguish-sweat His own Son lay,
> And prayed 'O God, take this cup away'?
> Did God take from Him then the cup?
> No, child, His Son must drink it up."
> —*Ibsen, Brand.*

"More than half beaten, but fearless,
    Facing the storm and the night,
Reeling and breathless, but fearless,
    Here in the lull of the fight.
I who bow not but before Thee,
    God of the fighting clan,
Lifting my fists I implore Thee,
    Give me the heart of a man!

What though I stand with the winners.
    Or perish with those that fall?
Only the cowards are sinners,
    Fighting the fight, that is all.
Strong is my foe who advances,
    Snapped is my blade, O Lord;
See their proud banners and lances.
    But spare me the stub of a sword."

CHAPTER XXIV

MUSIC IN THE SOLITUDES

During the summer months of 1917, it was our privilege to be with the village evangelists who were then itinerating in the mountain districts of Northern Japan. As we were going from the lowlands up to the heights, amidst the wilds of mountains, wood, and forests, a distant sound reached us—a plaintive weird melody, with touches of brightness here and there fading into a sadness that was indescribably sweet. What was it, and where did it come from?

Not for long did we have to wait for the answer, as there in the midst of the mountain solitude, under a tree, sat a native musician. He held in his hand an instrument made of bamboo which he moved gently to and fro as he blew through it, making strange melodies, which reverberated from rock to rock and peak to peak in the most wonderful echoes—tender and soft, loud and deep, dying away after a time into the most intense silence. There was a strain of melancholy about these notes as they were all in the minor key. As the sweet sound reverberated on, filling the whole air with echoes, we asked each other these questions:

"Does God speak in the solitudes? Can He make His voice to be heard in the lonely places?" Yes, God has often talked to His own in desolate places and revealed Himself to them in the solitudes, as He could not have done in the midst of busy crowds. He knows the wilderness and solitary places,—every step of the way amidst its rocks and stones, and He can utilize the barren wastes as sounding-places for His own voice.

How often during the years that followed was the incident recalled, and once, after an unusual battle with pain, Charles Cowman said to the one sitting beside him, "God gave me a song in the night and I have found sweet music even in the solitudes of the sick room."

Why not leave the story of his life just as it stands, bright, beautiful, full of life and glow? I would be untrue to my subject were I to omit the shadows which give to the picture balance and tone. But why record this? For one reason only, that some dear missionaries away from their flocks, shut up in sick rooms, or in lonely deserts, may catch the echo of a wonderful note of triumph, and through it may also learn to discover streams gushing forth in the desert place.

Charles Cowman was great as a business man; he was great before his audiences; he was great on the mission field; but he was greatest when shut away alone with God in the loneliness of the desert. All the interests that had been so dear to him were shut out from his life, yet he never lived so deeply, so triumphantly, as during those six pain-filled years. I shall ever thank God for the privilege which He gave me in being close by, to witness the anointing of that life in the twilight hour. The measure of the cost of withdrawing from the work which he so dearly loved can only be understood by knowing the fervor of his spirit. A small bungalow was now the sphere to which he found himself restricted. The keen, active man, ever ready to be on the march for His Lord was now suddenly halted. Many battles were fought within the narrow confines of that home, but they were not battles against the will of God. It was a bitter schooling, a long siege and a dreary one; but he triumphed and won his trophy, a tranquil mind conscious of power and heroic calm. He wrung a proud tribute out of sorrow, but it yielded him all its treasures. The steadfastness of his faith, revealed in the days of his tireless activity, stood out still more conspicuously during the days when he walked through the furnace of pain and agony. There are at times, glorious, heroic martyrdoms associated, not with the momentary flash of sword or kindling flame, but with the slow dreary agony of shattered nerves and throbbing brain and sleepless nights. May we not look upon such a life spread out before us as a trophy of his triumph? "I find it difficult to realize," he wrote to a heart-friend, "that I am a real prisoner, but thank God, a prisoner of the Lord. This trial may turn out to the furtherance of the Gospel and I am resting in Romans 8:28."

His friends saw him growing in patience and grace while paying the price of spiritual power and fruitfulness. Like the man named Simon who shared with Jesus the burden of the cross, he knew not what he did. He carried what he did not comprehend, he only felt the weight of the heavy load, but we who stand in the after-glow of his beautiful life can see that it was the load that glorified it. Things come to us marked in gloom and black; but Time, the Revealer, strips off the disguise and lo! what we have is blessing.

In Scotland, there is a battlefield on which the natives and their Saxon foes met in deadly conflict. No monument marks the spot, but there and only there, tradition tells us, a little blue flower grows. It is called the flower of Calodon. The baptism of blood, again tradition avers, brought the flower into fertilization. The choicest flowers found anywhere are always Calodon flowers. They spring only from the soil on which the life-blood of a brave heart has been built.

> "The mark of rank in nature is capacity for pain,
> And the anguish of the singer makes the sweetness of
> the strain."

My pen utterly fails in describing the six shut-in years, as it was an experience when all the powers of darkness seemed bent on destroying faith in God's love. Charles Cowman seemed to be in the center of a furnace seven times heated, but thanks be unto God, "even there," God held his hand and "kept that which had been committed to Him." The refining fires never raged beyond His control. The billows, which in their approach, threatened to submerge him as they came on, lifted him up to the heaven he was bound for. All the waves were crested with God's benediction.

One of the things for which he prayed more than another was that he might be "rich in faith," and God sent him to the school where the lesson is taught. He answered his prayer in His own way, permitting him to be shut-in with Himself that he might find the treasure of darkness, delivering him with such a mighty Hand that he was glad that the tempest arose, for the furious winds and tumbling seas revealed to him "What manner of Man this is."

Every morning was a miracle of resurrection and the beginning of a new day was like rising up out of death. To dare that sense of death and to launch forth morning after morning with what seemed an impossible effort, needed a faith that the reader can scarcely realize. He had never a night of whole, unbroken sleep throughout the six years, and added to it, unutterable agony when the heart attacks would seize him. It was a great furnace for a great soul, walking with death always in sight, yet his pain-lined face was aglow with the Master's joy all the time. Bloodmarks stain the steps that lead to the throne and scars are the price of scepters. Grief has always been the lot of greatness. It is an open secret.

There is a prevalent idea that the power of God in a human life should lift it above all trials, conflicts. and suffering. The fact is, the power of God always brings a conflict and a struggle. One would have thought that on his great missionary journey to Rome, Paul would have been carried by some mighty providence, above the storm and tempest and enemies; but on the contrary, it was one long fight with wild tempests, with venomous vipers, and all the powers of hell, until at last he was saved, as it seemed, by the narrowest margin, and he had to swim ashore at Malta, on a piece of wreckage and barely escaped a watery grave.

Was that like a God of infinite power? Yes, just like Him. We find St. Paul engaged in a constant conflict that never ended, a pressure persistent, but out of which he always emerged victorious through the strength of Jesus. The language which describes this is most graphic. "We are troubled on every side, yet not distressed; we are perplexed, but not in despair; persecuted, but not forsaken; cast down, but not destroyed, always bearing about in the body the dying of the Lord Jesus, that the life also of Jesus might be made manifest in our body." What a ceaseless, strenuous struggle! It is impossible to express in English the forcible language in the original. There are five graphic pictures in succession. In the first, the idea is crowding enemies pressing on every side, and yet not crushing him, because there was a way made wide enough for him to get through. The literal translation would be, "We are crowded on every side, but not crushed."

The second is that of one whose way seems utterly closed, and yet he has pressed through; there is light enough to show him the next step. The revised version translates it "Perplexed, but not unto despair." Rotherham still more literally renders it, "Without a way, but not without a by-way." The third figure is that of an enemy in hot pursuit while the divine Defender still stands by, and he is not left alone. Again we adopt the fine rendering of Rotherham. "Pursued, but not abandoned." The fourth figure is still more vivid and dramatic. The enemy has overtaken him and struck him, knocked him down, but it is not a fatal blow; he is able to rise again. It might be translated, "Overthrown, but not overcome." Once more the figure advances, and now it seemed to be even death itself, but he does not die, for "The life also of Jesus" now comes to his aid and he lives in the life of another until his life work is completed.

The texts of Scripture meant much more than others to him during those days of conflict. They were his anchors in the time of storm, anchors which firmly held. To a friend who called to see him daily, he said, "I thank God for the faith He has given me apart from His outward dealings with me. The King of saints will explain His ways." 2 Chron. 35:21, was an oft quoted text, "Forbear thee from meddling with God." To another friend he remarked, "I am in the University of Quietness, under the Master Teacher." How truly did he fulfil the qualifications of Kipling's IF.

> "If you can force your heart and nerve and sinew
> To serve their turn long after they are gone,
> And so hold on when there is nothing in you
> Except the will which says to them: 'Hold on.'"

There was absolutely nothing of the morbid invalid about him for he never allowed himself the luxury of retrospect. He was never able to brook the thought of invalidism! He went out daily for a short walk. Someone in the neighborhood saw him passing slowly by, and they inquired who he was. A neighbor's lad replied,

"Don't you know who he is? He is the *smiling invalid* who has heart trouble and faith in God." His most prominent characteristic was radiant cheerfulness and joyousness, which was both a gift and a grace. He had set his face toward the sunrising, refusing to look on the dark side, and even when pain had made its deep marks upon his body, he still claimed the title of "smiling invalid." When pain was at its height, not a murmur would escape his lips, but at such times he would often attempt to sing, and if he failed, he would ask the one who sat by his side throughout the nights to sing to him.

How little we know what unlimited service this suffering meant to prepare him for! After six shut-in years we hear him saying, "these have been the best years of my lifetime and I believe the most fruitful. Doubtless more has been accomplished for my Lord than when I was in my most active days."

Pilgrims from the army of noble workers who turned from life's fret and fever to seek an hour apart in the little home, will remember the sunny room which all looked upon as the chamber of peace. Its tranquility was the atmosphere exhaled by the sweet spirit of the self-sustained, optimistic soul, whose quietness and assurance were his strength. On his desk lay his Bibles, letters, and articles on which he was working, intending to further the cause of missions.

The little brown bungalow became a real missionary center, its influence reaching the ends of the earth. Missionaries were coming and going frequently and meeting them was one of his great joys, but these were times of pain as well, when the parting time came and they were waved off at the steamer. None but the blessed Master knew how his heart was yearning to be off with them. To those who stood by during those days there was given a fresh revelation of how much a saint could suffer and yet be silent unto God, as never a word of complaint was uttered.

> "I asked for strength; for with the noontide heat
> I fainted, while the reapers singing sweet,
>   Went forward with ripe sheaves I could not bear.
> Then came the Master, with His blood-stained feet,
>   And lifted me with sympathetic care.
> Then on His arm I leaned till all was done,
> And I stood with the rest, at set of sun,
>   My task complete."

He took the cup that God gave, quaffed its bitter dregs and stood calmly beneath His chastening rod, subdued, but not cast down. During those years, although extremely broken in body, he kept an oversight of the home office and every department of the work on the field; and in the midst of suffering was dictating letters by the hundreds. They were so full of old time fire, cheer and enthusiasm, that the recipients little imagined that they came from a hopelessly sick man. With his exceedingly limited strength he was making an appeal to the strong to keep the missionary vision; not to grow cold or lukewarm in the task of evangelizing the Orient.

Nothing cheered him more than letters from his fellow-workers on the mission field, although they added fresh fuel to the flame that was already consuming him. Letters from Brother Nakada ever added fresh fire, the old longing to be back with him again returned, and usually it was some time after receiving his letters that he would be able to settle down again to relaxation and rest. His heart was in the fight, and no far-flung battle-line struggled and swept on, without his eyes scanning the dispatches and his supply of funds and faith sustaining the fighters, for he knew that the battle was on and he was not in the van with the fighters.

While many were praying that he might be healed, one of our dear missionaries wrote to him saying, "How gladly I would die in your stead and offer myself up to God for that purpose, if He would but spare you to the work." This letter very deeply touched his heart, but he was not to get well again. The hard work, the overwhelming burden that he carried for years had sapped his vitality until there was nothing left. It was grievous to watch him during those days at the work to which he clung in spite of all his pain and our remonstrances, but the Orient with its appealing needs was graven upon his heart and he could not forget it. The really great thing in the midst of all the weariness and pain was that he never lost the missionary vision; it went right down with him to the gateway of death. Once I found him in his study with his face buried in his hands, weeping bitterly. On his desk was a map of the Orient and tears had dropped upon it. He handed me these lines of a poem he had been reading.

> "Let me go back! I am homesick
>   For the land of my love and toil,
> Though I thrill at the sight of my native hills,
>   The touch of my native soil.
> Thank God for the dear home-country,
>   Unconquered and free and grand!
> But the far-off shores of Japan for me
>   Are the shores of my Promised Land.
>
> "No longer young—I know it—
>   And battered and worn and grey
> I bear in my body the marks that tell
>   Of many a toil-filled day.
> But 'tis long to the end of a lifetime
>   And the hour for the sun to set;
> My heart is eager for years to come;
>   Let me work for the Master yet!"

There was a fresh battle and a fresh victory. Again He was enabled to say "Not my will but Thine." Oh, the blessedness of an accepted sorrow, of seeing no hand but

God's hand, of saying "The cup which my Father hath
given me, shall I not drink it?" This was greater than to
calm the seas or raise the dead. To do and suffer God's
will is still the highest form of faith, the most sublime
Christian achievement. To have the bright aspirations of
life forever blasted; to bear daily a burden and see no
relief; to be fettered by some incurable disability—to be
able to say in such a school of discipline, "It is the Lord.
Let Him do what He will:" this is faith at its highest,
and spiritual success at the crowning point. There are few
more severe tests of character than pain, but while the
suffering we cannot change, we can be conquerors. Between the pages of the book he was reading, a card was
found bearing a few lines in his handwriting. It had the
appearance of being well-worn and the words revealed
what must have been uppermost in his mind. They were
these: "He endured as seeing Him who is invisible."
"Endure when there is every external reason not to
endure."

How often during those pain-filled nights he would
walk the floor softly singing:

> "Shelter me, Lord! for the blast is strong,
> Shelter me, Lord! for the way is long;
> Cover me, Lord! for the night is cold.
> Hush me to rest, in Thine Arms enfold.
>
> *There* can I rest, without fear of ill,
> *There* find new strength, for the waves are still;
> Under Thy blood, I am cleansed from sin,
> Light evermore! Thy deep peace within.
>
> "Succor me, Lord! for the way is steep,
> Succor me, Lord! for the tide is deep;
> Strengthen me, Lord! in the path of pain,
> Jesus! draw nigh, and my soul sustain.
>
> "Shelter me, Lord! from the fiery blast,
> Shelter me, Lord! till my life is past:
> Cover me, Lord! when the night is cold,
> Hush me to rest, in Thine Arms enfold."

The memory of his low sweet voice singing, "The Song of Hope" will forever linger in the hearts of those who heard it.

> "I hear it singing, sweetly singing,
> Softly in an undertone;
> Singing as if God had taught it,
> 'It is better farther on.'
>
> "Farther on, yes, farther on,
> It is better farther on;
> What tho' life has many a sorrow,
> Why should we new troubles borrow?
> Faith can claim a bright tomorrow,
> It is better farther on.
>
> "By night and day it sings the same song,
> Sings it while I sit alone;
> Sings it so the heart may hear it,
> 'It is better farther on.'
>
> "It sits upon the grave and sings it—
> Sings it when the heart would groan;
> Sings it when the shadows darken,
> 'It is better farther on.'"

Another favorite was,

> "A charge to keep I have, A God to glorify."

He would often sing during such times of testing, "My Faith Looks up to Thee."

Like a weary child he would pillow his head on the back of an easy chair and fall asleep for a few moments, but when pain was at its height, he would say to me, "Hold my hand and sing one of the sweet old hymns for I do not wish to moan." A favorite hymn was "Take the Name of Jesus with you." Often he would translate it into Japanese and try to sing it. He had lived for them and now he was dying because of his labor for them.

To one very dear to him he wrote:

"This is the fifth year of my prolonged illness. The inward man has been wonderfully sustained and enabled to triumph day after day. How blessed is Full Salvation in such times of extremity! With every nerve quivering in agony, I can testify, 'The blood of Jesus cleanseth me from all sin.' Yes, the best hours of my illness have been when the fierce fires of suffering were kindling and scorching all around me. How soothing in the midst of suffering to feel hour after hour, the soul-cleansing blood of the Lamb! I find the Word very full of admonition to the suffering child of God and have prayed continually that He would hold me steady when the fire burned hottest. I believe He has answered this my cry."

To another he wrote:

"The surface of my soul is often furiously agitated; but I praise God who helps me to hold fast and keep still. The enemy suggests to me at times that God's promises will fail, and nothing quells the tumult like a fresh dedication of myself. This valley has been planned for me, provided for me, and is the very best place, for the Lord is with me even here and I can stake my all upon God's faithfulness. I could give you a thousand proofs of His reality and real presence. In His moment He will say, 'It is enough.'"

His faith in God's power to heal never wavered throughout the six years, a perseverance so characteristic of the man. He fought day and night with what was considered unbelief that prevented the healing touch and felt that something must be lacking in his prayers. Days and weeks were spent in searching the Word, and he kept on praying; indeed his every breath was a cry for life for his broken body. When the best physicians told him plainly that he could never hope to recover, he only smiled and replied, "But they do not know that God can heal when the case is impossible. Most of the people whom Jesus healed during His earthly ministry were impossibles." Nothing staggered his faith.

It was not merely that he desired to live, he desired to be out in the service of the King and often remarked, "If an angel should be dispatched from heaven with a message telling me I was to live twenty years longer, I would say, Praise God! Now let me return to the Orient and be spent to the very end." Often he attempted to act out his faith, and taking a few feeble steps, he would walk slowly for a block or so, when the heart weakness would seize him and he would sit on the curbstone for an hour or more waiting for strength enough to return home. After such attempts there would be added weakness for days and even weeks. It was plainly not God's will to heal him.

Thousands of people were praying for him and nothing was a greater stimulus to his faith than the letters received during those years. Several times when life seemed to be ebbing away and he was being tested to the uttermost concerning his recovery, a message would be received that would give a momentary lifting; hope would revive and a fresh grip be taken upon the promises for healing. A letter was received from a beloved missionary in South Africa. It read: "Last Sabbath I asked my congregation of Zulus to join with me in prayer for your healing and one after another prayed. One big black chief who has been recently converted prayed with tears rolling over his cheeks and it almost overwhelmed me."

Another letter was received from Korea which read: "We have spent a day in prayer for your healing. The precious Koreans fasted and prayed that health might speedily be restored to the one who had been the instrument in causing the light of the glorious Gospel to shine in their hearts." The Japanese brethren also were praying daily for his recovery and their simple prayers were answered in a measure, many times death having been held back because some one had prayed.

A prominent physician said to him, "Brother Cowman, God is keeping you upon earth a while longer because of the intercession of His children. We cannot let you go just yet." Another physician said: "I cannot conceive how Charles Cowman has lived these years. It is his indomitable will-power that has helped him to hold on so tenaciously." While this may be true from a physician's standpoint, we believe his work was unfinished and God kept him upon earth until the last line had been written, the last prayer uttered, and the blessed "finis" could be written over all. Then "God's finger touched him and he slept." Why was he not healed? We must allow God to keep some of His own secrets. "He kept the faith" which doubtless was more glorifying to God than His healing would have been. I do know that he triumphed in death and can say as did the woman who, when asked, "Is it well with thy husband?" answered, "It is well."

One night the enemy came in like a flood, suggesting to him that God did not care and that he had been signally picked out as a target while ungodly men walked about free and well. There was not a word of murmur or complaint but a great pressure rested upon his spirit. Not a word passed between us throughout the long night, but silent prayer went up to God unceasingly and near the dawning of the morning these words were illuminated. "I have prayed for thee that thy faith fail not." It was as if the Master Himself slipped into the room and reached down His own loving hand to His sick child. He wrote the words on a plain card and tucked them in a corner of a lovely picture which hangs over his desk, the picture of Christ in the Garden praying alone.

The prayer of Christ was abundantly answered and Charles Cowman's faith did not fail, although it was placed in a furnace seven-times heated. A quick fire would have been much easier to bear than the long slow fire that burned and burned on steadily for years. Thank God he kept the faith in the midst of the furnace! We often seem left to ourselves as if God did not know or care. This condition is graphically described by George McDonald:

"To trust in spite of the look of being forsaken, to keep crying out in the vast, whence comes no returning voice, and where seems no hearing, to see the machinery of the world pauselessly grinding on as if self-moved, caring for no life, nor shifting one hair's breadth for all entreaty, and yet believe that God is awake and utterly loving; desire nothing but what comes from His hand; to wait patiently, ready to die fearing only lest faith should fail—such is the victory that overcometh the world, such is faith indeed."

"Our faith," wrote Spurgeon, "is the center of the target at which God doth shoot when He tries us; and if any other grace shall escape untried, certainly faith shall not. There is no way of piercing faith to its very marrow like the sticking of the arrow of desertion into it; this finds it out whether it be of the immortals or no. Strip it of its armor of conscious enjoyment, and suffer the terrors of the Lord to set themselves in array against it; and that is faith indeed which can escape unhurt from the midst of the attack. Faith must be tried, and seeming desertion is the furnace, heated seven times, into which it might be thrust. Blest the man who can endure the ordeal!"

"Blessed is he whosoever is not offended in Me," was the word of Scripture that greatly comforted Charles Cowman's heart and which he often quoted.

In many ways our confidence in God is tested; amongst others, by the multiplication of occasions when it is possible to be offended in Him. God can bring us into strong faith only by taking great liberties with our confidence. John is in a miserable prison and hears that Jesus is raising the dead and healing the sick. Most naturally he must think that if Jesus can do that He can surely get him out of this prison. Why does He not do it? What grace it must have taken not to question why He who possessed such mighty resources should leave him there undelivered in that dungeon! But Jesus left him right there with no explanation. One word would have opened those doors and let him free. If we are to enjoy a close walk with God, we have to leave many things unexplained. We do not understand everything, but "what I do Thou knowest not now, but thou shalt know hereafter." God could take burdens out of our lives and yet He does not. These are the hours which peculiarly fit us for the inheritance of the saints in light, when Jesus puts all around us the message: "I can do it; but trust Me, though I do not do it." That is just the point where hearts break. He has all power and yet He does not mention one word to you of deliverance. These are the hours that we will study with delight and amazement in the light of eternity: no explanation; faith nourished; the prison doors left closed; and then the message, "Blessed is he whosoever is not offended in Me." That is all!

Christ did not deprive John of the unspeakable blessedness to which those come who take no offence. Had He explained He would have robbed John forever. Let us never press God for an explanation. John did much for Jesus but the greatest thing he did was his willingness to remain right on in that prison *an unoffended* soul. That will probably be his supreme honor.

The length of our life in this world is in the hands of God. We have no independent lease of life, so that we may decide of our own accord that we will remain for a year, or ten, or twenty years on earth. We have only a lease at the will of God. Elijah went when God called him. The record does not say that when Elijah saw that his work was done, he decided that it was time for him to go to Heaven; there is nothing of the kind. It is, "when the Lord would take Elijah up to Heaven."

Our lives are just as certainly at the disposal of God as was Elijah's and we have no power that Elijah did not have to stay the hand of God when He would call us away.

There were many very tender touches during this season of sorrow.

All was not shadow under the discipline of daily dying. Sorrow and joy walked hand in hand. He was "shut up to faith" and was in a place to prove the faithfulness of God. True Christian friends are among the Lord's choicest gifts in the pilgrim's path. A rich man is he who stands possessed, not of lands, or gifts, or gold, but of the love of noble souls. Although Charles Cowman was one of the busiest of men, he found time to build up friendships which were apparently as close as ties of flesh and blood, and these friendships had the seal of perpetuity. He loved his friends and true worth always found in him a sincere admirer. His friendliness had a heartiness which made itself substantially felt by those who shared it; far from an artificial, capricious, and vanishing sentiment, it became one of the realities of his life and theirs.

Throughout his long illness, kind friends kept his desk covered with cheery, comforting letters. On anniversary days his room would be filled with flowers, among them the deep red California rose, which was known as his favorite flower. What a beautiful thing is true Christian love! It means much in this busy life, when through days

23

of silences and separations, we are able to count upon true and sympathetic hearts!

Often was his heart comforted by a letter or visit from his friends, and when the cross grew too heavy to be carried alone, God sent friendly helpers to him. Even the Lord Jesus sank under His own cross and had to be helped with it by a passer-by on the way to Calvary.

His closest earthly friend was Ernest Kilbourne, his colleague. God in His tender love sent him to America six months before his Home-call and his presence was like flint to steel. What promises they claimed together, what plans they made for the furtherance of the kingdom in Oriental lands, what precious seasons of prayer they enjoyed, as unitedly they took the work so dear to their hearts and presented it before the throne!

Edwin Kilbourne also occupied a large place in his affections and a true heart's love existed between them. Charles Cowman prayed daily for him and the three "little buds" of his family.

Mr. Charles E. Sawtelle, of Cincinnati, Ohio, was one of his closest American friends. He was a former fellow-telegrapher, who later became president of a large steel plant. Not only did he bring the standards of Christ into contact with his business relations, but established a chapel and other institutions which are radiating centers of the pure and unadulterated Gospel. This kind Christian brother was one who never failed and throughout the years distributed many a strain by taking part of the load. It can be safely stated that not a day passed in thirty years that he did not mention in prayer the name of Charles E. Sawtelle.

Mr. W. J. Clark was a Los Angeles business man and when he and Charles Cowman met, a friendship began which continued for twenty years. Two brothers could not have been more alike and for years they worked together in the most loving fellowship, Mr. Clark giving his service as a love-offering to the Home Office in California. It was this kind friend who stood by his side throughout his entire illness. It seems a bit strange that just a year after his Home-call, Mr. Clark joined him in the Glory-land. They are there together, two perfect knights of God, perhaps on some fresh noble quest.

In his heart was a peculiar affection for A. I. Berninger, M.D., of Indianapolis, who was a great soul-winner. A very tender friendship which never died existed between the two men, and when Charles Cowman's life was hanging in the balance, it was this kind doctor who crossed the country to lend a hand and whisper words of consolation and hope.

The brief visits of his friend, John Shober Kimber always left a fragrance of brotherly love and sympathy. Rev. W. A. Prescott spent nights in prayer for his recovery. Mr. A. N. Clark he nicknamed "dear old faithful," because he so frequently ministered unto him. He stood at his side when the summons for his Home-call came to him. He was a "millionaire" in friends, but space forbids mentioning but a few.

What about the fulfillment of the Word, "If any man will leave houses and lands for my sake and the Gospel's?" Did this poor "Faith Missionary" come to want when he lay broken and helpless, no longer able to serve? Ah, no! It was then that the Master came forth and "carried him all the day long." When the break came, we rented a house in Los Angeles where for seven months the battle for life was waged. One day a notice was received that the house had been sold and we would be expected to move in a few days. But where? God only knew the storm that broke so suddenly upon our defenseless head. Yes, He did know, for the following day the bungalow on 256 South Hobart Blvd., was in our possession, and Charles Cowman said in his daily prayer, "God bless my beloved friend, Charles E. Sawtelle."

God never leaves us in His debt. He takes care to pay for His entertainment royally and divinely. He uses Peter's fishing-smack, and gives it back, nearly submerged by the weight of the fish which He had driven into the nets. He sits down with His friends to a country marriage-feast, and pays for their simple fare by jars brimming over with water turned into wine. He uses the five barley loaves and two small fishes; but He fills the lad with an ample meal. He sent His prophet to lodge with a widow, and provided meat and oil for both of them.

A friend sent him a gift with which to purchase an automobile. Being unable to walk more than a block or two, the car was purchased. Four months later a letter was received from a native worker which told of a great need at one of the interior stations. As he prayed and wept, he saw a way of meeting the need. The Ford automobile was sold and the station in Japan was supplied with a native worker; however, the short trips which Charles Cowman had enjoyed every day out in the fresh air were discontinued. A true missionary will challenge us with his sacrifices.

God tenderly cared for him through those broken years and nothing touched his heart more than the outpoured love of the Japanese brethren. They feared that he would lack some of the comforts of life and occasionally sent him a gift to help cover his expenses. The dear Japanese friends in Los Angeles kept him supplied with the choicest and the most beautiful flowers. How deep and genuine was their love!

A well-ordered life was drawing to its close and in his usual systematic manner, quiet preparations were being made for the harmonious adjustment of the change. When the strain of responsibility rested too heavily upon his weakened body, he called two of the trustees, Ernest A. Kilbourne and W. J. Clark, and laid the bank books together with his last signature in their hands. "The cross is not greater than His grace" and the Lord seemed to lift the burden right off his shoulders. Often he had said to me,

"As there is yet much hard work to be done, let us do with our whole heart what we can do, and what we cannot do, place in the hands of others whom we can fully trust, and then put all of it with absolute faith upon the Lord, who can and will attend to it. The time is coming when I must leave you, but the work must go right on to the glory of God." A few lines in his diary under this date express his deepest heart feelings. "My heart is kept in perfect peace as I lay down the work which has been so dear to me. It was God who raised up the work, enlarging it year after year; it was God who supplied its great need for twenty-one unbroken years; and God, our infinitely rich Treasurer, is still leading the band. As He was with us in the yesterdays, so will He be with us in the tomorrows,—the God of the changing years. The work is His, not ours, and because of that fact it cannot fail. Luther in the day of his great crisis cried out, 'Lord, thou art imperiled with us.' God has enabled us to lay the foundations, 'to lengthen the cords and strengthen the stakes' and although it shall not be my privilege to be upon earth mingling with the reapers in garnering the harvest, I shall look over the battlements of heaven and shout to my fellow-helpers now and again, 'Sail on! Sail on!'

Lovingly I turn it over into His Hand, the pierced Hand, the safe Hand. I trust Him utterly."

"There are two ways," wrote Henry Drummond, "in which a workman regards his work—as his own or as his Master's. If it is his own, then to leave it in his prime is a catastrophe, if not a cruel and unfathomable wrong. But if it is his Master's, one looks not backward, but before, putting by the well-worn tools without a sigh, and expecting elsewhere better work to do."

There seemed to be a very peculiar completeness to his days. He had no anxiety about the future of the work, it was so wholly committed into the Hand of God.

This word of admonition was given to those left behind. "I am so convinced that the work is God's that nothing from without can by any means harm it, but you must stay very close together and at the foot of the cross, where there is none of self but all of Christ. You can harm it if you allow disunity among yourselves, looking after your own personal interests and failing to be true to the vision God has given us. Read often Psalms 133. '*There* the Lord commanded the blessing.' Have fervent love among yourselves. Pray for fresh baptisms of love. Disunity cannot live in an atmosphere of love."

Was Charles Cowman's task unfinished, was his life-work incomplete? Who will dare say that it was?

ALL IS WELL

"So short the time—so much to leave undone,
Frets my impatient heart,
Hush, for with God is time. Though I've begun,
To end is not my part.

"Perfect or broken, is not mine to say;
  I can but do my best
 Until the Master bids; Leave work today
  For new work and rest.

"Rest He will give, and labor He will give
  In that day as in this,
   And love, and nothing miss."
 For life is both, and on through death we live

"Let the victors when they come,
When the forts of folly fall,
Find the body by the wall."

"Let me die working,
Still tackling plans unfinished, tasks undone
Clean to its end, swift may my race be run.
No laggard steps, no faltering, no shirking;
Let me die, *working!*"

"Anywhere provided it be forward."—David Livingstone.

CHAPTER XXV

HIS CALL TO CHINA

Charles Cowman's call to China was as definite as his call to Japan or Korea. While the work in Japan was still in its cradle days, he made a trip to China chiefly for the purpose of studying the working methods of other Societies. Ernest A. Kilbourne was his traveling companion on this quest. They made an extensive journey to inland China and on their return home spent a week in Shanghai. One day, when quite alone in a hotel, a very distinct impression came to both of them that sometime in the future, the Lord would ask them to extend their borders into China. They did not tell each other, but a very definite call for this forward movement was plainly revealed by God in giving both men the same word of Scripture at the same time. It was difficult for them to comprehend the meaning of this call and during the following eighteen years frequent comment was made upon this strange experience. No further light was received, but God kept the call before them, bidding them wait for the vision which was for an "appointed time." While waiting for marching orders they prayed.

Oftentimes through the years it looked as if the time had arrived for entering China, but each time when the door seemed to open, it closed almost as quickly and the Lord would whisper, "My time is not yet." There were tests, hindrances and times of waiting. Often during his last years, a question would arise in his mind as to the meaning of the call, now that he was a hopelessly ill man, there was no possible chance of ever seeing China. Amidst weakness and suffering, in the quiet of the sickroom, definite plans began to form themselves and the Lord's servant was able to grasp God's Hand for the advance into China.

Letters were received from the workers in Japan and Korea which told of the young Chinese students who, having heard of our Bible Training Institutes, had sought admittance in order to study the Word and to carry it back to their own countrymen. His child began to trace God's hand. Something whispered to him that God's time was near, God's rain cloud, already larger than a man's hand, could be seen on the horizon. A map of China hung on his study wall, but it also hung in his heart and he would take province after province, walled cities, destitute districts, villages and hamlets, and pray believingly for them. He was dealing with God for these places and people. Hours and hours were spent in praying for China's millions and a foundation was being laid for the new work in prayers and tears. To the one who pens these lines he would often remark: "We must 'give Him no rest' till the whole of Japan glows with the rays of the sun of righteousness, till poor deserted Korea shall arise from the dust and sing, yea, until thousands shall come from the land of Sinim (China) arrayed in white garments, redeemed by the Blood."

Added to his prayers were faith and works and although unable to walk across the floor he would sit for hours dictating letters to prayer-partners, urging them to lay hold of the promises of God for the speedy evangelization of China. In the stillness of his forced retirement, his inventive genius discovered new channels for usefulness. Instead of relaxing his efforts, or abating his desires on account of what he had achieved, he pushed forward with unabated zeal to win greater trophies. Like the devout Xavier, he prayed with unsatisfied longing, "Still more, O Lord, still more!" The time did not seem propitious as China was war-torn, yet the urge of Jehovah was Forward.

> "Columbus found a world and had no chart,
> Save one that faith deciphered in the skies."

We who looked on saw that he was overworking far beyond his limited strength. We would often feel like remonstrating with him, but he belonged so wholly to God and we realized he was not ours to keep. God in His tender love had permitted us to have such a beautiful character by our side for so many years that we did not hold him back from the God called tasks, but endeavored to lighten his loads throughout those weary days and nights and to keep pace with him. In one of Carlyle's letters are these words, "Do not pity me, rather, as a runner, that though tripped down, will not lie there but rise and run again." Christ's grace gloriously triumphed in Charles Cowman. Though placed in circumstances which might easily have turned him into a self-centered invalid, he became one of the noblest and largest hearted men. He was well aware that death might come to him at any moment. This fact, however, did not cast a cloud over his spirit, and far beyond his strength, his happy tasks for his Master were pursued with the same wonderful zest and wholeheartedness that had always characterized him. There is no more perplexing situation than one in which strength does not keep pace with spirit, yet it is an unanswered question of how much God's Hand may not be outstretched in this mystery of pain. There will be a lighting up of mysterious providence in the dear Homeland according to the Saviour's promise, "What I do thou knowest not now, but thou shalt know hereafter." The cloud which now lies so dark before us will be stricken through with beams of light from the inner glory.

Diary notes during these days are expressive of the man. "I feel so unequal to the task allotted me, but the work is God's and I can only look up to Him that He may glorify His name, in His own way. China's age-long night must end. Christ has begun to besiege this ancient and strong fortress and the work to which He has set His hands will assuredly prosper. We shall reap if we faint not. The Bible Training Institute will be built, though I may never see it.

"Was much impressed this morning with the thought that although the desire to build the temple of the Lord was strong in David's heart, he was not permitted to carry out the work himself; he was allowed to make preparation for it, but his son Solomon was appointed to build it. God will raise up and incline others to carry out our various plans. Often a believer is called to his eternal reward without being permitted to see the fulfillment of that which God's promise made him bold to take, but there can come no loss or denial to those who actually "die in the faith not having received the promises."

In 1924, he wrote to a friend, "I have the fullest faith in God that He will enable us during the coming year to launch forth and plant the banner of Holiness on China's soil." In his vision he walked over those unbuilt walls, traversing the length and breadth of them; his eyes had seen room after room before one stone was set upon another for he had prayed clear through for the building of the Bible Training Institute. Those prayers are doubtless the greatest work of Charles Cowman's life, the "finish" of the work to which God had called him. How much the work of intercession is discounted, when it is

THE COWMAN MEMORIAL BIBLE TRAINING INSTITUTE, SHANGHAI, CHINA.

by far the most important of all the dealings with God for men!

Prayers are deathless. The lips that uttered them may be closed in death, the heart that felt them may have ceased to beat, but the prayers live before God and God's heart is set upon them. Prayers outlive those that utter them, outlive a generation, an age, a world.

Two promises were continually made spirit and life to him. "Go ye into all the world—Lo! I am with thee alway" and "For I the Lord thy God will hold thy right hand saying unto thee, Fear not; I will help thee." With this rod and staff he felt secure and protected. We would often wish to take a look from Heaven's side to see how the advance of the work was connected with the suffering days, with the prayer burdens during such times, for we do know that the Holy Spirit was mightily at work.

Six months before his Home-call, he sent out a special letter to the friends telling them of the increased purpose and farther-flung plan of campaign which had widened to an undreamed-of scope, challenging them to come up to the help of the Lord against the mighty. "We are not working against uncertainties, nor afraid of the results. We have tested the power of our weapons," was a sentence in a letter. This was not a mere passing enthusiasm, but the new passion of a life. He longed to give to China the soul quickening Scriptures and his heart went out to the unreached millions.

> "And I am His—O! heart be faithful still!
> Still let Him lead me as it seems Him best!
> With Him to combat, or with Him to rest,
> March or encamp according to His will."

And what of the outcome of the vision and the call? In September, 1925, a year after his Home-call, the Oriental Missionary Society rose up to follow its beckoning

Lord and the work was launched in that great needy land.
Were you to visit Shanghai today you would find a beautiful compound of three acres covered with buildings.
On the cornerstone of the Chapel these words are
inscribed:

"The Cowman Memorial
Bible Training Institute."

Some one said, "How beautiful if he were here to
witness it all!" How do we know that he is not witnessing
it all? And more, that he is not having a hand in it all,
a hand, even greater, perhaps, than when we *saw* him
here.

Unanswered yet? Faith cannot be unanswered,
  Her feet were firmly planted on the Rock;
Amid the wildest storms she stands undaunted,
  Nor quails before the loudest thundershock.
She knows Omnipotence has heard her prayer,
  And cries "It shall be done" sometime, somewhere.
                                      —Browning.

"Take your Bible, and carefully count, not the chapters or verses, but the *letters* from the beginning of Genesis to the 'Amen' of the Revelation; and when you have
accomplished the task, go over it again and again and
again—ten times, twenty times, forty times—nay, you
must read the very letters of your Bible *eighty times over*
before you have reached the requisite sum. It would take
something like the letters of eighty Bibles to represent
the men, women, and children of that old and wondrous
Empire of China. Fourteen hundred of them have sunk
into Christless graves during the last hour; thirty-three
thousand will pass today for ever beyond your reach.
Dispatch your missionary to-morrow, and one million and
a quarter of immortal souls. for whom Christ died, will

have passed to their final account before he can reach their shores. Whether such facts touch us or not, I think they ought to move our hearts. It is enough to make an angel weep."—Rev. Silvester Whitehead.

"A stick once fire from end to end;
Now ashes, save the tip that holds the spark!
Yet, blow the spark, it runs back, spreads itself
A little where the fire was."
—*R. B., A Death in the Desert.*

"Then said Christian, 'I am going to my Father's house and
though with great difficulty I am got hither, yet now I do not
repent of all the trouble I have been at to arrive where I am.
My sword I leave to him that shall succeed me in my pilgrimage,
and my courage and skill to him that can get it. My marks and
scars I carry with me, to be a witness for me that I have fought
His battles, who will now be my rewarder.' When the day
that he must go hence was come, many accompanied him to the
river-side, into which as he went down deeper, he said, 'Grave,
where is thy victory.' So he passed over and all the trumpets
sounded for him on the other side."—Bunyan's Pilgrim's Progress.

"Whensoe'er it comes—
That summons that we look for—it will seem
Soon, yea, too soon!—Let us take heed in time
That God may now be glorified in us!"
—*H. Hamilton King.*

"Think of
Stepping on shore and finding it Heaven!
Of taking hold of a hand and finding it God's hand,
Of breathing a new air and finding it celestial air,
Of feeling invigorated, and finding it immortality,
Of passing from storm and tempest to an unknown calm,
Of waking up and finding it Home!"

"Thou hast borne . . . . and hast not fainted."

CHAPTER XXVI

IN THE THICKENING SHADOWS

"Carry me over the last long mile,
Man of Nazareth, Christ for me."

After several years of testing by pain, it seemed as if a calm and sunny ascent to the "Golden Gates" must be at its close, but instead of that it was given to the tested servant to tread a long avenue of suffering before they were finally reached. The "abundant entrance" was not yet to be. The suffering had been very acute for several weeks, the muscles of the heart were fast losing tone. How suddenly the water deepens sometimes in one's life! How little one knows the depths that lie beyond, or whether the currents be swift or still!

A few penciled notes in his diary tell of some of the dealings he had with the Lord on July 15th, 1924. "It looks as if the Lord had forbidden my return to the Orient. He was peculiarly present with me this morning about daybreak. Just what He meant to tell me, I am not certain. It may have been my healing, or it may be that He was trying to tell me that the time of my departure is at hand. I would rather remain upon earth a while longer, if it be His will, but if He wants me in His presence, I can but say, 'Thy will be done.' I am perfectly willing to leave the work I love so well in His Hands, perfectly willing to leave with Him my unanswered prayers, perfectly willing to let my body return to the dust—dust that He will watch over till the resurrection morning."

The King of kings was giving him a call. He could not clearly interpret the summons at first. How the "even

24

so Father" must have pleased Him better than to have heard praises for his healing. In every accomplished life, there comes an hour, which is, sometimes not fully understood by the suffering one or the surrounding friends. There is the natural struggle, the fervent prayer, and the deep disappointment when it does not seem to be answered. But we are sure that if we wait upon the Lord, the heart will be able, with quietness and confidence, to understand enough of God's will to triumph even in death itself.

The day following, we could scarcely speak to each other, as an unspeakable burden rested upon our hearts. There had come the intimation from the Homeland afar that he was being summoned and any attempt to speak of it brought on great heart weakness. He sat quietly by his desk and penned the lines which he could not speak. He was willing to go, but leaving me was the crucial test. However, when the hour really arrived very tenderly God's great arms of love were folded about him and marvelous grace was given.

It is hard "to take down the folded shadows of our bereavement" and hold it even to the gaze of friends and there has been some hesitancy in placing excerpts of his last messages in the biography; however, at the request of friends I have done so.

"July 16th, 1924. I thank God for you, my loved one, as for no other gift of His bestowing. You cannot know what you are to me, no words will express it. God's blessings to me have been very marked and I desire to rear a memorial to Him for His love and tender care over me, since I left all to follow Him. Everything in our lives has gone like the unwinding of a golden thread.

"I have never been more certain that my Redeemer liveth. There has been a ripening of circumstances for the event that is just ahead of us. It is a providence that seems to have been gathering for months, and now the hour has arrived. You will have no one but God, after I am gone, my dearest, but 'lean hard upon God.' As you enter the pathway of heart-loneliness, grace and comfort will be given.

"The work will need your ministry as never before. Dedicate yourself to it anew and keep close to Jesus. Complete my work and yours. The Lord has raised you up to be a witness to the ends of the earth. After a time you should go out to the Orient and see how our brethren do. Encourage their hearts and strengthen their hands. They will need you there. Live in Japan awhile and keep in close fellowship with dear Brother Nakada. I dearly love him.

"Do your utmost for the evangelization of China. See to it that Bible Training Schools are established. That is God's method. Let nothing turn you aside from it. I have prayed through for these Schools, so just follow the Lord as He leads step by step and His plan will unfold and funds will be given. 'Jehovah-Jireh.' Hold fast to the old truths and walk in the old paths. Be brave, dear heart!

"After my departure you will have to find comfort first of all, before you can administer it. Read often 1 Thess. 4: 13-18. God will comfort in His own appointed way, which is to watch for His appearing and the resurrection of those who sleep in Him. I would not advise you to spend too much time at my grave as it will only keep open the wound. I will not be there, you know. The Lord will bring you triumphantly through. He assured me yesterday that He would and there will be the sweetest reunion in the Summerland.

"You will be all alone when the beauty of the summer is gone, but there is an eternal summer. Heaven will be exceedingly beautiful and we shall dwell together there.

"Don't let the song go out of your life, my love, for your sake, for others' sake, and maybe I, too, shall hear it and be glad."

Over the real romance of his life, over the tenderest, loveliest passages in his letters a veil must be thrown, but it will not be lifting it too far to say that Charles Cowman fulfilled the ideal of a most true and perfect husband to the one woman blessed with a love that never failed. His last letter was written literally with tears and bears impressive witness to the deep affection for her who is now waiting on the earth side.

On the evening of July 17th, the Master whispered to us both, "Tonight I am going to lead you through the valley of the shadow." It was as real as if He had stepped into the room in bodily form and had spoken to us. Charles Cowman called for his friends and a little group of those very dear to him to come quickly. Among them were Ernest A. Kilbourne, W. J. Clark and A. N. Clark. When they entered the room he said to them, "I am going to Heaven tonight and wished to see you and bid you farewell." He thanked them for their ministry of love. To Brother Kilbourne he said, "What comrades we have been throughout the years! Our hearts have been knit together, no, *knit* is not the word, our hearts were *burned* together. What a glorious time we have had out in the Orient! I have no regret that my life is slipping away because of what I have done for my heathen brothers. I am glad, oh, so glad!

To each of his fellow-missionaries a message was given, then a word to the native workers. To dear

Brother Nakada and the Japanese brethren tender messages were sent. After them the Koreans were remembered. None were forgotten. He sent words of appreciation and love to his friends in England, the Misses Crossley and Hatch, elect ladies who had stood so nobly by the work for more than twenty years. To Mr. David Thomas he sent the message, "Press on." To Mr. Geo. Wooster, "Walk in love as dear children." These were Holiness leaders greatly loved by him.

To the "Revivalist Family" he sent special thanks for all their outpoured love throughout the years of his missionary career; to the trustees he sent special love; to his greatly loved friend, Charles E. Sawtelle, he sent a word of tender thanks; to The Oriental Missionary Society family scattered throughout the earth he sent a loving farewell message, exhorting them to press the battle to the gates until Jesus comes. His message to the friends of "The Little Brown Church" was, "Tell them that Charles Cowman dies a witness of the saving power of those precious truths which have been taught and believed and experienced among us from the beginning."

Following farewells came the plans for the work so dear to him. The Orient was uppermost in his thought and it will take years to completely execute the plans so clear in his mind to the very last. Full and complete suggestions have been left for those who were to take up the work where he left off. How beautifully God arranged it that Brother Kilbourne could be near him during his last six months upon earth! We read of Jonathan and David in the last interview they had together, that "Jonathan came to David *there* and strengthened his hand in God." All that text means is not easy to write, but our hearts interpret the words and the readers can imagine the holy encouragement.

The entire evening was made glorious by his utterances. Now and then he would shout out, "I feel so clean, the Blood of Jesus cleanseth me from all sin. The water is getting deep, but my anchor holds." There were sweet personal messages, which may not be given to the outside world. These are kept among the sacred private treasures of memory by those for whom they were spoken. God did not permit the pathos to overwhelm us; on the contrary, all present experienced a lifting in spirit and none could shed a tear. It seemed like a farewell service to some missionary who was bound for a far-off clime, and we were standing on the shore waving him off.

There came sweet peace to our hearts and we knew that the Master had a great work to be done by his death which could not have been accomplished in any other way. We do not know what or how; perhaps never shall, but it is even so, for He worketh His own will; yea, and will work. Charles Cowman was calling back to us that the end was worth all his toil. What a wonderful thing to shout back from the grave and say, "I have not a regret. It was worth it all." We felt as though we had been on the Mount of Transfiguration and had caught a glimpse of Paradise through the Gates Ajar.

For more than two hours he talked until he seemed satisfied. He then turned to me saying, "I must now bid you goodbye, the last one of all." Permit me to draw a veil over the scene. It was a beautiful, peaceful, loving parting and God did not fail us in giving great grace. After this farewell he said, "Now I am all ready to go. Please Jesus, take me at Thy moment." We looked on with breathless awe at the blood-washed saint as he started down the lone valley. We had paused at its entrance for the farewell when there came a conscious moment and each one felt that he had taken the last step with him. Literally placing his tired hand into the hand of the Good Shepherd, he said, "Now I am off alone, yet not alone, for Thou art with me." He then started to sing with a rich clear voice,

> "'Tis so sweet to trust in Jesus,
> Just to take Him at His Word,
> Just to rest upon the promise,
> Just to know thus saith the Lord."

We joined him in the song and helped to sing it clear through until we came to the last line which he finished alone.

> "For I know that Thou art with me,
> Will be with me to the end."

What was at the further end of the valley through which we were not permitted to travel with him? How very little we know, we cannot even surmise, but his Shepherd was with him and he wished us to sing, sing all the time. What victory! What triumph! Being very weary he pillowed his head on his chair as he had not been able to lie down in many months. And there he slept quietly throughout the night. Oh, what a picture of perfect peace! When the day dawned he was still upon earth and he exclaimed, "Oh, how strange it all seems! I thought I would surely be in Heaven this morning! In his face was a look of keen disappointment.

A saintly minister once said, "If the feet of a child of God were nine tenths through Jordan, he would bring him back again, if his plans were unfinished." God had another testimony for him to give. His dear aged mother who was in the East had been summoned and was enroute to California, praying earnestly, "Oh God, spare my boy until I see him and have just one more conversation with him. Let me hear him again speak the word, 'Mother'

before Thou dost take him Home." She arrived on July
17th and God gave strength for the answer to her heart-
cry, but the Charles Cowman we knew was changed,
utterly changed from that day. He lived and breathed,
but did not belong to earth.

A severe lesson to be learned was yet in store for this
tested servant. Dear heart of fire! His lamp had to burn
down to the last drop of oil. On the night of July 17th,
there came a stroke, which paralyzed his entire left side
and the doctor said he could only live several hours, but,
in that low valley he lingered throughout the month of
August and greater part of September. They were mystery months and the suffering was very keen. Often
came the question to our hearts, "Does the Lord mean to
raise him up? Is He taking him down to the very brink of
the grave to show him that He is able to raise him up,
almost from the dead?" We did not know just how to
pray after that memorable night when the Lord led us
so wondrously. Occasional rallies took place, raising
hopes which were quickly abandoned. These occurred at
frequent intervals, followed by a condition of increased
weakness and suffering.

There is something divinely pathetic about a soul that
stands upon the border of a great new country beyond.
There is always something that strikes a tender key about
a life that is so soon to be merged into the fuller life of
immortality. It is only when the leaves have left the tree
and the bare arms are lifted against the clear winter sky
that you can see how every tendril, every twig turns
Heavenward and, looking upward through the bleak and
bitter blasts, waits to be clothed upon with immortality.

One thing above all else that Charles Cowman feared
was that in some tremendous hour of testing, he might
be tempted to doubt the promise. It was not deliverance

from pain that he asked for, but that he might be able to stand in the midst of wreckage and say, "I believe God." This desire was gloriously fulfilled for frequently he whispered, "I am trusting Thee, Lord Jesus."

When the first stroke came and he lay in a low valley, the doctor said, "There is danger of another stroke which will paralyze the right side also." He drew me close to him and whispered, "Never mind even if the other side does paralyze, that will be nothing to God. If He wishes to heal me, He will do so in His own moment so let us trust Him." Smithfield's fires did not make martyrs, they only revealed them.

One morning after an unusual night of suffering, his nurse went to the victrola and played the record "Carry your Cross with a Smile." He looked at me pleadingly and said, "I cannot." Assuring him that throughout his entire illness he had been able to smile at pain, I sought to encourage him, even though my own heart was breaking. The day wore on, there came again another long, long night. In the morning the nurse said to me, "Mr. Cowman has been smiling all through the night." He called me to him and whispered, "I can." His faith was triumphant and his courage unweakened. What a triumph!

Often he was in a delirium and he was always moving among his friends in the Orient,—the dear native people, preaching to them, living out his old heroic role; or else he was most earnestly addressing his fellow-workers, urging them to a life of constant waiting upon God, that their labors might become more fruitful. Once he imagined that he was among the native preachers arranging for a great Yearly Convention. He said, "If our native brethren drink deeply of the living water, then according to the sure Word of promise, out of them shall flow rivers of

living water, and the entire land will feel the power."
His last intelligible words as he addressed this imaginary
gathering was, "Sail on, my brethren! God is with us and
we cannot fail."

During his waking hours he exhorted us as he had
never exhorted before and in the delirium of sleep he would
break out in the most impassioned appeals to the church
to awaken from her sleep, and stand by the cause of
foreign missions. When we did not know whether he was
with the angels or with us, with one foot on the other
shore, he shouted back to us, "Tell the people not to let
the warmth go out of their hearts." One night in a
delirium he spoke for a full half hour on the need of
God's children taking advance ground in sending the
Gospel to the heathen. He said to me, "Help me to get up,
I am going to preach tonight." Asking him to what
church he was going, he replied, "I am speaking at Christ
Church at a missionary meeting and my text is Eph. 5:14,
'Awake thou that sleepest, arise from the dead, and Christ
shall give thee light.'"

He then added, "From now on in every meeting where
I shall speak, I expect to combine foreign missions and
the Lord's coming." He loved His appearing and said on
that particular night, "Mother, are you ready for the
coming of our Lord?" She replied in the affirmative. The
nurses were then questioned, and he finally said to me,
"My dearest, is His coming more than a doctrine to you?
Is His coming a living hope? Assuring him that it was, he
then requested me to sing his favorite hymn,

"It may be at morn when the day is awaking,
 When sunlight thro' darkness and shadow is breaking,
 That Jesus will come in the fulness of glory
 To receive from the world His own.

O Lord Jesus, how long, how long
Ere we shout the glad song,
Christ returneth, Hallelujah! Hallelujah! Amen!
Hallelujah! Amen!

He tried to join in the chorus repeating "Christ returneth Hallelujah!"

On September 15th, a great change became apparent.
I lingered near his side and asked him for a word of
Scripture. He quoted passage after passage, clearly indi-
cating that they had entered into the very fibre of his life.
He lay feeble and languid and in the afternoon asked for
hymns and we sang another favorite,

> "Hail, thou once despised Jesus,
> Hail, thou Galilean King.
> Thou didst suffer to release us,
> Thou didst free salvation bring."

He then requested us to sing, "All Hail Immanuel."
He joined with us in singing the words, "King of
Kings and Lord of Lords." When the last verse was
ended he remarked, "I love that hymn and shall soon see
Him face to face." He rallied again and his friends were
summoned. His mind wandered on old themes and he
especially requested the reading of Gal. 2:20. He paused
awhile before he passed on into the glory that awaits. It
was as though his boat had sailed out of the storm,
under the lea of a sheltering clift, and had a bit of sea yet
to pass before it came into the final harbor.

Again and again it came to us in the day watches and
in the night watches between those memorable dates Sept.
1-24, the words of Scripture, "And sitting down they
watched Him there." It was about all that we could do.
Singing was all that we could do to rest him while the
dear, great heart was ebbing out to sea. "Lead Kindly
Light amidst the encircling gloom, lead Thou me on, O'er

crag and torrent till the night is gone!" We knew that he was passing over crags and through torrents and the old familiar hymns soothed and quieted amid the paroxysms of pain.

To those who stood by watching as he lay in the deep mists of the valley of the shadow and saw the earthly lights dimming more and more, there came the thought that his work for China had come to an abrupt ending, but there were found in a small notebook on his desk a few scribbled notes dated June 12th, 1924. "I have had definite dealings with God today. He spoke to me about China, assuring me that we would open a Bible Training Institute and that thousands of Chinese would be trained and sent out through the length and breadth of their land. 'Hath He spoken and shall He not make it good?' There shall be a harvest in China and if He calls me Home before its accomplishment, He may have something for me to do from the Heaven side."

Death closes the doorway upon earthly service, but whatever door it may open to other forms and spheres of activity, we have but an intimation. We know that "they rest from their labors," the toils and tasks that left marks of weariness upon their bodies,—"but their works,"—activities for God—"do follow them," for "His servants shall serve Him day and night in His temple." We shall awake to find that the future life is a grand consummation of the present, and Heaven with its higher service is ours in Jesus Christ. I cannot think of Charles Cowman as being inactive, although he has gone to his everlasting rest. I think of him still working for the evangelization of the Orientals.

On September 23rd, in the evening, his friend, W. J. Clark, called, bringing an exquisite night-blooming cereus.

It had reached perfection that very night and the sight of that fragile but beautiful flower, that blooms but once and then dies when it has reached its height of beauty, spoke volumes to our hearts, but there was an inbreathed peace.

> "Peace—perfect peace shadowing us and ours?
> Jesus hath vanquished death and all its powers."

Oh, there were breaking hearts around him as he lay there so still with pulse fluttering and heart beating rapidly, but in the midst the peace which passeth understanding kept our hearts.

"I have felt the death-chamber," wrote Bramwell Booth, "to be like unto an artist's studio, in which the last touches of beauty were added to the glowing canvas before exhibition, and the judging of the honors. A finishing—maybe in agony and with all the marks of physical humiliation, but a finishing none the less, of a great work already done and a gentle yielding of life's labors and its fruit into the hands of God, amid calm assurance of faith alone.

"Life would be incomplete without death. Waiting on the frontiers of the eternal world, they often do more in a few hours in the light which falls upon them there than by years in the twilight on this side. Instead of a crumbling past, we see already something of the works which follow them. And so death is not only conquered, but made to aid their triumph, harnessed to their chariot wheels—in short, swallowed up in victory."

"More pilgrims upon the road, more pilgrims came to town, and so many went over the water and were let in at the Golden Gates today."

Wednesday, September 24th, was a typical California day. Nature clothed hill and dale with life and beauty, and the brightness of the upper courts seemed reflected upon the earth. A fleecy cloud floated through the heavens. The birds sang on, just as if the world had no grief in it. Flowers filled the sick chamber, gifts of those who loved him. In hundreds of towns, villages and hamlets in Japan and Korea, the people were wending their way to churches that he had been instrumental in giving to them. Many of the dear native people had never seen his face, and little realized how blessing and salvation had come to them, because for a quarter of a century he had planned, prayed, worked, with their faces ever mirrored in his heart and with their salvation uppermost in his mind. They went to their houses of worship while their friend and missionary was gradually sinking into the sleep which has no earthly waking.

Slowly the sun went down behind the mountains, flooding the valley of life. Twilight fell and deepened into a perfect autumnal evening. In the gloaming we watched, waited until the midnight hour. Ebbing out to sea—dear, great heart! He looked like a picture of peace. How we yearned that he might be able to tell us when he caught sight of Heaven's glory! How we longed for just one more word, but we only had the reflection of the glory through the fragile clay and it said plainly to us, no need of light there, for the glory of God did lighten it. The clock tolled half past twelve, the eternal gates were open, and all the weariness, the painfulness, the watchings, the fastings, the hunger and thirst, were passed. Charles Cowman had reached Home. His warfare was accomplished. God had lifted his cross and given him his crown. In faith he went down to the shadowy river; in this faith he passed over to the other side.

I knew that my earthly anchorage was gone; that the little brown home in the west was henceforth a house, and not a home; that I was alone. "It was too hard for me; until I went into the sanctuary of God." Psa. 73: 16-17. What shall I do? I can only say that I go forward to fill up the measure of service required of me; to take up the thread that he was weaving, when his dear, tired hands were folded, for the consciousness of fulfilling his wishes is one of the chief joys of my life.

> "So long Thy power hath blest me, sure it still
> Will lead me on, o'er moor and fen, o'er crag and
> torrent, till the night is gone."

"I thank Thee, O Father, there is here a memorial to human friendship, I thank Thee that Thou hast suffered Elisha to be swayed by the memory of a departed friend; it is Thine own imprimatur on the sacredness of earthly love. Thou wouldst tell me that the fire of death cannot burn up the mantle of earthly influence. Teach me that Elijah can finish his work from beyond the grave. Teach me that a departed life may hold in my heart an empire which no present life can claim. So shall I learn the immortality of love."—George Matheson.

"O God of Love! prepare us who are groping our way, catching glimpses of shining feet that mock our haste, searching for loving hands we may not clasp, prepare us for the immortality and blessed companionship, when life's work is done. We shall overtake those who are gone. There must be healing in the glorious future; we can wait 'earth's little while.'"

Those passing by the home, noticed on the door, not the black crepe symbolic of mourning, but a bouquet of lovely flowers, and they knew that the "smiling invalid" had slipped Home. In accordance with his wish, there were no tokens of death to be seen. He also requested that his relatives should wear no mourning. Especially did he ask that his companion wear white for he had said to her: "It will be my coronation day and why should you be dressed in black, symbolic of death."

The day following dawned in splendor and stillness. Birds and flowers vied with each other for supremacy, the haze of a lovely Indian summer rested on the golden hills.

The service was held in Trinity Missionary Church, a church he had helped to pray into existence, and one which he greatly loved, as it was a live missionary church. Many had been the times when he had stood in the pulpit telling the crowds of the great, white harvest fields. Many times had he attended farewell missionary services for outgoing missionaries. It was a hallowed place to him for his dearest earthly friends were members there,—true friends who loved not only him, but the work for which he laid down his life. It was in this pulpit that he had given his last missionary message, one which ended with a strange outburst. When he concluded his message, someone started the grand coronation hymn,

> "All hail the power of Jesus Name,
> Let angels prostrate fall
> Bring forth the royal diadem,
> And crown Him Lord of all."

There was such a paean of praise bursting forth from every heart that it seemed as if the whole wide world must have caught the echo. All present sensed something heavenly and spoke of it later.

The funeral service was exceedingly simple, all ostentation and show being avoided. Friends covered the casket with their choicest wreaths. The pulpit was banked with California's loveliest flowers. The service was at 2:00

o'clock and the church was filled with friends, who had come from surrounding towns and suburbs. Rev. Jos. H. Smith, President of the National Holiness Association, and a warm friend of Charles Cowman had charge of the service.

Two of his favorite hymns were sung, "It may be at morn when the day is awaking that Jesus will come" and "The Home of the Soul."

Earth-life is but a tent life after all. Our real home is in the many mansions yonder, while the years of eternity roll, never ending. Heaven is not a prison with tier upon tier of cells; but a HOME. And what is home without the recognition and love of fond hearts? So long as we read of David going to his child; of Paul anticipating the pleasure of meeting again his converts; of the women and the disciples being able to recognize the Saviour amid the glory of the resurrection body—we are prepared to believe, with the patriarch, that dying is re-union with those to whom in the deepest sense we are related. Spiritual affinities are for all time and eternity, and will discover themselves through all worlds.

Brother Kilbourne attempted to speak about his departed comrade, but could not finish as the heart-wound had been too deep. He read the telegrams and cablegrams which had come from many distant friends. The cablegram from the Japanese church read, "Our deepest sympathy," from Korea, "Child of my love, lean hard." The Chinese students' message read, "Joshua 1:9." A note of triumph was dominant and it seemed more like a rousing missionary meeting than a funeral service. That would have been in accord with his deepest wish. To many the Word came with fresh meaning, "There is no death" for death "has been swallowed up in victory."

25

Those who were present will not soon forget the tribute paid to the still form wrapped in its death sleep. How full of gratitude and loving reminiscence! What reference to the self-sacrificing life! One spoke as follows: "None present today can but say that something irrepressible and invisible, prompted and guided this remarkable missionary to the scene of his labors in the Far East, among the heathen. Upon that scene he stands in competition, I am glad to believe, with many saintly, holy men. I am glad that from the Church of our day there have gone forth such men as William Taylor to Africa, Morrison to China bearing upon their labors a very heroic and apostolic stamp. But I rejoice not less unfeignedly to recollect that they have competitors and rivals in that noble race of Christian warfare, among whom was Charles Cowman. Let no man envy them their crown which they have earned, but let everyone know that they now stand in the presence of God before Whom we shall all appear. Rejoice that they have fought a good fight, that they have run their race manfully and nobly.

"It was a marvel to those who were close enough to our Brother Charles Cowman to know the high tension under which he worked, that he stood the strain as long as he did. He never let up. Day and night, month in and month out, year in and year out, he kept up the terrific pace. For several years before his breakdown, his friends knew the pace he set for himself was telling on his health and strength. They urged him to adopt a more moderate pace, but Charles Cowman pushed on. The one word that best describes his character is—*intense,* and he was so in a large and fruitful way. Many men at seventy have not accomplished what he did at the age of fixty-six. During all the years he was in the work he stood in the blaze of that fierce light which beats against the throne, but it can

be said of him as of another that 'the fiercest ray found
no flaw in his armour, no stain on his shield.' The
Charles Cowman of intense application, of furious work,
of highest ambition, was such because he wanted to be
the Charles Cowman of completest service. 'Ich diene' was
the motto emblazoned on his banner. He fulfilled it to the
uttermost measure.

"His work will go on. God will raise up an army of
men and women who will 'carry on.' There will be no
backward steps because a great leader has fallen. Great
as was Charles Cowman the cause for which he gave his
busy life is greater than any man. God reigns and will
produce others who will lead the great missionary army
to yet greater victories. If he could speak to us today, I
am quite certain he would say, 'Sail on! Your Captain
leads the way!'"

Another spoke as follows:

"How unutterably complex are the ways of Providence! How unprepared is the world to dispense with
the services of such a worker as Charles Cowman! It
seemed that he must be spared a few years longer to
travel over the world stirring up young and old to their
duty to the heathen. It looked from the human standpoint
as if he could not be spared from the Missionary Society
of which he was the founder and president, just at the
time when China is ripening to which he looked forward
with the keenest joy in entering. But we must allow God
to keep His own secrets. All the mysteries of His providence God himself understands, and this ought to be enough
for our peace. There are no broken columns in cathedrals
God builds—no unfinished arches. Who knows but that
by his death, our dear brother may be even a greater
blessing to the Oriental Missionary Society than had he
lived. Who knows but that he will be doing a greater

work for China than had he continued to live on imprisoned in a suffering body. God's way of dealing with us cannot be traced for His footsteps are in the trackless sea,
but He surely leads and He surely loves.

"If someone asks 'Why did he die?' I would reply, 'I
cannot tell.' I can only say that God knows when men
ought to die. It would seem wise to leave the matter with
Him. Nay, it would be strangely unwise to intermeddle
with His disposal of His own. Some life-tasks are completed in a few quick, pulsating years, and the laborer
may fitly rest. Some can only be accomplished in the
course of a long weary struggle. To some it is appointed
that they should traverse 'the great way round,' while
others may take a direct pathway to the goal. But God
knows. There are those who have lived most who have
done least and those who have done most have lived, in-
years, the least.

"The influence shed forth by Charles Cowman's life,
example, and teaching was never greater than it is today
and it will be even greater tomorrow. His sun went down
in all the splendor of a glowing faith and self-sacrifice
and just how far reaching the influence of his life was,
none of us can possibly estimate. It is not how long a man
lives that counts; it is what he puts into life while he is
living. Charles Cowman has lived about three times longer
than any other missionary of his generation, for he surely
put into the last twenty-five years three times as much as
the ordinary worker. His name is on the honor roll of the
world's history. The faithful warrior is home to-day
'waiting for the morning.'"

The closing note was as the opening one, praise to
God for what He had made of His humble servant and
for what He had wrought through him for the evangeliza-

"Still on the lips of all we question,
  The finger of God's silence lies;
Will the lost hands in ours be folded?
  Will the shut eyelids ever rise?
O friend, no proof beyond this yearning,
  This outreach of our hearts, we need;
God will not mock the hope He giveth,
  No love He prompts shall vainly plead.
Then let us stretch our hands in dark-
    ness,
  And call our loved ones o'er and o'er;
Some day their arms will close about us,
  And the old voices speak once more."
                              —*Whittier*.

"TILL THE DAY BREAK."

tion of the Orient and the quickening of missionary interest in the homelands.

The body was taken to beautiful Hollywood Cemetery. A number of ministers were there, leaders of missionary societies, old friends, a host of godly Christians who knew that a great missionary was being laid to rest.

At the graveside Rev. Joseph Smith said, "A precious worker has been removed from our midst and the responsibility has fallen upon us to stand in the breach and fill up the gap. More than ever do we need to pray for the work which this dear brother has laid down. I shall ever remember him as the missionary with the map of the Orient as I found it in every meeting where he was speaking on missions. Let us give ourselves afresh to the work; let us pledge ourselves to pray for it and around this newly opened grave may our interest in the missionary work be revived. God bless the Society bereft of its founder and raise up scores of young men and women to step into the breach."

The cemetery was bathed in sunshine and amid sunlight and flowers and the throb of human sympathy, the brief service ended. The grave was covered with flowers and he was laid where the shadow of a great cypress tree lies each afternoon. There California holds him close to her heart,—precious dust over which He will watch until the resurrection morning.

We left him under the lilies, a covering no more stainless than the one who lay beneath it. The sun was westering when we left that sacred mound. There was a soft afterglow and the hush of Heaven rested on vale and hill. Here then, we leave him, and we go forward inspired by the light of the life which, like a star serene and inextinguishable, "flames in the forehead of our morning sky."

His grave is a place which may well quicken the consciences and purposes of those who desire to "occupy" with their talents, "while it is day."

Immediately, friends wrote saying: "By all means let us have a memorial to him. But where? Not in painted window, nor a great pile of stone, but out in China, a Bible Training Institute, where the prayers of his suffering years will have an answer."

Shall it be thought strange that two days after the funeral, a letter was received addressed to him? It was from a beloved fellow-worker who knew nothing as yet of his translation. It read thus:

"Dear Brother Cowman:

"My heart is burdened over China and I wish to do something to assist you and will send $25,000 (£5000) soon for the erection of the Bible Training Institute."

How I wished that it had been received earlier, but I am sure the Lord would never have kept it from Charles and into my sore heart there came a consciousness that he knew and there was rejoicing in Heaven.

—o—

"One night, lying on my couch when very tired, my children all around me in full romp and hilarity and laughter, half awake and half asleep, I dreamed this dream: I was in a country. It was not in Persia, although more than oriental luxuries crowned the cities. It was not in the tropics, although more than tropical fruitfulness filled the gardens. It was not in Italy, although more than Italian softness filled the air. And I wandered around looking for thorns and nettles, but I found that they did not grow there; and I saw the sun rise and watched it set, but it set not. And I saw people in holiday attire, and I said, 'When will they put off all this, and put on workman's garb, and again delve in the mine or swelter at the forge?' But they never put off the holiday attire.

"And I wandered in the suburbs of the city to find the place where the dead sleep, and I looked all along the line for beautiful hills, the place where the dead might most blissfully sleep, and I saw towers and castles, but not a mausoleum or a monument or a white slab was to be seen. And I went to the chapel of the great town, and I said; 'Where do the poor worship, and where are the benches on which they sit?' And the answer was made me, 'We have no poor in this country.'

"And then I wandered out to find the hovels of the destitute, and I found mansions of amber and ivory and gold; but not a tear could I see, not a sigh could I hear; and I was bewildered, and sat down under the branches of a great tree, and I said, 'Where am I and whence comes all this scene?' And then out from among the leaves and up to the flowery paths and across the shifting streams, there came a beautiful group thronging about me, and as I saw them come I thought I knew their step, and as they shouted I thought I knew their voices, but they were so gloriously arrayed in apparel such as I had never before witnessed, that I bowed as stranger to stranger. But when again they clapped their hands and shouted, 'Welcome! Welcome!' the mystery all vanished, and I found that time had gone and eternity had come, and we were all together again in our new home in Heaven.

"And I looked around, and I said, 'Are we all here?' And the voices of many generations responded, 'All here!' And while tears of gladness were raining down our cheeks, and the branches of Lebanon cedars were clapping their hands, and the towers of the great city were chiming their welcome, we all together began to leap and shout and sing, 'Home, home, home, home!' "—*T. Dewitt Talmage.*

APPRECIATIONS

From a fellow-telegrapher, Mrs. Fannie E. Ham.

"While working in a testing station for the Postal Telegraph Cable Company early in the year 1904, I received a sample copy of 'Electric Messages,' the paper then published by the Oriental Missionary Society. I read it through with great eagerness and immediately forwarded my subscription.

"A short time before a friend had gone to Japan as a missionary under the Presbyterian Board and because of that fact I was intensely interested in everything pertaining to the Sunrise Kingdom.

"Very little was published in the daily press regarding Japan in those days and it seemed to me a land very far away whose people were quite unknown to me; therefore a paper published monthly in the city of Tokyo was a prize well worth securing.

"There was another reason for desiring that little paper regularly; it was published by telegraphers and was full of little telegraphic touches. I had not then heard of the Mission Band in the Chicago office and had never known a missionary to 'evolve' from a telegraph operator.

"Such development was interesting, and, as I entered my office each morning, I cut a plug into a spare wire to represent the new prayer line to Tokyo.

"That old switchboard was long ago discarded for a more modern one and the office has been twice moved, but communication with Japan has never ceased and the invisible current still flows on.

" 'Electric Messages' had started on its second year of publication when I subscribed, but all the previous numbers were sent me so that I have a complete record of Oriental Missionary Society activities, first in 'Electric

Messages' and later in 'The Oriental Missionary Standard.' "

"I never knew to whom I was indebted for that first sample copy; therefore the Lord has had all the credit.

"In 1906 I had the pleasure of hearing Brother Cowman and his wife speak of their work at a near-by camp-meeting and a few years later had the honor of their presence in my home when they spoke in neighboring cities.

"I cannot tell all the Society has added to my life these past twenty-two years.

"There has been the joy of having a small part in a great work; the knowledge that a new light is shining in the dark places of earth, giving 'beauty for ashes, the oil of joy for mourning, and the garment of praise for the spirit of heaviness,' a new and deeper interest in *all* missionary work; the blessed fellowship of prayer and the richness of rare friendships which are to be eternal.

"He who is in the Celestial City, receives honor from God (1 Sam. 2:30. John 12:16) and needs not the praise of earth.

"His loyalty to the highest standards of spiritual life and experience was helpful to many in the homeland 'In the midst of a crooked and perverse generation' and his influence is still active in their lives."

—o—

From a Presbyterian Minister.

"My dear Mrs. Cowman:—

"I wish to express to you my deepest heartfelt sympathy in this your greatest loss. Not *your* loss alone, but the missionary world has lost one of its great men. I have followed with intense interest yourself and Mr. Cowman throughout your entire missionary career and have daily prayed for you. I loved your husband in a manner that I do not think I ever loved another man. He was very lovable and while we differed very widely in doctrine, and I have never been able to see sanctification in the way he taught it, yet *he* saw it in the Book and 'adorned the doctrine.' Every honest-minded man is bound to be extreme, and by extreme I mean definite. I admired him for his faithfulness to what he saw in the blessed old Book, the Bible. I admire his firmness, his steadfast spirit. We had some very precious and hallowed seasons of prayer together, and when I reach Home, and by God's grace I intend to reach that happy place, I expect to meet my beloved friend and brother. His life influenced me in a way, a peculiar way, which I cannot quite express in words. I wanted to live closer to God after being with him for an hour and I longed for the deeper life which he ever lived."

—o—

A fellow-missionary wrote: "It will be difficult for those of us who were so closely associated with Brother Cowman to believe that he is actually away. His kindly, wise, and yet firm spirit will brood over our committee meetings and will have a part in every plan and program, looking forward to the time when every creature shall have heard the Gospel message. He has handed us a torch which he could no longer carry, and we must carry it until every man, woman, and child from the vast Orient has been told the story of Christ."

—o—

From Mr. C. E. Sawtelle:

"To the biography of my very dear friend, Mr. Cowman, I would like to add a few words of tribute.

"We were associated together in the telegraph office

at Chicago for a few years where I learned not only to respect him, but to love him, as did many others.

"Two things were very conspicuous in my dealings with him, and in watching his personal work. First, his persistency in aiming at and shooting at his game, gun always loaded, cocked and primed. Among the other men, several hundred, was one of his superior officers, a man who had been reared by a Christian mother, but who had wandered away into worldliness.

"At times when there was a 'let up' in the work, which occurred for a few moments, Charles Cowman watched for his opportunity. Nothing daunted, he proceeded to his desk and asked for a few moments' chat—never fearing the possibility of a discharge. He was greatly repulsed by some such comment as 'I know what you are about to say. I'm not interested,' but Charles Cowman had a new tactic for each rebuff. The last case so far as I know, before he left his position to go to Japan, was when he asked directly, 'What would your old mother think if she knew of your life and wickedness.' Shortly after this, their courses diverged and God alone knows the final result.

"The other thing in Mr. Cowman's life which made a strong impression upon me was his *energy*. There were a dozen or more men in the same or similar duty in the office, but of them all he was the conspicuously energetic man. *No man could accomplish as much in as short a time*.

"He was booked for a much higher official position with the company, but was in no way interested, greater things being on his heart.

"After he started in his missionary work, with the two above factors, is it any wonder that I expected to see results? If energy, zeal, and persistency permeated his life, when devoting his time to the affairs of the world so necessary and justifiable, though his heart beat with desire for labor in the Master's field, is it any wonder that my eyes followed the work in which he was engaged with such interest and rejoicing?

"And how many times have I referred to his case when talking with young people, as an example of what can be accomplished from a business point of view as well as religious.

"His faithfulness was never questioned. Carrying Charles Cowman's qualifications in the business world, to that for the Master's work, who would dare gainsay the remark once made to me, 'His accomplishments have never been equalled since the days of St. Paul.'"

From a Fellow-worker:

"The most lovable, the most beloved, and the most loving member of our Society, was Charles Cowman. No one could find anything unkind to say about him. The only fault we had with him was the way he entered into hard work, but we will keep in mind that Epaphroditus was 'nigh unto death for the work of Christ,' and it may be we are too dilatory and slow. He manifested always such a transparency and purity of character, that the very few times when it was necessary to rebuke wrong, the censure was most keenly felt. He was one of those rare characters who are all unconsciously a conscience for men; petty meannesses and selfish acts that ordinarily passed unnoticed, appeared in all their true ugliness in his presence."

From the Japanese Conference:

"It is a sweet and proud recollection for us that the late Brother Cowman was ever among us and his distinguished figure is still lingering with us.

"Hardly is it necessary to account this fact to his credit that he has set the solid foundation of our work by his undaunted will and sacrificial services. And we now fully appreciate his labor of the past twenty-five years.

"At the present we have more than one hundred and thirty churches thriving under the Almighty's blessing, and we come pretty close to the epoch-making achievement in our church annals, that is, our churches begin to be able to stand on their own feet, supporting themselves. Praise His precious name! We are sure that he would have been glad to have lived and to have seen these days with us. But, alas! he has gone to his reward. We are not slow to convince ourselves that we have been abruptly bereaved of our beloved brother by his travailing sufferings for the establishment of the present blessed Holiness churches in this country."

Excerpts from letters:

"It would be difficult to find in the whole range of modern missions another man to whom God has awarded an equal measure of visible results in so brief a ministry."

"A blameless and beautiful character, whose saintly spirit exhaled so sweet a fragrance that the perfume lingers with me yet; and who went to his heavenly home like a plumed warrior, for whom the Everlasting Doors were lifted and who had nought to do, but mount in his chariot and ride in glory to triumph."

"May it not be too much to hope, too much to ask, that the inspiration of our brother's earnest spirit may pass into some other who may take up the sculptor's fallen mallet and chisel and yet finish the masterpiece of life which he begun so well?"

A native brother wrote: "We have lost our kind, loving shepherd and the flock is bleating."

"As the mountains round about Jerusalem, so he stood a veritable Matterhorn of strength to the society of which he was the founder. 'He fought a good fight, kept the faith, finished his course,' and he waved the victor's palm and wears the conqueror's crown today."

"He was not only a missionary-statesman, administrator, and executive, not only a missionary editor, and missionary traveler, but above all else, he had a real and true missionary heart. He possessed so much real 'missionary sense.' He loved the native workers and preachers and their work was his very life's blood."

A missionary wrote: "It was my great privilege to know Mr. Cowman for one brief half hour, but those moments have left an indelible memory. We went together to Kudan Hill overlooking the densely populated city of Tokyo. He pointed out to me the districts where the Society's mission stations were located. Suddenly his countenance grew sad and he said with much emotion, 'Oh, when will these millions be won for Christ!' For a time neither one of us could speak, our hearts were so moved. He then said, 'Let us claim this city for Christ.' He took off his topee, (sun hat) bowed his head, and prayed. His eyes were wet with tears and I could not but think of the Master who 'beholding the city, wept over it.' "

FROM LOUIS CASPER, AN OFFICIAL

"He was one of the most efficient and fastest workers in this branch of the telegraph profession I have ever known, and I have known a large number.

"I received a great deal of instruction from him in this line of work, and owe a great deal to him for my knowledge in this particular line of work.

"He plainly evidenced the fact that he received inspiration from a high Source. One thing that impressed me was the practicability of his religion. His faith was sublime, therefore, whatever he did was invariably successful. He believed in the promise 'That when ye pray, believe that ye already have it, and ye shall receive it.' He exemplified that faith in his contact with his fellows and always did it tactfully, never creating the impression that he was preaching to anybody or that he considered himself superior spiritually to anybody else.

"With the tremendous advance made in the telegraph business since the time Brother Cowman left for his chosen and higher calling, he undoubtedly would have advanced with it and probably would have been one of the leading officials in the telegraph service had he remained with the company.

"He has, however, chosen that which is permanent and lasting, of serving and leading his fellow men of the Orient into the Light."

Dr. A. I. Berninger writes of his friend:

"My acquaintance with Brother Cowman began in 1893. I went to Chicago to work for the Western Union Telegraph Company and Charles E. Cowman was chief of the New York division. He was active and accurate in his work, and beloved of those who worked under him. At that time he was not converted. I went away from Chicago for two years, and when I returned in 1895 was rejoiced to find that he had been converted. It was genuine, too. Everybody around the office knew it. He had been beloved before his conversion; now he was revered.

"He was a tireless personal worker. There were some five hundred men working in the office and he tried to see and talk with every one of them about his soul's welfare. Some undertaking that, when you remember that big corporations do not hire one to talk, but to work. However, he was always buying up the opportunities and 'redeeming the time' (Eph. 5:16).

"He was winsome in his labors for Christ. His approach was genuinely whole-hearted, cheery and earnest. He was like a good salesman,—he did not leave the case with closed doors, but always with a way to return and talk about it some more.

"At that time there were from twelve to twenty men in that office who were Christians. These he banded together in a little organization to pray for missions. It was called the 'Telegraphers' Mission Band.' I have often thought of this as the beginning of the Oriental Missionary Society.

"Shortly after his conversion Brother Cowman took up systematic Bible Study in the Moody Bible Institute, working nights in the telegraph office to make a living for himself and wife, attending the Institute and studying in the day time. This he kept up for six years.

"I shall never forget the day when he told me on La Salle Street, just north of Chicago Avenue, of his call. 'Unless the Lord stops me, I am going to Japan. And this is the promise God gave me.' He took out his Testament and turned to Matt. 20:6.

"Before the call had come to him to go to Japan, he had opened a mission at 35 North Chicago Avenue. He was a wise fisherman and believed in using bait, which was truly effective in his mission, for he had many converts. The room which he rented was a store-room on the ground floor, with basement below. This basement room was cleaned up, the walls white-washed and a stove put in for heating. Then announcement was made that any man might come and stay all night *free* in the basement, if he would attend the preaching service upstairs and be orderly. The one who came early and thus secured chair No. 1 in the meeting room could have choice of the place below for spreading his newspaper to sleep on. A janitor was employed to keep up the fire at night and keep order. This was very effective bait, and gave a respectful hearing. These men knew they could sleep at the police station, but they preferred this place. The result was, as stated above, many conversions.

"He was on fire for souls. I do not know that he ever took a vacation from the time he went to the mission field until the fatal breakdown came. To the end, he was reaching out to the fields beyond that are white unto harvest. Among my last conversations with him, the subject was the evangelization of China—the Bible Institutes that are now becoming a reality—and then on to Annam. Between paroxysms of suffering, he was, in his spirit, away out in China and Annam, a typical apostle.

"The writer is glad to be among those who knew and loved Charles E. Cowman, a man led by the Spirit of God. Rom. 8:14."

BROTHER COWMAN, A MAN OF PRAYER

A tribute from his co-worker, Rev. E. A. Kilbourne:

"Looking back twenty-five years I can hear Brother Cowman pouring out his heart to God for missionaries. One hundred missionaries was the burden of his prayer. Those were days when we thought of missionaries as white folks, and God's larger purpose and plan had not penetrated into our minds. But those prayers were inspired; they were earnest, they were fervent, they were answered. Not as we thought, however, but in God's way, beyond all we could ask or think, yea, even ten fold beyond, God has answered. White folks? Yes, but not many, God's thought was not our thought, at least not then, and better than we knew God was answering and that answer has meant a thousand missionaries, Japanese, Korean, and Chinese, and as we look back now, we see how much better than we realized God answers prayer.

"Again, we hear Brother Cowman pleading and now the burden of his soul is the Village Campaign. To visit every home, to reach 'every creature' in Japan was the desire of his heart. 'Impossible' the enemy insistently whispered. Just think of the millions of homes in this empire of 60,000,000 people; just think of the congested cities with their interminable alleys; just think of the great mountains everywhere to be crossed; just think of transporting the literature to the innumerable villages of the far interior; just think of the thousands of homes hidden in the fastnesses of the snow clad mountains; just think of the impassable roads and paths to be traversed; just think of the inhospitable reception one must meet among fanatical idolaters; just think of the lack of hotel accommodations to be found for the workers in the country districts and especially in the mountainous parts; just think of a hundred other difficulties that presented themselves to that pleading soul and how they were magnified into mountains! But Brother Cowman knew God, as the God of the mountains and of the valleys, he knew Him as the Author and Fulfiller of all His promises. Mountains must be cast into the sea, trees rooted up, every valley exalted and every hill made low before this man on his knees, and thus it was. How he delighted in the Word! And when he prayed he ever pleaded those precious promises. He took especial gratification in pleading that series of promises containing those remarkable and illimitable words, 'Whatsoever,' 'Anything,' All things,' and entered into the realm of impossibilities to seek God and found Him ever there.

"Again he prays. This time for China, a worthy object for a man of great faith. China loomed great in his vision for years, and especially since that day in 1907 when in a hotel in Shanghai he and the writer were definitely called to that field. Although years of inaction passed, the vision ever held and never dimmed; contrariwise it brightened. The patience of faith was tested even unto the very end of his earthly career, and on his death bed China was not lost sight of. Indeed it was his immediate expectation to see our work started there and a Bible Training Institute erected. He did not live to see it, but died in this hope and the Cowman Memorial Bible Institute has been built.

"Does God answer prayer? A foolish question, a query of the unbelieving. Such a question never entered the mind of Brother Cowman, for from the day of his conversion his prayers were answered, and he lived as in the presence of Him whose ear was ever attent to the heart cries of His children. He who bent low, who 'hearkened and heard' and recorded in His book the pleadings of His faithful child, was well pleased."

THE TIME TEST

"There was an enlargement . . . . still upward."

> "The centuries go by and now they say
> The age of miracles is wholly past.
> When did it pass, we ask,
> And who are they?"

Isaiah 54:2 was definitely given to Charles Cowman by the Holy Spirit in 1902, a year after his arrival on the field. It was God's command as well as promise.

> "Enlarge the place of thy tent, and let them
> Stretch forth the curtains of thine habitation.
> Spare not,
> Lengthen thy cords, and
> Strengthen thy stakes;
> For thou shalt break forth on the right hand and
>   on the left; and
> Thy seed shall inherit the Gentiles, and
> Make the desolate cities to be inhabited.
> Fear not."

"In the month of April we shall celebrate the twenty-second birthday of our work in the Orient and it has been laid upon our hearts to make it a special season of thanksgiving and praise, inviting you to participate with us. Would it not be a joy too deep for words to express if all of the precious friends who have prayed, and worked with us throughout these twenty-two years to give the Gospel message to the heathen, together with the thousands who have been saved through your sacrifice, could meet for a great birthday Rally? Can you imagine how your heart would throb with unspeakable joy to hear these dark-skinned men and women tell how they emerged out of heathenism into the glorious light and liberty of the children of God, and you knew that it was through your prayers and your tears that they received the Gospel Light?

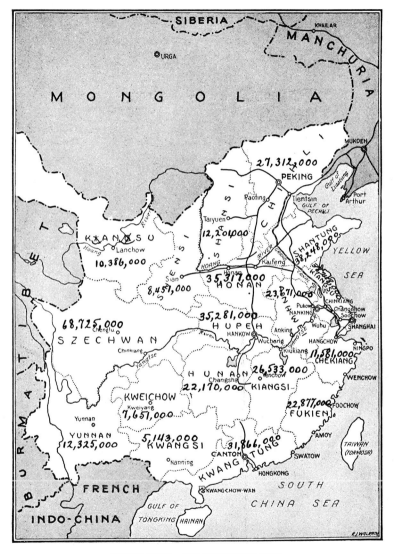

MAP OF CHINA. THE UNFINISHED TASK.

"Many—yes, the majority of those whom you would meet at this birthday Rally would tell you that they had never heard one word of the Gospel until twenty-two years ago, although their hair would be snowy white and their forms bent with age. They would doubtless plead with you to send the Gospel faster that others nearing the dim valley of the shadow might also find peace.

"You would meet the Loo Choo Islanders and hear them tell of the gladness that came into their hearts when messengers of the Great Village Campaign came to their lone island. When you heard them pronounce the name of Jesus with their soft, sweet accent, methinks you would say you never heard anything so wonderful in all your lifetime.

"The Ainu would be at the Rally from their far away villages in the northland where they live in tribes by themselves. They would testify of the transforming power of Christ and tell you how before the Gospel came to their tribe that often murderous night raids would sweep entire villages and the air would be filled with the yells of the heathen in their drunken orgies, but now, praise God, peace reigns and songs of praise of the true God ascend from hundreds of hearts and hundreds of homes. Then when one of their own clan comes forward to greet you and tell you that he was a heathen Ainu but Jesus has saved him and called him to preach, methinks your heart would be too full for words.

"Would you not just love to shake hands with the seven hundred preachers and Bible women who have graduated from our Bible Training Schools and who are now scattered in all parts of the country? Your joy would know no bounds when you met all the dear Christians from the seventy-five interior stations in Japan, the

forty in Korea, besides the scores of itinerary points.
And the dear Koreans! They are coming by the hundreds
from their mud huts and when they come forward to take
you by the hand and you hear them trying to stammer out
a deep heartfelt 'Thank you for sending to us the sweet
story of Jesus,' you will be like the Queen of Sheba—
'have no more spirit left in you.'

"But 'who are these that fly as doves to the windows?'
They are the thousands of precious little children who
attend our Sabbath Schools and who will never again
bow down to idols, for the Gospel has reached them in
time. There are others who will be at the Birthday Rally,
but alas, they will not be permitted to shake hands with
you for they are our leper Christians. Yes, this Birthday
Rally will include those from the snow-covered northland
to the tropical southland; from the lone mountain village
and hidden away hamlet; from the islands of the sea and
from the various tribes; 'They shall come from the North
and from the South, from the East and from the West,'
once heathen now Christian, one fold and one Shepherd."

> "Coming, coming, yes, they are,
>   Coming from the fields afar;
> All to meet in plains of glory,
>   All to sing His praises sweet;
> What a chorus, what a meeting,
>   With the family complete!"

In 1924, the year of his Home-call, after twenty-three
years of service for his King, Charles Cowman could write
his remarkable and oft-quoted summary: "Not a day has
passed since the opening of the work that some souls have
not found Christ. One of our Tokyo Missions has aver-
aged more than a thousand souls a year, since its inception
twenty-three years ago. The Oriental Missionary Society

has 21 mission stations in Tokyo, 130 inland stations in Japan, 50 in Korea, with numbers of outposts; 10,320,000 homes were visited by the Japan Village Campaign Bands, thousands of Bibles were put into circulation; yearly conventions that are influencing the religious life of the entire Empire are a special feature of the work; beginnings have been made in China and Russia; and all this in heathen lands! It is far beyond my comprehension, and there is only one solution to it all and that is that God has answered prayer!"

Not one year since its beginning has there been a retrograde; rather, each year has seen stations opened and districts entered which were heretofore closed, but every gain in the growth that reads so easily today was purchased at a tremendous cost. The growth is but the final triumph of the "seed buried in the ground" which has borne fruit throughout the years. And since his call to his Heavenly Home, it has developed faster than he ever dreamed. The foundation has been well laid, and if our Lord tarries, the next quarter of a century should witness the answer to Charles Cowman's heart-cry,—for one thousand inland stations in the three countries of the Orient. It is not the spurt at the start, but the continued, unresting, unhastening advance that wins the day. Although the work is now but a little more than a quarter of a century old, we thank God for a consecrated army of hundreds of native preachers whose supreme watchword is

"The evangelization of the Orient and Holiness unto the Lord."

A parting message which he sent to his fellow-workers ere he slipped into heaven was, "Let us ever keep in the plan of the Lord, seeking to please and glorify Him in everything small as well as great and there need be no concern about the advancement of the work. It cannot help but grow and expand. And as to the funds for its maintenance the God who has supplied the need thus far will still continue to be the unfailing One."

The supreme test of any movement is "The Time Test." Centuries ago, Gamaliel said, "Let these men alone, if the work be of men, it will come to nought; but if it be of God, ye cannot overthrow it" (Acts. 5 :38-39).

Life stripped of its essentials offers two alternatives to the man of action. He may work for himself alone, building little selfish walls across the path of civilization and making them stumbling blocks in the way of progress. Then, however successful he may be, ultimately the stern mill of the gods will grind him and his structures to dust, and he and his work will vanish from earth. Or, having the eyes that see, he may place his effort parallel with those eternal forces that mark the purposes of God, and then what he builds will endure. An oft quoted sentence by Charles Cowman was: "Let us build for the years we shall not see." It was usually coupled with a favorite Scripture text, "And his fruit shall remain."

Charles Cowman's work has stood "The Time Test" and it has been the necessary factor in understanding its meaning and advance. Year after year it has gone on with increasing results. This is proved by the fact that the four years which have passed since he was laid to rest have been the most prosperous in the history of the work. With such a record behind it, such a foundation under it, and such promises before it, this work of faith may hope to stand until the King Himself appears, and drives sin and heathenism out of the world.

How did the Home-call affect the hundreds of precious native workers? Their brother and friend who had loved them even unto death, that churches might be planted in their soil, was no longer with them. Would their faith fail? Nay! Of them it might be truly said, "In the year that Charles Cowman died, the Japanese and Korean Christians saw also the Lord." And what of the beloved fellow-missionaries? Their brother and leader who had furnished smiles, courage, hope, and a thousand other blessings, and whose very presence was a benediction to them, was gone. And what were they to do? They met together, wept, prayed, and covenanted anew to go forward, relying on the One Who faileth not. The company left behind have the same spirit which possessed his entire life, and are still in the same glorious battle. They preach the same old-fashioned glorious Gospel; they have caught the same vision; they have still the same altar services with weeping sinners by the hundreds. Upon their banner is inscribed, "On, on to the ends of the Orient with the Gospel of Christ." Standard bearers may fall, but not standards. God is not through with the message of the Oriental Missionary Society and He Himself will stand behind the work He has called into existence. His comrades are marching on with the same pace, with the same message, with the same vision, and with increasing victory.

Just as Lutheranism did not perish at the death of Martin Luther, or Methodism with the passing of John Wesley, nor the Society of Friends through the death of George Fox, so this Society will ever be perpetuated by men and women who have the same vision as their leader, Charles Cowman. The man has fallen, but his work lives.

"THOU REMAINEST."

THE AFTERGLOW OF A SUNLIT LIFE

One evening, some years ago, we were standing on the balcony of a little native inn in the heart of the Hakone Mountains, watching the play of light and shade upon the great grey peaks. We had come up from the valley that day to meet our Village Campaign bands, who were distributing the Scriptures in that region, and to spend a day or two away from the crowded city. These times of withdrawal from all the world's turmoil and distraction, these spiritual breathing-spaces for uninterrupted communion with God, seem necessary now and then to those upon whom He has laid a heavy responsibility.

The evening was perfect. One has to live under the spell of the twilight and evening bell, the soft moonlight, the music of the waterfall, to comprehend fully the fascination of a summer's evening in the mountain heights. Poets come here to dream, and to write; tired folk come to rest; and artists climb the hills to obtain charming views of the sunset.

Our arrival was late in the afternoon. The sun had just dropped behind Mount Fuji, the most beautiful mountain in all the world. Stretched out before us was a panorama of exquisite loveliness. The hills seemed to be bathed in heavenly glory, and the hush of heaven rested upon forest and glen. Silhouetted against the sky was a mammoth cathedral, built of peaks, its spire reaching up into the clouds till it seemed to meet the stars; and,

> "In the little pause in life while daylight lingers,
> Between the sunset and the pale moonrise,"

the time for the "Quiet-Hour Tryst," it was easy to be transported in thought to this strange house of worship, far from the haunts of men, to hear the sweet strains of the wonderful organ played by invisible hands, and listen to an angelic choir chanting an evensong; for it is in such surroundings as these we catch the mystic notes that issue from the soul of things. Such scenes have power to quiet the restless pulse of care.

> "If peace be in the heart,
> The very trees and stones all catch a ray of glory,
> If peace be in the heart."

Mr. Cowman was pacing to and fro on the veranda, lost in this matchless vision, for he loved the mountains, the flowers, the trees, the rocks,—God's own handiwork. Presently he came to my side, and I felt his strong arm stealing around my shoulders. We had been lovers from childhood, and this evening we talked of God's tender dealing with us since first we met,—the lad of fifteen and the girl of thirteen,—and of His marvelous leading since the day we had stood together at the marriage altar taking the solemn vow "Till death do us part." We recalled the hour when the hand of the Lord plainly pointed to the mission fields of the world. Oh, how full were our hearts with praises to Him for counting us worthy to bear His Name before the Gentiles!

And then, we fell to musing. Long had we hoped and prayed that it might be the will of God to let us finish our earth work together, and go to our Heavenly Home *together*.

We talked of the blessed ministry He had given us in beautiful Japan, Isle of the Morning; and in Korea, the Land of the Morning Calm; and then our conversation drifted to the evangelization of China's millions. China was included in our call, but as yet our work for that land had consisted only of prayer: we were awaiting the moment when He would bid us launch forth into that great field.

Tonight a strange question arose in our minds,—a question doubtless prompted by a letter that had just been received from a dear fellow-missionary in China, telling of the sudden Home-call of her beloved companion. At the bottom of the little missive which bore the news was this tear-blurred sentence: "We had hoped, always hoped, that we might finish our work out here *together*, but now I am all alone,—alone in China!" We breathed a prayer for this precious woman so bereft, so broken-hearted, sensing something of the depths of her loss and utter aloneness in the heart of a great heathen land.

But her letter had raised a question, which was persistent and troublesome,—"Shall *we* be permitted to walk through China *together?*" Neither gave expression to the thought although each was conscious that it was in the mind of the other.

Again the subject of our conversation was China,— great, unreached China,—her vastness, her lostness, her ringing challenge to the Church,—when suddenly Mr. Cowman exclaimed, "Oh, look! Look! What a wonderful color is shining on the great white cloud that is floating over Mount Fuji! What is it?"

We went to the farther end of the veranda, where we could secure a more favorable position, and there before us was a picture that will never fade from memory. Beautiful Mount Fuji, clothed in its uppermost garments of thick white snow, had caught the most brilliant light, and shone in it like melted gold, with shadows of pure soft grey across it here and there, flickering and changing continually. A deep crimson cloud hung gently over its crest, or above it at a little distance; and one, of the softest grey, divided the golden peak from the mass of cold blue snow and some shadowy rocks beneath; so that alone, in its pure, silent glory, stood the upper summit of the mountain. And then the other rocky heights seemed gradually to share its warmth of color, until they looked as if they were on fire, and glowed in the most intense flame-red. Having no snow upon them, they failed to catch the amber light of the Hakone peaks; but they served to increase the wonder of the scene.

We looked on in silence, which was suddenly broken by my loved one's exclaiming, "It is but an hour after the sunset, and this,—why, this is *the afterglow*. It is growing brighter! How beautiful! Oh, how rare! Marvelous afterglow!"

And then we were silent and watched until the gold had faded into silver, and the silver had changed into snowy-white, and all the flame-colored rocks had put on an ashen-grey, and the wonders of that radiant scene had faded into the night.

But can the memory of it ever fade! We went to our room in the inn to live over again this lovely scene, and our precious talk together in the glory and glow of the sunset; but hours later, in the silent watches of that memorable night, Someone seemed to say, "Child, you *shall* walk through China, *but not together*." There was a cry of agony on my lips, "Anything but *that* cross, O Lord! Anything but *that!*" Somehow the vision of it never dimmed, although throughout the six pain-filled years, when battling with death itself, we tried to tell ourselves that this was but a dream, the result of tired nerves caused by the overstrain of the heavy days out on the far-flung battle line, or the impression made by the letter we had received that day. Often we attempted to tell our loving Lord that Charles Cowman was needed in the Society which he had founded, that he could not be spared, and to go on alone in a heathen land was an utter impossibility.

The *alone* walk through the Orient and China is now a reality; but, thanks be to God, we are witnessing the marvelous afterglow of His servant's blessed ministry,— the Lord's own touch of glory upon the work of the one who literally burned out for His dear Name's sake. The question, "Why, Lord?" has been answered. *God finishes the work by noble souls begun.*

"Just and true are Thy ways, O King of Saints!"

Spiritual work cannot be measured by man. How can one measure a thing of which he can see only one end, the other stretching into eternity! And who can estimate the influence of the life of Charles Cowman?

Nearly nine years have come and gone since he was summoned into the presence of the King. The pages of the Missionary Warrior, with its *finis,* "Thou Remainest," have been read by thousands of people both old and young. The story of his work, his passion for missions, has floated over the world. A thrill of missionary interest has gone through the Church. The cause of the world's evangelization has received an impulse second to none since the early days of pioneer missionary effort. The work which the Lord called into existence through His servant is looked upon by almost every existing missionary society as the model for missions, and has constituted the call to a forward march for hundreds of societies in every part of the world. His slogan and watchword, "A Trained Native Ministry, self-supporting native churches, the Gospel to 'every creature,'" has been caught up by thousands. The point for discussion has been, "If it can be done in the Orient by *one* Missionary Society, and that one a *Faith* Society, why cannot it be done in every field?" The question is unanswerable, except in the affirmative.

The story of Charles Cowman's passion for the speedy evangelization of the Orient almost oppresses the ordinary Christian. His courage and consecration of purpose make our lives seem so weak and disconnected—like water spilled on the ground compared with the torrent that turns a hundred factories.

> "A short life in the saddle, Lord!
> Not long life by the fire"

If it be asked what lies at the bottom of the success attained by The Oriental Missionary Society, or what makes it preëminent in the field of missions, it seems to me that the secret lies mainly in two things: *first,* that there has never been anything countenanced by its leaders but simple preaching of the Gospel, unheralded by sensational announcements and advertisements, and unmixed with worldly leaven; and, *secondly,* that from its inception there has been set up in the native churches the simplest and purest type of apostolic worship. Hindrances either to the Gospel's power or the Spirit's working have been practically reduced to a minimum.

Charles Cowman laid the foundation of the Society so securely and wisely,—planned the Church staffed by natives and launched it forth on its God-given mission, feeling strongly that for this very purpose the Society had been called into existence,—that for all essentials there has been nothing to undo or to modify. In all these years the O.M.S. has never swerved from the doctrinal basis or the governing purpose of its Founder. It still stands firmly on the integrity of the Scriptures as the Divine revelation, on the Deity and atonement of Jesus Christ, the necessity of the new birth, justification and sanctification by faith. And it still has as its objective the training of a native ministry in practical methods of Christian work, with special reference to soul-winning.

The quality of the trained native workers is of the utmost importance, and is one of the most searching tests of the vitality of the church in the Orient. It is a joy to state in this year 1933, that never in the history of the Society have there been better and more efficient native missionaries than those who in recent years have been raised up in our fields of labor; and it seems as if it would yet be seen that the missionary zeal of a native church, while it can only come as the expression of the loyalty and love of devoted Christians to their Divine Master, may also be the salvation of the Church at large.

The work of the Oriental Missionary Society has been blessed of the Lord, and under His multiplying touch "a little one has become a thousand." Let the figures tell the story.

In the year of Charles Cowman's Home-call the mission stations of the Society numbered between three and four hundred. Today, less than nine years after, they number 1200. More than 2500 native preachers and Bible Women have received their training for active service in our Bible Institutes. The students now in training number 340, and this number will doubtless be increased by 100 at the beginning of the fall term. During one year, in our mission stations, there were 86,000 seekers after God; and last year approximately 100,000 bowed at our altars, seeking to know Christ as their personal Saviour.

Were these people actually converted? Do these statistics have any real meaning, or are they simply figures? Does the Gospel actually reach the heart of the heathen? Recently we were asked this question: "Are the people *really* converted, as *we* call converted? Are they not all raw heathen who have to be taught much the same as we teach our little children?"

There is *something* that reveals very plainly whether the converts from heathenism are really converted in our sense of the term. It was my privilege this year to attend the great yearly Convention of the Oriental Missionary Society held in the heart of Tokyo. Between four and five thousand people were in attendance. The days were crowded from morning till night with meetings of all kinds; and never in my life, in any period of old-time camp-meeting fervor have I heard more illuminating sermons and exhortations and prayers and experiences on the subject of the gift of the Holy Spirit, witnessing to present salvation and enduing with power, than I heard under the tent in the five days of this wonderful Convention.

Were these people really converted?

During our missionary tour of the fields we went one day to a large heathen temple. Acres of ground in the heart of a great native city were dedicated to the worship of pagan gods. In the center of the courtyard was a small pool called the Fountain of Life. To this fount came worshipers by the hundreds. They dipped their fingers in the water, then touched in turn their hearts, their tongues, and their foreheads, hoping thus to find favor with the gods. We saw hundreds go through this performance, but not one face revealed by its expression that the blessing of peace had been bestowed: the blank hopeless look of paganism was still there.

Later in the day we went to our Compound, where the native Christians were assembled. We arrived during the closing moments of the afternoon service. The congregation was standing, heartily singing the familiar old hymn:

"There is a fountain filled with Blood,
Drawn from Immanuel's veins;
And sinners plunged beneath that flood
Lose all their guilty stains."

Every countenance wore an expression of joy and gladness, plainly revealing that the invisible realities of heaven had found a place in the soul. The "born again" marks were unmistakable. How the Christians of the Orient love to sing the grand old hymns! The poetic instinct that lies deep within the heart of the Oriental people is easily touched with the divine fire, and the music bursts forth when the great themes of God, the Savior of the world, and deliverance from sin, are sung. The Gospel works in hearts here just the same as it does in the homelands.

At the close of this great "feast of fat things" I journeyed on to Korea to attend the yearly Convention in Seoul, our Korean headquarters. I had been charmed with the Tokyo Convention, and had wondered if anywhere in the Far East such a company of saints could be gathered in one place; but in Seoul also we found the crowds. Day after day to the commodious hall on the compound came hundreds of believers, wending their way up the steep hillside, long, long ere the break of day. Some of their greatest services were those of the very early morning. At 5 o'clock I have entered the building at the rear door, and there before my gaze were five or six hundred Korean Christians prostrate upon their faces engaged in fervent prayer. The hall was packed at every service till there was not standing room.

One of the marks of their conversion is in the way they sacrifice to give to the Lord's cause. In 1932, the year of depression so deeply felt all over the world, when funds were scarce, and the gifts which flowed into the missionary treasury were small, this company of Spirit-filled Koreans were informed that, because of a depleted treasury, the twenty-four graduates of the Bible Training Institute, who had expected to go out into untouched districts and open new mission stations, would be unable to do so. The enemy of souls sat by that empty treasury boldly declaring, "Now the work will fail, for I have power to close doors and to lock up funds!"

But Another also sat "over against the treasury,"— the One with Whom nothing is impossible. Still He proves to His own that He is the "God Who is able" to step into desperate situations and deliver His own who follow Him to the ends of the earth in obedience to His "Go ye!"

The news of this testing of faith became known to the hundreds of Korean native Christians and workers while the yearly conference was in session. They received the news in their usual calm manner, saying, "We must talk to God about this!" And they talked to Him. Prayer was made without ceasing; for hours a steady stream of intercession went up to the throne. They refused to be denied. They held on in faith until they believed the answer was on the way; then they sang praises to the God Who alone doeth great wonders. The hall echoed and re-echoed with their shouts of faith. They had "prayed through."

The answer could not be delayed. Out of their deep poverty they came and laid gifts of love on the offering plate, which was altogether too small to hold their contributions to the work of the Lord. At a time of year when the weather was cold, the men took off their warm, wool overcoats, and carried them to the platform as an offering. Leather shoes, brief-cases, watches, spectacles, blankets,—every available thing that these dear people possessed was freely given. The women of the congregation—hundreds of them—took from their hair the one silver pin which held their long dark tresses together, and put these pins in the offering. One precious little Bible Woman, whose station was away off in the mountain fastness, a distance of three hundred forty miles, walked down the aisle and laid her return railway ticket on the offering plate. Most gladly would she walk home, for the joy of the Lord was her strength. There were those present who were owners of an acre or two of land, or of a yoke of oxen, and these were joyfully given in order that trained laborers might go forth to glean precious sheaves for the Master.

This "giving meeting," which began at two o'clock in the afternoon, continued until after ten o'clock that night, when a missionary who was present, and whose heart by this time was well-nigh breaking, went to the platform and commanded them to give no more, saying, "I can bear it no longer!" Thus the sacrificial but hilarious giving was brought to a close; and with great joy and rejoicing the blessed company of Korean saints wended their way through the dark, narrow streets to their little mud huts, called homes, sweet peace, the gift of God's love, filling their hearts.

The Convention closed in a flood-tide of blessing. All the workers returned to their inland stations, and the twenty-four graduates were sent into new districts far inland to "break up the fallow ground." Within a brief time the offerings were converted into money, and the amount received was nearly $3,500 (£700).

No one will need to be reminded that this splendid offering represented actual sacrifice. It is an encouraging disclosure of the fact that the spirit which gave the movement birth, continues in our midst; the Rock still follows us, and the song and staff ministry awaits exercise as the desert wastes, common to our earthly pilgrimage, are one by one overtaken.

We feel after visiting these brethren and sitting with them in these Conventions, that we have been filling ourselves with spiritual oxygen and ozone, and are exhilarated and refreshed. There is something Pauline in their faith in the message, something Elijah-like in their confidence in prayer, something Napoleonic in their audacity.

We speak of the heroic missionaries, but we should not overlook the heroic element in the church we are developing among the heathen. If there be any of our readers who have been tempted to lose faith in the old Gospel and its simple ways of reaching men, and have been inclined to think of the methods of the apostles as a range of extinct volcanoes, we advise such to find in this work a new *elixir vitae* to quicken and revive their confidence in God's eternal truth and Spirit.

The year of depression has been one of the greatest years in the history of the Society. Not a station has been closed, not a worker sent away; on the contrary, one hundred thirty-two new stations have been opened. These times of shortness are for the proving of our faith.

> "Tell of His wondrous faithfulness,
>   And sound His power abroad;
> Sing the sweet promise of His grace,
>   And the performing God."

Yes, through the power of the Omnipotent One we can achieve! Queen Victoria declared, "We are not interested in the possibilities of defeat. They do not exist."

Our Lord and King has given the blessed assurance, "Whatsoever ye shall ask in my name, that will I do.—All things are possible to him that believeth."

28

We are happy to testify that "our EXPERIENCE in the past hath worked HOPE for the future."

> "Faith, mighty faith, the promise sees,
>   And looks to that alone;
>   Laughs at impossibilities,
>   And cries, 'It shall be done!'"

"Beat a retreat," said Napoleon to his little drummer-boy. The boy replied, "Sire, I know not how. I was never taught a retreat, but I can beat a charge."

Nor has our God, Who led us forth thirty-two years ago, giving us one bare word of promise as a basis for our faith, ever taught us to retreat though the battle were long and hard. What miracles we should witness, and what glory would come to Him Whom we delight to honor, if our faith were but more simple, and we dared to move forward in His strength without question or delay. It is for us to blind ourselves to every obstacle, and say with one of God's saints of old, "Let us go up at once and possess the land, for we are well able to overcome it."

If Charles Cowman were here now I am sure that his Spirit-filled words to us would be, "Forward! Forward, Crusaders for Christ! into the whitened harvest fields! Our Great Commander's orders read, 'Go ye!'"

There has been a long, criminal delay of the Church in taking up the enterprise of a world's evangelization. While we have been "playing missions," fifty generations have come and gone, without one generation of them all being overtaken with the Gospel. Oh, with Paul, *"Let me be ambitious to preach the Gospel where Christ has not been named."*—(Romans 15:20 R. V.).

It is remarkable when we stop to think of the devotion of men in Oriental lands to their rulers. One cannot help wondering how rapidly Christianity would spread if we, who profess His Name, were as willing to go and die as are the soldiers.

A celebrated Japanese statesman said, "We do not worship our Emperor; we love him"; and certainly there is plenty of evidence that this statement is true.

The commandant before Port Arthur called one day for volunteers to cut the barbed wire entanglements. "You will never come back," he said; "you cannot carry a gun, but will take a pair of pliers and cut one or two wires and fall dead. Others will take your place and cut one, two or more wires, but you will know that over your dead bodies will the armies of your Emperor march to victory." Whole regiments volunteered for these death parties. The Japanese who related this incident added, significantly, "If you Christians loved your God as we love our Emperor, you would long since have taken this world for Him."

How much do we love Him? Beloved, the record is not yet complete. The recording angel is waiting to put other names on the list of love's crowned ones. Oh, shall our names be there?

Have Charles Cowman's longings, for which he breathed out his life in prayer been lost sight of, or been forgotten by God?

Have his pleadings passed unnoticed?

Was Charles Cowman a dreamer? Were his life's sacrifice and his visions of God's wonderful workings in the Orient in vain?

No, God has heard. God has answered. God has not forgotten.

> "He answered prayer so sweetly that I stand
> Amid the blessings of His wondrous Hand
> And marvel at the miracle I see,
> The favors that His love hath wrought for me.
> Pray on for the impossible, and dare
> Upon thy banner this brave motto bear,
>   'My Father answers prayer.'"

It is a radiant day in June, 1933. These lines are being penned in the Missionary Home of the Oriental Missionary Society, Shanghai, China.

The Cowman Memorial Bible Training Institute, the *first unit* of a chain of five, opened its doors in 1925, the year after His servant was called into His presence; and already numbers of precious Chinese men and women have received their training for life service and are out in the great white harvest, gathering in the sheaves.

Down in South China, in one of the world's largest cities, Canton, the *second unit* has been providentially given in answer to prayer. There, at the very heart of a population of more than one hundred million, the Bible Training Institute is established for the training of the Cantonese to reach their own people. The mind fairly reels when speaking of China's millions, for each unit represents some soul for whom Jesus went to the Cross. Who, oh, who is sufficient to solve the problem of their evangelization!

Come with me, today, and we will take a walk through China's old Capital city, Peking, North China. It is one of the most fascinating cities in the world, and boasts of a history covering more than 4500 years. Let us walk through the streets until we come to a large gateway over which is hanging this sign:

THE ORIENTAL MISSIONARY SOCIETY BIBLE TRAINING INSTITUTE

This is our *third unit* in China. Its doors were opened in September, 1932. God—our wonder-working God—has given to us fourteen old palace buildings of purely Chinese architecture, arranged to the minutest detail for our Bible Training Institute. The old ancestral hall serves as a splendid chapel, and the various buildings on the compound will easily furnish accommodation for one hundred fifty students. Already a number have been accepted, fine Mandarin-speaking Chinese who have heard the Master's call, "Come, follow Me, and I will make you fishers of men."

God is thus preparing the way in the Orient for the master stroke of modern missions,—the raising up and enlisting and equipping of a *native agency* in the young men and women of these lands who shall constitute a home missionary contingent on foreign missionary soil, to carry Christ's banner among their own countrymen and take possession of these Oriental empires in His Name.

Charles Cowman being dead, yet speaketh. Five monuments more lasting than brass, and more precious than gold, stand to his memory in the centers of three great nations, and lift high the flaming light of a testimony that flashes its beams over the Far East.

Finis cannot be affixed to this, the added chapter of "Charles Cowman, Missionary-Warrior," without sounding out another note of praise to the One Who has been so utterly loving and faithful to her who walks in the afterglow of that rarely beautiful life.

Oh, how sweet, how painful and sweet it is to stoop and bend, day after day, over the common dust-heap of our past experiences, and humming old tunes to ourselves, and thinking of our lost hopes and buried loves, to pick out the little diamonds of memory and put them into our bosoms! And we may do this without *living* in the past. Yes, thank God! there is rest—many an interval of rest, sweetest rest, even here, when it seems as if evening breezes from that other land, laden with fragrance, play upon the cheeks and lull the heart. How singularly such moments are the epochs of life—the few points that stand out prominently in the recollection after the flood of years has buried the rest, submerging all the low shore, and leaving only a few rock points visible at tide.

In the lovely springtime of 1933, during the yearly Convention, something beautiful happened, no, not happened, for it was planned by none other than the loving Lord Himself for her who pens these lines. It is He Who has formed the mysterious chords within us, that thrill or sadden with a touch, and that are discerned by none but Himself; nor is He Who rules the world unmindful of the least want of the soul that He died to save. He understands the human in us. Wonderful, wonderful Jesus!

On the day of Charles Cowman's coronation, September 25, 1924, this promise was definitely given me:

"Said I not unto thee that if thou wouldst believe, thou shouldst see the glory of God"—(John 11:40).

For nearly nine years I have pondered over that word, often asking my Lord to reveal to me its meaning. "I had fainted unless I had *believed to see* the goodness of the Lord *in the land of the living.*" At last the answer to my heart-cry has been given.

It came at the hour of twilight, when the huge tent on the compound was filled with believers who had gathered for the evening service. The day had been a very crowded one, its hours fully occupied from early morning with services and greetings to the workers and Christians who had come up from their stations. There was but one secluded spot where one could withdraw from the crowds and be quite alone, and that wee corner was at the farthest end of the compound,—the garden at the rear of my sweet, old home. Often in other years had I gone to that little spot with Mr. Cowman to watch the setting sun, as it had been our custom to spend together those few moments at the close of each day. Such still moments in the midst of crowded days seem to leave a magic touch upon body and soul.

On this particular evening, the atmosphere was so clear that the mountains stood out in bold relief. Not a cloud floated across the heavens. Some moments before the great red ball had dropped behind the distant range. Then came memories! Memories!

> "Ah, golden yesterdays now laid to sleep,
> What everlasting fragrance still ye keep!"

The evening was an exact replica of the one in the long ago when together, in the heart of the Hakone Mountains, we watched the sunset. For one brief moment the heart cried out for the

> " . . . . touch of a vanished hand
> And the sound of a voice that is still."

Ah, *human* comfort! None but the loving Lord Himself is great enough for loneliness!

A Voice softly whispered, "Look up! Look beyond!" Instantly I obeyed, and there in the far distance I saw Japan's loveliest mountain bathed in a color as soft and dainty as the blossoms that make the springtime a fairyland. Gradually the soft color changed to a deep crimson; rivers of glory wound through meadows of gold; mountains of glory reared themselves to the heavens with their cloud-capped summits tipped with the splendor of the dying day; and there, in the lavish glory of the sunset,—the faint foreshadowing of the glory of the Father's House,—I watched the afterglow, the beautiful, the exquisitely beautiful afterglow.

It was an hour for retrospection. Time turned backward in her flight, and together with my loved one I was once more walking over mountains and vales seeking the "other sheep" which He said He MUST bring. Memory brought back again the years when the life of excess consecration had paid its martyr penalty. And then, then this question stole into the mind unbidden. Had Charles Cowman received his Home-call too early? Had he been defeated? Had death robbed him of his inheritance as a missionary?

Was Henry Martyn, the scholar of Oxford and Cambridge, who buried himself in the sands of Arabia for Jesus' sake, defeated? He went down into territories where no white man had ever been, and at last he lay down to die on the desert sand, and they buried him in an unmarked grave. Was this great hero defeated?

"Go to the old burying-ground of Northampton, Mass., and look upon the early grave of David Brainerd, beside that of fair Jerusha Edwards, whom he loved but did not live to wed.

"What hopes, what expectations for Christ's cause went down to the grave with the wasted form of that young missionary of whose work nothing now remained but the dear memory, and a few score of swarthy Indian converts! But that majestic old Puritan saint, Jonathan Edwards, who had hoped to call him his son, gathered up the memorials of his life in a little book, and the little book took wings and flew beyond the sea, and alighted on the table of the Cambridge student, Henry Martyn.

"Poor Martyn! Why should he throw himself away! . . . . To what purpose was this waste? Out of that early grave of Brainerd, and the lonely grave of Martyn far away by the splashing of the Euxine Sea, has sprung the noble army of modern missionaries."

Was Martyn defeated? No, a thousand times. Put a stone at the head of his grave and let some angel carve upon it with eternal letters. It is victory.

Was Charles Cowman defeated because he finished his course years ahead of his time? A thousand times, no! The strings of the harp are snapped, but the harp is not broken: it has been handed to a Truer Minstrel, who will bring out the richness of its hidden music. The torch which he bore aloft is not quenched,—it still shines with all the brilliance of the sun,—and thousands, taking that torch from his hand and carrying it aloft into every corner of Japan, Korea, and China, will light a vast multitude Home.

My reverie was broken by the sound of a bell. It was time for the evening service to begin. Entering the tent I witnessed a never-to-be-forgotten sight. The crowds! The crowds! On the long platform in the front were one hundred native preachers, numbers of them having been with the Society since its inception. Faithful men! Saints! Hundreds in the audience were the delegates and workers who had come from the nine hundred thirty-five stations and outstations. There were representatives from the Russian work in China, the Korean work in Japan. Devoted workers came from their stations along the Manchurian border. The Ainu brother was there from the cold northland, and the converted and sanctified Headhunter from the Formosan jungle. A dusky-faced Celebes Islander, our own worker, was also among the number.

As I entered the tent that vast throng were standing with hands uplifted while they sang that grand old hymn our fathers loved so well:

> "Amazing grace, how sweet the sound,
> That saved a wretch like me.
> I once was lost but now am found,
> Was blind, but now I see.
>
> "Through many dangers, toils and snares,
> I have already come.
> 'Tis grace hath brought me safe thus far,
> And grace will lead me Home.

"When we've been there ten thousand years,
　　Bright shining as the sun,
We've no less days to sing His praise
　　Than when we first begun."

This glorious company of Blood-washed saints, keeping time to the music with uplifted hands, reminded me of a great field of golden grain, waving to and fro in the summer's breeze. I do not expect ever to witness a lovelier sight. But, whence came this golden harvest? *From a single buried grain.*

"Except a corn of wheat fall into the ground and die it abideth alone; but if it die, it bringeth forth much fruit"—(John 12:24).

Methought I heard again that precious promise, *"Said I not unto thee that if thou wouldst believe, thou shouldst see the glory of God?"* And *then*, yes, *then*, I understood its meaning.

At that moment I beheld *another* afterglow,—the afterglow of the beautiful laid-down life of

CHARLES COWMAN, Missionary-Warrior.

"And I heard a voice from heaven saying unto me, Write, Blessed are the dead which die in the Lord from henceforth: Yea, saith the Spirit, that they may rest from their labours;

AND THEIR WORKS DO FOLLOW THEM."

HOW FAR TOGETHER

"How far together? Till the road
   Ends at some churchyard wall; until the bell
Tolls for the entrance to the lone abode;
   Until the only whisper is 'Farewell'?

"How far together? Till the light
   No longer wakens in the loving eyes;
Until the shadow of the final night
   Has swept the last star-glimmer from our eyes?

"How far together? Past the end
   Of this short road, beyond the starry gleam;
Till day and night and time and space shall blend
   Into the vast Forever of our Dream."

───────────

"But are they dead? our hearts may ask.
They lived, performed their glorious task,
Spent and were spent, and now they bask
      In Gloryland.

"Fill up the ranks depleted so!
To us from falling hands they throw
The torch; be ours to hold it high—
If we break faith with those who die
On us the shame! For grasses blow
      In heathen lands."

The Oriental Missionary Society

The Late Rev. Chas. E. Cowman—Founder

THE ORIENTAL MISSIONARY SOCIETY, an incorporated, interdenominational Missionary Society, founded April, 1901, by the late Rev. Chas. E. Cowman, has work in what we believe to be the ripest missionary fields of the day—Japan, Korea, China, and India. It is called to do but one thing in these fields—EVANGELIZE.

From its very inception the Society's main objective has been the training of native workers for the evangelization of their own people, and the establishing of native churches in neglected districts. Seven splendid Bible Training Institutes have been given us in which to train native preachers, teachers, and Bible women. These are located in the following centers: Tokyo, Japan; Seoul, Korea; Shanghai, Canton, and Peiping, China; Allahabad and Sholapur, India. More than three thousand native workers have already been trained. The Society has established over twelve hundred seventy-five mission stations.

We have about nine hundred trained native workers so devoted to the Lord and so diligent in His service that during one year they were instrumental in leading one hundred thousand souls to Him.

We are old-fashioned believers in the whole Bible, the Trustees and Missionaries being obliged to sign a contract which insures the continuity of the "faith once for all delivered unto the saints." (Jude 3, R. V.)

THE ORIENTAL MISSIONARY SOCIETY was the first organization in the history of missions to go to every home in a nation (10,320,000 homes in Japan) and leave in each a Gospel portion. We praise God for giving us this great honor and privilege. A similar campaign is now being carried on in Korea, where over half of the 4,000,000 homes have been systematically visited by our workers. Five dollars will purchase Scripture portions, and send a messenger of the Cross to every home in a large village.

A native student in training may be supported for $5 per month; a trained Bible woman, for $8 per month; a native pastor, with a family, for from $12 to $18 per month.

This is a faith work, dependent on God for its maintenance, and only through believing prayer can it be maintained. The free-will offerings of God's people have made possible all that has been accomplished by the Society. Our yearly budget amounts to approximately $350,000 (£70,000)—an amount which constantly increases as the work grows.

Our properties are valued at approximately $750,000 (£150,-000). The policy of the Society is never to go into debt.

For further information please write us, and thus get into touch with one of the most aggressive missionary societies of the day—a Society that does but one thing—*direct evangelism.*

Address: THE ORIENTAL MISSIONARY SOCIETY
900 North Hobart Blvd.   Los Angeles, Calif., U. S. A.

Publications of The Oriental Missionary Society

THE ORIENTAL MISSIONARY STANDARD, a sixteen-page magazine, published in Peiping, China, in the interest of The Oriental Missionary Society, operating in Japan, Korea, China, India, and Formosa, is sent free to all donors to the work. It is alive with fresh news, and all lovers of missions should have it in their homes. Send a post card for a sample copy.

Books by Mrs. Chas. E. Cowman

STREAMS IN THE DESERT, a companion volume to *Springs in the Valley.* Over 300,000 copies have been printed to date, and its daily messages have been read around the world. Price: Cloth, $1.50; Limp Leather de luxe, $4.00, postpaid. English currency, 6/6 and 16/6.
Spanish Edition. Price: Cloth, $1.50 postpaid.
Other foreign translations in preparation: *Swedish, Russian, German, French, Finnish, Estonian, Greek, Arabic, Afrikaans* and *Korean.*

CONSOLATION, another compilation of comforting and encouraging daily messages, especially for the sorrowing who have been bereaved of loved ones.
Price: Cloth, $1.50 postpaid; Limp leather de luxe, $3.00 postpaid; English currency, 6/6 and 12/6.

CHARLES E. COWMAN — MISSIONARY WARRIOR, life-story of the founder of *The Oriental Missionary Society.* This story grips and thrills the reader as he follows the trials and triumphs of a young business man who heard God's call to the regions beyond and "rose up and followed." 400 pages. Price: $1.00; English currency, 5/— postpaid.

SPRINGS IN THE VALLEY, Mrs. Cowman's latest compilation, a companion to "Streams in the Desert."
Price: Cloth, $1.50 postpaid; English currency 6/6 postpaid.

Address: THE ORIENTAL MISSIONARY SOCIETY
900 North Hobart Blvd.   Los Angeles, Calif., U. S. A.